BARE FEET,

Stories from the Other Side

By James G. Zumwalt

Jacksonville, Florida—Herndon, Virginia

Bare Feet, Iron Will

Stories from the Other Side of Vietnam's Battlefields

By James G. Zumwalt

ISBN 978-0-9777884-3-9

Library of Congress Control Number: 2009913982

Published by Fortis Publishing

Jacksonville, Florida—Herndon, Virginia

www.Fortis-Publishing.com

Manufactured in the United States of America

DEDICATION

- To my brother Elmo, whose belief in duty, honor and self-sacrifice for country, led him to volunteer for service in Vietnam, where the seeds of his demise were sown.
- To the 58,000 Americans who made the ultimate sacrifice for their country in the Vietnam war.
- To the estimated one million North Vietnamese and Viet Cong soldiers who fought for what they believed in—a reunified Vietnam—enduring immense hardship, suffering and tragedy in the process, winning their final victory at the sacrifice of their own lives.
- To the 254,000 South Vietnamese servicemen who, believing in a right and just cause, fought and died beside their American comrades.
- To the estimated two million Vietnamese citizens who, either as participants or victims of the war in Vietnam, paid the ultimate price, hoping one day their descendants would enjoy a life free from the ravages of war and its suffering.
- To my daughter, Thea, whose continuous love and support have brought great joy and happiness—more so than she realizes—into my life.
- To my son, James, who epitomizes the family creed of duty, honor and self-sacrifice for country, risking life and limb to save the lives of others as he defuses explosive devices on battlefields of a new era.
- To my wife, Karin, who has taught me so much about the power of love and the healing process—and who continues to give me strength.
- To my mother, who suffered the ravages of war in the first decades of her life, to see it claim a father, and in later decades, to see it claim a son.

- To my father, who taught me by his sterling example to believe in duty, honor and self-sacrifice for one's country.

I dedicate this book.

Contents

Provinces – North Vietnam i

Provinces – South Vietnam ii

Acknowledgements iii

Prologue 1

Section One: Medical Care **17**

Into the Belly of the Beast 19

Healing the Wounds of War 45

Doctor Pain 55

The Fight Ends But the Real Battle Begins 62

Section Two: Survivor's Luck **66**

A Run for Life 67

Buried Alive! 69

Freedom Flight 71

A Near Fatal Mistake 74

Section Three: The Civilian Toll **78**

The Reunion Not to Be 79

Child of the Jungle 88

Digging Deep for Higher Education 100

Hanoi's Christmas Nightmare 105

Section Four: Patience **125**

By the Dawn's Early Light 126

Hello, Dolly! 133

Section Five: Ingenuity **136**

Flying the Unfriendly Skies 138

Shoot Out over Noi Bai 150

Contents (continued)

Section Six: The Missing-In-Action **154**

The Fallen Eagles 155

Hope Springs Eternal 161

First to Know, First to Die 177

Section Seven: That's Entertainment **183**

The Show Must Go On 184

Section Eight: The Unexpected **195**

The Assassin 196

The Capture That Was, Wasn't 204

A Novel Approach to War 210

The Shifting Sands of Cua Viet 215

Section Nine: "Iron Will" Personified: The Ho Chi Minh Trail and Cu Chi Tunnels **220**

The Always Invincible (sometimes invisible) Ho Chi Minh Trail 222

The War Down Under 295

Going It Alone 317

Epilogue: "Lest We Forget" **326**

ACKNOWLEDGEMENTS

It had long been a dream of mine to write this book. I discovered, however, there were enormous challenges involved in taking this task on. While it may take a village to raise a child, it takes a team to write a book. I discovered the challenges in writing mine were greatly eased by having the right team assisting me.

I would be remiss in not mentioning those team members who made it possible for me to achieve my dream.

-   Phu Van Nguyen, my Vietnamese brother. The war that claimed an older brother also gave me a younger one. Phu's family escaped from Vietnam and was taken in by mine. Phu later returned to Vietnam where his help was invaluable in dealing with the Vietnamese government, helping arrange interviews and translating them, etc. Together we traveled the length of the country twice in our search to talk to veterans wh provided us with fascinating insights as to what the war was li e from their side of the battlefield.

-   Dennis Lowery, my friend and colleague. While writing a book is often a constant journey of starts and stops, Dennis provided the motivation and expertise to get me over my last 'stop." Having finished the manuscript for **BARE FEET, IRON WILL**, I had lost steam in my efforts to get it published. Dennis, understanding the importance of the message the book contained, pressed me to get it out—and provided the ultimate vehicle for my doing so.

-   Le Do Huy, my photograph researcher. Huy spent endless hours combing through photo archives to find many of those that appear in **BARE FEET, IRON WILL**. His dedication in locating those most representative of the stories shared therein was relentless.

- Chuck Searcy, a fellow Vietnam veteran who resides in Vietnam. When I was in need of independent verification to document a never-before-told aspect of the war related in the chapter "Going It Alone," Chuck became the "go to guy." He refused to allow barriers—even physical ones—get in his way to ascertain the truth.

A team is only as good as the sum of its parts. I was fortunate and blessed to have some good "parts." I could not have completed this book without them and thank each team member for his dedication and contribution in helping me realize my dream.

PROLOGUE

The Vietnam war left an indelible mark on America.

Not since the American Civil War has a conflict so divided her people. More than a generation after the war in Vietnam ended; many Americans remain haunted by its memory.

For some, the haunting may be the loss of a loved one. For others, it may be the loss of a comrade, a limb, or a part of one's life. It may be an internal conflict of struggling to understand the war and why, having answered America's call to arms, one who served failed to receive a Nation's gratitude.

That the Vietnam war left a deep wound on the very soul of the American psyche cannot be denied. That the wound still festers is evident from the controversy generated by events occurring long after Saigon's fall. From the late Secretary of Defense Robert McNamara's mea culpa—**IN RETROSPECT**—to President Bill Clinton's decision in July 1995 to restore full diplomatic relations to Vietnam after a forty-year hiatus, the controversy rages on.

BARE FEET, IRON WILL will be received with similar discord. It is my hope; however, those still haunted by the war or struggling to understand it will read what follows with an open mind. I feel many of us have been remiss in failing to accept a fundamental principle about the Vietnam war—one we adopted in the aftermath of all other wars in

which America fought. This principle has enabled us, as a people, to embrace former enemies, to build a bridge of friendship and heal the wounds of war. It is one of which we lost sight, perhaps, because Vietnam was the first war in U.S. history we failed to win.

In warfare, it cannot be denied that both sides suffer. Neither the victor nor the vanquished emerges unscathed. Tragedy, hardship and suffering are universal to the warrior regardless on which side of the battlefield he stood; they are universal to the family awaiting the warrior's return; they are universal to the civilian population supporting the warrior's cause. "Universality" is a simple principle—it recognizes the commonality of suffering so that, once the fighting ends, a fertile ground can be plowed in which the seeds of friendship are then sown. It is a principle of which I, in my own sense of loss, lost sight.

Let me share my motivation for writing this book.

I think there are Vietnam war veterans who have had difficulty accepting the suffering that conflict visited upon them. It was my return to Vietnam in 1994, however, in which I was able to come to terms with the internal struggle of my own personal tragedy of the war that inspired me to write **BARE FEET, IRON WILL**.

I fully recognize there are many Americans who suffered far greater tragedies from the Vietnam war than did I. One's experiences in life are always unique to the individual—and so are one's losses. In that context, the loss suffered by my family and me affected us deeply. It was this profound loss, and the bitter irony of the circumstances surrounding it—in that the military orders given by my father were ultimately responsible for my brother's death—with which I sought to come to terms.

❋ ❋ ❋

Our family has long enjoyed a proud military tradition: a Zumwalt has served in almost every major war since the American Revolution. It came as no surprise to friends aware of the history that every male member of my immediate family volunteered to serve in Vietnam.

From 1968 to 1970, my late father, Elmo R. Zumwalt, Jr., a Vice Admiral at the time (pictured at right), commanded the naval forces in Vietnam. As "COMNAVFORV" (Commander Naval Forces Vietnam), all U.S. Navy coastal and riverine craft committed to the war effort in South Vietnam fell under his command.

Upon my father's arrival in Vietnam, his immediate superior, General Creighton Abrams, made known his dissatisfaction with the role the Navy was playing in the war. He wanted the Navy to be more assertive. Accordingly, my father mapped out a very aggressive strategy, ultimately turning South Vietnam's canals and narrow rivers, long used by the Viet Cong as uncontested highways along which to ferry troops and supplies throughout the south, into battlefields. (The term "Viet Cong" was a pejorative description used by the Saigon government, and later adopted by the U.S. military, to describe those communist rebels in South Vietnam seeking to overthrow the government. While it is more appropriate to use the term "People's Liberation Armed Forces" {PLAF}, I use the term "Viet Cong" only because Americans are more familiar with it. No disrespect to the PLAF is intended by so doing.)

My father's new strategy resulted in major reversals for the Viet Cong as their use of the canals and rivers for resupply and infiltration (from Cambodia) was significantly reduced. U.S. Army casualties in the Mekong Delta region (the "Delta") dropped as Viet Cong supplies dwindled. Maintaining a more stable presence in the area, the U.S. was able to accelerate its pacification efforts in the Delta, gaining increased support for Saigon and the U.S. Government among the Vietnamese people.

The strategy's success did not come without cost. While U.S. Army casualties decreased, U.S. Navy casualties drastically increased as riverine personnel experienced a six percent per month casualty rate. This meant personnel serving "in-country" (the term applied to service within the Vietnam combat zone) on the patrol boats stood almost a three-out-of-four chance of being killed or wounded during a one-year tour. My father immediately searched for ways to improve their odds.

The Navy's extraordinarily high casualty rate was due to the terrain in which they fought—one consisting of narrow waterways paralleled by banks overgrown with thick vegetation. For the Viet Cong, it was an ideal environment in which to ambush the boats during their patrols; for the Americans, it was a nightmarish setting in which to mount a defense. The heavy vegetation along the banks gave the Viet Cong cover and concealment for ambush, allowing him to spring it within very close range of the U.S. Navy boats. With the element of surprise, the Viet Cong left boat crews with little time to react to an attack.

Among these brave U.S. riverine warriors, serving in the "Brown Water Navy" (the term applied to the forces operating on South Vietnam's inland waterways) was my brother, Ltjg. (Lieutenant Junior Grade) Elmo R. Zumwalt, III. Assigned earlier to the relative comfort of a guided missile destroyer in Norfolk, Virginia, Elmo felt an obligation to serve in Vietnam. He never consulted with my father about his decision to do so as he knew Dad would give a logical explanation as to why he should not. (In both high school and at the U.S. Naval Academy, my father won numerous debating awards. Elmo and I learned early in our lives not to try to debate him as he always prevailed, relying on something with which we were not as equipped to deal—logic.) Had he been consulted, the logic my father would have used would not have been to discourage Elmo from serving—for my father well understood my brother's sense of obligation. The logic applied would have targeted Elmo where he was much more vulnerable, i.e., *"Why cause your mother the additional worry of having a son exposed to the dangers of combat when the safety of her husband is already at risk?"* Elmo knew my father would make the case that he should at least wait to volunteer until after our father's own tour in Vietnam had ended. It was a logical consideration. But, Elmo knew he was not planning on making the Navy a career. Thus, if he failed to volunteer now, he knew he would lose his only opportunity.

The image above is a commemorative bas-relief at the U.S. Navy Memorial honoring U.S. riverine forces. PCF-35, commanded by LTJG Elmo R. Zumwalt III, is the craft in the background.

Elmo arrived in Vietnam to take the only command of his brief naval career—a riverine patrol craft or "swift boat"—the PCF-35 ("Patrol Craft Fast"). As a swift boat commander, Elmo fell within my father's COMNAVFORV chain of command. That personal relationship never resulted in any special favors flowing from father to son or any sought by my brother. It was not in character for either man to do so.

Left to right: Elmo R. Zumwalt III, James G. Zumwalt, Elmo R. Zumwalt, Jr. in Vietnam, 1969.

(In a candid moment, my father later admitted to one deviation from standard practice as a result of Elmo's service in the combat zone. Although an insignificant deviation, my father still felt a twinge of guilt for doing it. *"Each morning,"* he confided, *"when handed the casualty list from the previous night actions, in which names were listed alphabetically, I began reading from the end forward."* With the last name "Zumwalt," were Elmo a casualty, his name would prominently have been visible at the end of the list. I do not think any one could fault my father for such a deviation.) My father was a man of great compassion and intelligence. I do not think he ever implemented a military decision without first considering its impact on his men. No amount of forethought could have prepared my father for the personal impact of one decision he made early in his Vietnam command. While that decision achieved its intended purpose—significantly reducing U.S. Navy casualties—he never could have foreseen it eventually would claim the life of his son and namesake.

Weighing the available options to reduce U.S. casualties, my father realized there was but one way to offset the Viet Cong's advantage of surprise—by denying him the concealment of the heavily vegetated riverbanks. In 1965, the U.S. Army used a chemical defoliant to help clear jungle areas near Saigon, suspected of concealing enemy activity, of their heavy foliage. Its use was expanded as the army established

bases further out in the jungle. Chemical manufacturers of the defoliant assured the U.S. Government their product was not harmful to humans. Aware of those assurances, my father ordered it sprayed along the riverbanks where his boats operated.

The impact was immediate— U.S. Navy casualties dropped more than fivefold—to less than one percent per month. From a military standpoint, the decision to use the defoliant was a good one. Its use enabled tens of thousands of sailors, who otherwise might have fallen victim to the high casualty rate, to return home.

It would be several years before many of these men would discover their fight for survival was far from over. They returned home with a chemical time bomb ticking inside them. The defoliant to which they had been exposed, Agent Orange, proved—contrary to manufacturers' assertions—to be carcinogenic. (Sixteen years later, my father would not only learn the manufacturers were wrong about the effects of human exposure to the chemical, but—in some cases—had intentionally misrepresented what they knew.)

Heavily exposed to Agent Orange throughout their tours in Vietnam, many veterans found the terrible health consequences of their exposures were time bombs with variable length fuses. For some, the fuse was rather short, as children they later fathered were born with a wide range of problems. For others, the fuse was longer—with the effects not appearing for another ten, fifteen, or twenty years—as various cancers, now recognized by the Veterans Administration as Agent Orange-related, attacked their bodies. Among those victims to Agent Orange-related cancers was my brother.

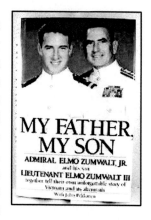

My father wasted no time in joining Elmo's fight for survival. Together they explored every option available. Initially, the focus was on medical protocols aimed at defeating the cancers; in the end, it shifted to protocols to delay the inevitability of its final onslaught. The bond between the two of them was remarkable. No father could have loved a son, or a son a father, more. That bond was perhaps best described in a letter Elmo wrote my father shortly before he passed away. In it, he said, *"Dear Dad...Both in Vietnam and with my cancers, we fought battles and lost. Yet, we always knew even when the battle was clearly desperate, that our love could not be compromised, and that however bad the odds, we were incapable of ever giving up...How I loved you. How I would have loved to continue to fight the battles by your side. You always made a difference. You made my last battle, the journey to death, gentler, more humane. I love you."*

On August 13, 1988, their final battle together ended. At age 42, following a valiant five-year struggle, Elmo died. Like the battles he waged in Vietnam, he bravely fought a hidden enemy but, in the end, lost to a more determined foe.

❉ ❉ ❉

After Elmo's death, my father championed a new cause—recognition by the U.S. government of Agent Orange induced health problems and financial compensation for those Vietnam veterans affected.

While my father's participation in this cause was motivated, in part, by Elmo's suffering, it also emanated from his longstanding belief that a wartime commander's responsibility to those who served under him does not end with the ensuing peace. The sacrifices brave Airmen, Soldiers, Sailors and Marines make in wartime cannot be ignored in peacetime by the commanders they dutifully served. My father's efforts, as well as those of others similarly dedicated to a resolution of the Agent Orange problem, led to a U.S. Government finding of a statistical association between veterans exposed to Agent Orange and a number of specific adverse health effects they suffered. Based on these findings, benefits were issued by the Veterans Administration to these veterans.

My father's involvement in the Agent Orange issue led, in September of 1994, to his return to Vietnam—the most senior military wartime commander to do so. I accompanied him on that visit—my first trip back to Vietnam since the war as well. My father's objective was to seek cooperation by Hanoi in conducting a joint study on Agent Orange.

❉ ❉ ❉

It was against this backdrop then—the pain and anguish of having lost a brother to the war in Vietnam still embedded in my mind—that we returned to the country where the seeds of Elmo's death were sown. As I headed for Vietnam, I realized the battle within me over his loss still raged. Try as I might six years after his death, I was unable to accept it.

Enroute to Vietnam in 1994, my thoughts turned to the war and a reunion I had with Elmo at his swift boat base in Danang in 1969. He was twenty-three; I was twenty. Youthful innocence had a way of making us feel invincible despite the obvious signs that death and danger lurked nearby: crews loaded their craft with ammunition and supplies in preparation for another patrol; boats, riddled with gunfire from earlier operations, were being repaired; new crewmen reported in, replacing those who had fallen just days before them. Yet the thought of death seemed so far removed from us at that time.

I had not seen Elmo for almost a year. It was the longest separation we had experienced. I remembered my excitement upon seeing him again. My initial instinct was to give him a hug; but I hesitated, remembering we both now were in uniform. I stopped, stepped back and executed a smart salute. He returned the salute—then we hugged. While our younger years had been full of the typical rivalries siblings experience, our high school and college years had brought us very close together.

Letting go of that memory, and returning to the present, I reflected on my trip back to Vietnam that day in September 1994. In doing so, I again felt the pain and emptiness over Elmo's loss...

❊   ❊   ❊

As we flew into Hanoi, my thoughts continued to focus on the deaths of my brother and thousands of our compatriots. I searched for some purpose in the loss.

Over the next few days, I met with our former enemies, veterans who had served in the North Vietnamese Army (NVA) and Viet Cong forces. I recalled feeling uneasy at first. My anger at the thought that these men had played a key role in the deaths of so many of my American comrades would not abate. In my mind, there was no doubt: in the Vietnam conflict, the forces of evil had clearly prevailed over the forces of good. Fifty-eight thousand Americans lives were lost attempting to contain communism and to keep South Vietnam free; roughly, twenty-five hundred more remained unaccounted for somewhere in the jungles of Southeast Asia. The tragedy, the pain, the suffering this enemy inflicted upon us was enormous. I remained convinced the war was a black and white issue—there was no gray— these people had caused America great suffering. They had caused me and my family great suffering.

While the Vietnamese veterans with whom I met were cordial and affable, I felt the anger welling up inside me. As I looked at them, I remember thinking they should not be standing before us as victors — for that was our destiny; that was the hand fate was to have dealt us. My perceptions, and anger, would undergo a quick change.

* * *

I recall the moment the change began. It was the third day of our visit. We were meeting with Major General Nguyen Huy Phan, who served in the medical corps and spoke perfect English. He was very soft-spoken. I remember feeling somewhat disarmed by his very gentle demeanor—a stark contrast, I mused, to the brutal image, I held of the stereotype NVA soldier.

Phan extended his sympathies over Elmo's loss. We talked about the war and its impact upon the lives of those who survived it. Dr. Phan (pictured at left) appeared openly affected by our discussion. As he became reflective for a moment, his eyes betrayed an internal anguish. As his eyes became misty, I sensed a personal tragedy loomed in his life as well. I felt an instant bond forming with him. Later, I learned the source of Dr. Phan's anguish—he had lost his father to the French in the first Indochina war and a brother to the Americans in the second. His pain over the loss of his own brother was heightened for many years by his family's inability to locate his remains—his brother becoming just another name on a long list of Vietnamese soldiers still missing-in-action. It took seventeen years of searching by Phan and his family to finally locate the remains and bring them home.

I was touched by Dr. Phan's story. As I reflected on it, I found myself looking at the war from an entirely new perspective. Overcome by guilt, I came to recognize the significance of a loved one's loss was not measured simply by which side of the battlefield on which he had stood. Obviously, Phan's loss of a brother to him was no less tragic than the loss of my brother to me. For the first time, I no longer saw the war in terms of "black and white" or "good and evil." For the first time, I felt my heart go out to an enemy for whom I no longer felt hatred, realizing he too had suffered from that war.

While the war claimed our brothers, I also came to realize I had been more fortunate than Dr. Phan—for at least I knew how, where and when my brother had died. I was with him as he drew his last breath; I knew his final thoughts; I knew he faced his death from cancer just as bravely as he had faced the enemy in battle; I knew his final moments of life were peaceful ones as he slipped quietly away in his sleep. Phan, on the other hand, had to wait seventeen years to discover some, but not all, the details of his brother's death.

✳   ✳   ✳

My experience with Dr. Phan was not the only one that caused me to undergo a change in my perspective of the war.

During the same trip to Vietnam, I also visited an amputee-care facility where many of those wounded in the war still bore the signs of their suffering. Some were double, some triple, some quadruple amputees maimed by an exploding artillery shell, bomb, or mine. Thousands of veterans still awaited delivery of an artificial limb to enable them to function independently again. Many had been waiting for these prosthetics since the war's end.

In 1992, my father became involved, at the request of a Vietnamese-American businessman, in an effort to establish a facility in Vietnam capable of providing Vietnamese veterans with artificial limbs and devices. During our September 1994 visit, my father presented an artificial limb to the 12,000[th] recipient under this initiative. It was a moving experience to see my father, then 73, lift a double leg amputee out of a chair and place him in the first wheelchair the veteran had ever owned.

✳   ✳   ✳

I felt it strange—as much as I had loved my father and as close as we were—the two of us had never really discussed how we, individually, were coping with Elmo's loss. I did not attribute such silence to the stoicism assumed to attach to male members of a family whose roots lie steeped in such a long and proud military tradition. The strict, detached figure of a military father portrayed by Robert Duval in the movie "The Great Santini" was a direct contrast to the father with whom I had grown up. I do not know why we never discussed Elmo's death. Perhaps a pact of silence existed, unconsciously accepted between us. Perhaps I feared the emotional response my father might have had were I to raise the subject with him or vice versa—although tears unabashedly have been shed by us over other family tragedies.

Of the many virtues, my father possessed during his life, one stood out above the rest—the immense compassion he had for those who were less fortunate. He exhibited this virtue towards others, whether friend or foe. A virtue further sensitized me to the great humanitarian he was.

※ ※ ※

As I watched while my father lifted that double amputee Vietnamese veteran into the wheelchair—both men smiling—it dawned on me that, despite the mutual pact of silence we had observed concerning Elmo's death, Dad seemed to have exorcized himself of any "demons" related to the tragedy. Whether the exorcism was a conscious one, I will never know—but I do know my father's compassion and humanitarianism provided him with a basis for putting the tragedies of this war behind him. I use the plural "tragedies" as I include not only Elmo's death but also the deaths too of those brave sailors under my father's command who failed to return home. (Reflecting upon the three wars in which he served, my father once observed that Vietnam was the most difficult for him personally. Unlike World War II and the Korean war where the risks of his combat decisions were shared equally by him and his men, in Vietnam they fell upon his men alone. Soon after his arrival in Vietnam, my father began accompanying his boat crews on their patrols and ambushes. One of his junior officer's years later wrote to him, "I so vividly remembered how you chose to be visible in the combat zone." It was a practice my father was forced to discontinue after General Abrams grew worried about the prospect of a theater commander's capture or death.)

※ ※ ※

The motivation for this book came from two sources: the compassion I witnessed my father exhibit during his life towards a former enemy and the bond of common suffering that arose out of my meetings with Vietnamese veterans like Dr. Phan—men who similarly lost a part of their lives forever on the battlefields of that war. I was not surprised by the inspiration I received from my father; I was surprised, however, by that received from a former enemy—for I did not expect to be so moved by their suffering.

⁂ ⁂ ⁂

My experience with Dr. Phan and observations of the Vietnamese veteran amputees in 1994 gave me cause to reflect—for the first time—on the principle of universality. For the first time, I saw the war's impact relative to the suffering by ALL its victims. The Vietnamese men and women, soldier, civilian, with whom I met, helped me understand the double-edged sword of war cuts both ways as both sides suffer. They helped me see there are no boundaries for suffering in warfare. It truly is universal.

In no way do I intend by this book to minimize the pain and heartbreak Americans suffered. As stated earlier, one's experiences in life are unique to the individual—and so are one's tragedies. But war, by its very nature, creates victims on both sides. And when the battlefields of a war encompass an entire nation—as did the Vietnam war—its entire population falls victim.

⁂ ⁂ ⁂

Neil Sheehan, a Vietnam war reporter, initially supported U.S. involvement. By 1967 that changed. Later, he wrote **A BRIGHT SHINING LIE** in which he ultimately denounced America's role. The book was awarded a Pulitzer Prize. As a strong supporter of America's participation in the war, I disagreed with Sheehan's criticism of the U.S. Government.

I now see Sheehan's book differently. While I still do not accept his denunciation of America's role in Southeast Asia, I have difficulty in blindly accepting the policies the U.S. pursued there. Sheehan's change in attitude towards the war was rooted, just like mine several years later, in his extensive personal experiences in the region and contacts with the Vietnamese people. It was this first-hand exposure to the other side that, eventually, led him to become an opponent of the war.

Having now spent the time to get to know the Vietnamese people firsthand, I can better appreciate the message Sheehan conveyed in his book. We must learn from his message and, hopefully, mine so that the mistakes of the Vietnam war are not visited upon a future generation of Americans.

Sheehan wrote another book about Vietnam entitled **AFTER THE WAR WAS OVER: HANOI AND SAIGON**. The book compares the country as he first saw it in 1962, on the brink of war with America, and in 1989, as its people were enjoying the longest era of peace known to them in the 20th century. He observed:

"We as Americans, who considered ourselves the exceptions to history, showed ourselves as fallible as the rest of humanity; we could do evil as easily as we could do good. We were all too humanly arrogant in the hubris of our moment in the sun.

"It was beyond us to put pencil to paper and understand that we were pursuing fantasies that would bring an immense tragedy to ourselves as well as on the Vietnamese and other peoples of Indochina."

Sheehan reaches a conclusion in total opposition to that preached by the American leadership during the war—that Vietnam never posed a threat to America. *"They (the Vietnamese) simply wanted us to go home, and they would not cease to resist, no matter what the cost to us and to them, until we did. It took me five years to understand that."*

It has taken me many years longer to reach a similar conclusion— reached only after taking the time to get to know the Vietnamese people.

In his book, Sheehan remembers a snapshot of the war that, I feel, sets the tone for mine. Returning to My Tho, located in the Mekong Delta, Sheehan noticed a volleyball court, which triggered a memory of the late Colonel John Vann who commanded U.S. troops there:

"It was late afternoon and the net was up. I could hear Vann's raspy voice calling, 'Come on, let's get those volleyball teams out there,' and the shouts of the American captains and lieutenants as they played. Those young men had been my contemporaries, and I had identified with them. They had been keen officers, the best the U.S. Army had to give, eager for battle, certain of their cause and their ideals. When we had clambered aboard the helicopters with the assault troops amidst the racket of the engines and the whirling dust from the rotor blades we had thought, 'Someday we will triumph, and this will be a better land for our coming.' We had not triumphed, and because of our coming Vietnam was a wounded land. In the twilight of the volleyball court I wondered what those young officers would have thought of the other brave men in the foxholes on the dike had they known the truth of the war they had been sent to fight."

❉ ❉ ❉

Brave soldiers fought on both sides of the battlefield in Vietnam. Likewise, tragedy and suffering came to both. For a generation, in book and film, we have heard much about the American side of the story; the time has now come to hear the Vietnamese side.

❉ ❉ ❉

This book represents the culmination of research from almost 200 interviews with former Viet Cong and NVA soldiers as well as a small number of Vietnamese civilians. Interviewees included General Vo Nguyen Giap (pictured to the right), commander of the NVA; General Tran Van Tra (pictured immediately below),  commander of the Viet Cong forces; General Dong Si Nguyen  (pictured on the next page), commander-in-chief of the Ho Chi Minh Trial; as well as dozens of senior and junior level officers and enlisted personnel. I was given free access to interviewees. While the same general line of questioning was pursued with each interviewee, it quickly became apparent each veteran had a unique story to tell. In spite of the

uniqueness of each story, a common thread was discernible: a mental strength was evident—one committed to victory by overcoming any challenge or hardship in its path. In the Vietnam war, Americans drew strength from vastly superior battlefield technology; the Vietnamese had to look elsewhere. They turned to their own rich history—one rooted in warfare going back a thousand years as one foreign invader after another violated their borders. Over this millennium, a spirit of nationalism and pride evolved, instilling within the Vietnamese people a determination to drive out all foreign invaders. This spirit of nationalism, pride and determination developed into their greatest strength—an **IRON WILL**—which made accomplishing the impossible possible. In the end, it was this **IRON WILL** that was able to defeat the technology of the world's greatest superpower.

Regrettably, we never really understood this quality about the Vietnamese people. We failed to recognize, in the final analysis, victory was not a factor of technology but of human determination. Their **IRON WILL** was never diminished by a lack of technology, i.e., their **BARE FEET**. Their superior technology was, in fact, an inner strength to endure the most demanding physical hardship and suffering, forcing America to fight the longest war in two centuries of its history. As World War II General George Patton once said, *"Wars may be fought with weapons, but they are won by people."*

More than three decades after the fall of Saigon, it is time to better understand the enemy we fought and the role their **IRON WILL** played in Vietnam's victory and America's defeat. The best way to do so is to share the personal experiences of the men and women who possessed it—empowering them to live, fight and endure Vietnam's war with America.

Section 1:

Medical Care

During the Vietnam war, a major concern of every combat soldier was the availability of medical support in the event he was wounded on the battlefield.

For the American soldier, support often was not far away. As emergency medical care affected morale, every effort was made to

make it immediately available. Medical evacuations (medevacs) of wounded from the battlefield by helicopter normally enabled American soldiers to receive care within hours.

While medical care was of concern to the Vietnamese as well, they lacked a similar capability to provide it. Care for

their wounded was often days, even weeks away—or, sometimes, never available. If and when it was available, shortages of supplies and medical equipment often hindered battlefield treatment. Medical staff improvised to compensate for shortages when they could and, when they could not, the wounded suffered.

BARE FEET, IRON WILL begins with a selection of stories providing insights into the nature of medical care available to the Vietnamese. These were selected for two reasons. First, they provide the reader with an immediate sense of the hardship endured on the battlefield. The second reason is personal, for I wanted to reserve the opening chapters for stories about two men who inspired me to write this book—Drs. Le Cao Dai ("Into the Belly of the Beast") and Nguyen Huy Phan ("Healing the Wounds of War"). The days I spent with both Dr.

Dai and Dr. Phan prior to their deaths, greatly enhanced my understanding of the war and the suffering it caused the Vietnamese. In so doing, it contributed significantly to my own healing process.

Here, then, are their stories...

Into the Belly of the Beast 19

Healing the Wounds of War 45

Doctor Pain 55

The Fight Ends But the Real Battle Begins 62

INTO THE BELLY OF THE BEAST

No one better understood the importance of medical support for a fighting force than Le Cao Dai. A medical student in Hanoi in 1946 when the war with France was in its infancy, he was pressed into service to provide medical support for Hanoi's fighting forces, the Viet Minh, due to a shortage of doctors.

Initially learning the skills of his profession by on-the-job training, Dai tended to the needs of General Vo Nguyen Giap's army over the ensuing eight-year period. As that army celebrated its final victory against the French at Dien Bien Phu, Le Cao Dai was still fighting to save lives of men who had fallen in that great battle.

❋ ❋ ❋

When war with America came, Le Cao Dai again answered his country's call. Serving as head of the surgical department at a military hospital in 1966, Dai, then 37, volunteered to serve in the south. He was ordered to organize and command a field hospital. Drawing on medical personnel from several other hospitals, Dai pulled together a 400-man staff for his hospital unit, designated as #211. While a hospital likes to maintain a one-to-one ratio of medical staff to patients, Dai well knew the ratio of patients to medical personnel drastically increased in the field. Although the army's medical corps had expanded significantly since the days of fighting the French, the realities of attrition, modern weapon technology, and battlefields situated far from home would all combine to take their toll, taxing his staff's capabilities to the maximum.

"When we were called to go south," said Dai (pictured to the right), *"everybody was very excited. We did not think then we would be there for eight years. I remember when I was preparing to leave the north with one of my friends; he and his wife came to visit my family and me. His wife asked me, 'How long do you intend to stay in the south?' I said I intended to stay there for about six months. She began to cry and told me, 'My husband said he will stay there for one year.' As*

it turned out, while I only planned to stay for six months, I ended up staying for eight years. The man who planned to stay for one year stayed forever. He died in the south."

(There was quite a dichotomy between the lengths of service tours in Vietnam for U.S. as opposed to Vietnamese soldiers. U.S. soldiers normally were limited to twelve months in country. The knowledge of a date certain upon which one's service in Vietnam ended was somewhat of a morale enhancer for American troops—for part of the mental exercise, each morning was to mark another day off the calendar, and

thus the number of days remaining on one's tour. Various "rights of passage" attached at certain key points in time, including the right to be called a "short timer" after serving the first half of one's twelve-month tour (U.S. soldier at left pictured with short timer calendar on his helmet). But among Vietnamese soldiers, there were no short timers. For them, their combat service time was unlimited. While individual length of duty tours varied, the experience of Le Cao Dai was not untypical.)

❋ ❋ ❋

To reduce the risk of losing the entire hospital staff in the event of an attack while transiting the Ho Chi Minh Trail (the secret jungle supply route, stretching thousands of kilometers through Vietnam, Laos and Cambodia, by which Hanoi kept feeding its war effort in the south), Dai split #211 Hospital into three groups. Two traveled by foot while Dai's group went by truck, at least until it reached Dong Ha (just south of the 17th parallel in Quang Tri Province). There they came under an air attack that destroyed most of their vehicles, forcing them to continue the journey on foot.

The #211 Hospital staff completed their transit with personnel intact. A few people became severely ill from malaria and other diseases, necessitating their return to Hanoi—but there were no combat fatalities. The outcome for their equipment, however, was much different.

"It was very heavy equipment," explained Dai. *"In total, almost one thousand boxes were transported by vehicle. I carried my own surgical instruments on my back (after the bombing at Dong Ha)...But most of the equipment was lost during the transit. Only about one-tenth arrived...and was incomplete...For example, the radio arrived with the tube missing and the generator and x-ray equipment arrived, but the latter without the lead protective apron."*

While most the equipment did not survive the transit south, there was some irony in what did.

"When we prepared to leave Hanoi, one of the female soldiers who wore Vietnamese clogs switched to wearing rubber sandals," Dai explained. *"So she discarded her clogs in a box."* (The rubber sandal is a very comfortable piece of footwear, the sole of which is made from an old tire and the cushion from the softer inner tube. It was the primary footwear of all NVA soldiers.) *Months later when she opened one of the few boxes to survive the trip, she found her old clogs inside."* Discarded shoes managed to survive bombings and numerous transfers at binh trams (geographic sectors of responsibility, separately commanded and each with its own military base) along the Ho Chi Minh Trail, but vital medical equipment did not.

⁂ ⁂ ⁂

Two months after their trip south began, the three groups of #211 Hospital linked up at Nga Ba Dong Duong, where the borders of Vietnam, Cambodia and Laos converge.

"We set up our hospital between the borders of these three countries and stayed there for about six months," said Dai. *"It proved to be too far from the front lines. So, we had to move closer. I moved many times during the war. The longest I stayed in any one place was about one year. But I could stay in most places for only two or three months, or until we were discovered. When the Americans kept defoliating (with Agent Orange) the jungles in which we were hiding, we had to move again."*

⁂ ⁂ ⁂

Moving a 400-man staff field hospital, including its average patient population of 1,000 to 1,800, was not easy. Besides the logistical demands such a move created, tremendous labor was required to establish the new site. While some hospital facilities were above ground, hidden from air observation by thick vegetation, most were underground. This involved digging a series of one meter deep, open-air bunkers, each capable of housing no more than four to five people. A bamboo or thatched roof was erected over the bunker, a half meter above ground, to shelter occupants from weather. An A-shaped bomb shelter, again capable of holding four to five occupants, was dug into the bunker wall at a depth of two meters. To house a hospital population of 1000 patients plus its 400-man staff required digging approximately 280 bunkers and bomb shelters. As most patients were unable to participate in this construction, responsibility fell to hospital staff personnel and the few infantry troops who could be spared. A new site took about a month to complete.

Regulations issued concerning construction of these field hospitals in the combat zone imposed further demands on staff personnel. Individual bunkers were dispersed, situated no more than thirty meters apart, to avoid destruction of more than a single bunker by one bomb.

Such dispersion made it difficult for Dai to conduct his daily rounds to check on patients and the needs of his staff. Dai explained *"We dispersed our hospital over a very large area. So, if I wanted to see a patient, sometimes I had to walk for almost an entire day to get there. It was one day's full journey from one side of the hospital to the other."*

❊ ❊ ❊

Security was a constant concern. While the hospital was usually located a safe distance from the battlefield, responsibility for security remained theirs since they were isolated from other units. Dai always established an observation post in a nearby tree to maintain constant vigil of the sky as the heavy jungle vegetation made it impossible to observe ground activity. He knew the enemy could insert troops by helicopter to gain quick and direct access to targets. Maintaining daylight vigil of the sky provided the hospital with advance notice enemy troops were in the area. This vigil became part of the hospital's daily routine.

When a helicopter was detected, the observer, communicating with Dai via wire telephone, provided its bearing and distance. The vegetation was so thick that many times it was impossible for the observer to even know whether the helicopter, screened from view by the foliage, had actually landed or was just passing through. But Dai never took a chance. He assumed every sighting was an effort by the enemy to insert a commando surveillance team in his area. After being given the helicopter's bearing and distance by his observer, Dai immediately took action.

"I would send a squad of men to protect the hospital," he explained. *"Sometimes they had to fight. Other times they just had to fire their weapons and the commandos immediately fell back, recalling the helicopter to extract them. I saw these commandos on many occasions. Since the aircraft could not land because of heavy vegetation, a rope was dropped from the helicopter, which the commandos then scaled down...Sometimes four or five men were seen hanging underneath an airborne helicopter.* (This was known as a SPIE rig—Special Purpose Insertion and Extraction rig—used to insert/extract troops very quickly, without having to land a helicopter. Commandos, wearing vest harnesses that allowed them to snap onto a line attached to the helo, hooked up in pairs. For insertions, they took off from their base, dangling on a line under the helo as it flew to the insertion site. Upon arrival at the site, the aircraft hovered, slowly descending to allow each pair of commandos to touch down, unhook their harnesses, and run into the jungle to provide security for the next pair of commandos who similarly detached themselves. The procedure was reversed for extractions.) *Sometimes I saw these commandos die because the trees were very high and, as the helicopter took off; they would get caught up in the branches and fall off. We had to protect ourselves. If discovered, I had to give the order to move. My motivation for moving was simple— inevitably, we knew a B-52 bombing would follow the same night our position was discovered."*

On one occasion, Dai's staff was credited with shooting down a U.S. helicopter that had flown too close to his position. Firing at the aircraft with small arms to drive it off, Dai was surprised when it came crashing to earth.

"I felt it had not been severely damaged," he reported. *"When I got to the crash site, I saw only one small hole from a bullet that came up from the ground. It may have damaged just one wire. The helicopter carried about six people. By the time we arrived though, no one was there. When it crashed, the Americans immediately sent several other helicopters to rescue the occupants."*

❊   ❊   ❊

Before departing Hanoi for the south, Dai recalled being given a very brief idea of what he should expect life in the jungles to be like. *"My director spent one year in the south before returning to the north,"* Dai shared. *"He told me you have to consider life there as being what it was for Robinson Crusoe on his island."* Dai soon discovered his director was not exaggerating. *"There was a shortage of everything. We did not even have knives to perform surgery."* Survival, and the unit's ability to perform as a field hospital, was linked to their ability to improvise.

Dai and his staff quickly adopted ways of replacing equipment shortages they suffered. He was pleased with his staff's ingenuity in discovering a practical use for the most impractical items. Ironically, the non-medical items they were able to put to medical use often times came from a most unexpected but accommodating source—the U.S. Government.

Among the shortages, #211 Hospital suffered from was a lack of surgical tools. Dai described how they addressed this: *"We used scrap metal, usually taken from unexploded American bombs. We used the metal from those bombs to make our surgical tools and, in some cases, other equipment. Or we used the metal from shell casings, or a piece of aluminum from a plane that had been shot down. All kinds of medical needs were met in this manner—to make surgical instruments, to make the boxes in which we sterilized our instruments, to make stethoscopes..."*

Dai reported, *"Nothing provided by the Americans went to waste."* Anything discarded was cannibalized and put to use in some functional manner. Such was the case with parachute flares, dropped by U.S. aircraft at night to illuminate the ground below to monitor NVA activity. These provided material for a wealth of medical applications: flare tube remnants were used to make stethoscopes; parachute lines were separated to provide surgical thread; parachute cloth was used to make tourniquets and bandages.

When an aircraft crash site was discovered, it was immediately scoured for salvageable material to be similarly applied. Electrical wiring was stripped from the aircraft and wire removed from its rubber insulation. This insulation was used for intravenous (IV) tubes.

"The Americans made up for a lot of our equipment shortages," chortled Dai.

The hospital faced a shortage of syringes too. Again, the staff relied on their imagination. *"Initially, there was no way to containerize the medicines so we could give injections,"* explained Dai. *"We had to use the glass syringe over and over again. After using an antibiotic or some other medicines, we retained the syringe to use it again. It was very difficult to recover all of them for such re-use...So we decided to manufacture these syringes at our field hospital...A new unit arrived from Hanoi and I asked the commander if he had any handicraft workers. He had three. They told me to produce syringes all that was needed was old glass or used bottles. From there, the process of making the syringes was very easy.*

"At this time—in 1967 to 1968—we started to liberate certain parts of Cambodia. In and around the many military posts in Cambodia were many empty soda and beer bottles that were readily available for our use in making syringes. But the most important aspect, these handicraft people informed us, was construction of the furnace for melting the glass. Fortunately for us, and I do not know why they were there, we had some bricks in the hospital's storage area. I do not know who ordered them, but we had about a dozen...so we made a furnace.

"The intensity of the heat was important too. It was simple to find wood to make charcoal in the jungle. But wood charcoal does not provide as

much heat as coal. One of my people involved in manufacturing weapons was very experienced in this area. He told me we could use charcoal, but not ordinary charcoal. It had to be charcoal burned in a special way—without any air. It would provide a higher temperature...We followed his advice.

"Having built the furnace and provided the high temperature charcoal, we liquefied the glass. The handicraft workers then blew the liquefied glass into syringes...So we used our imagination and were able to produce syringes for the duration of the war."

When the Americans failed to provide needed materials for the hospital staff to make up for certain shortages, Dai improvised again—e.g., when a shortage of alcohol created a critical medical problem—infection.

"We had some antiseptic from the north," recounted Dai. *"But we were experiencing a severe shortage of alcohol at that time. So I sent a team of my people to see the 'ethnic people.'* (The Vietnamese referred to native minorities living in the jungles as the "ethnic people" or simply "ethnics.") *They were known to make alcohol. They made an alcoholic drink—a rice wine. But the problem for us was we did not know how to ferment it. So we sent people to the ethnics to learn what plant leaves to use and how to make this kind of fermentation. Later, we grew manioc which provided flour for the process as well."*

The #211 Hospital staff also learned about medicinal applications of other plants from the ethnics. Some were used to induce sleep; some had application as a vitamin source.

"We also learned from the ethnics, ways to fight malaria—such as with worms," reported Dai. *"The worm was cooked and the juice used to treat the patient."* While such treatment methods might seem questionable, Dai suggested, the ethnics—despite their backwardness—were, in their knowledge of plant applications, on the leading edge of medical science. *"Recently,"* he pointed out, *"there was an article in a French medical magazine in which these properties of the worm were recognized by the medical community."*

A limited supply of electrical power also presented the hospital staff with challenges. If an adequate water source was present, a small hydroelectric power source was built. But more often than not, they relied on fuel-powered generators. Prior to 1967, Dai remembered, *"there was no fuel with which to run the generators so our troops ambushed enemy convoys for the specific purpose of obtaining fuel."*

But battlefield medical emergencies could not wait for generator fuel. Surgeries had to be performed immediately upon the arrival of the wounded, whether fuel for the generators was available or not. It was not unusual, therefore, for Dai to use an alternate power source built around an unlimited supply of energy—man. Stationary bicycles were connected to the generators. When Dr. Dai was ready to operate on a patient, an able-bodied soldier began pedaling the bicycle. Lights above the operating table flickered as the generator came to life. Once the soldier established a rhythm to his pedaling, indicated by the light's steady glow, Dr. Dai would begin to operate. The soldier on the bicycle became the patient's lifeline, providing electrical power for lighting as well as all necessary support equipment required during surgery. As one soldier grew tired from pedaling, another quickly took his place.

"Sometimes," related Dai, *"I operated all night long with the lighting provided in this manner."*

The lack of electricity presented other problems too, such as no refrigeration for blood storage. Healthy soldiers could not donate blood as needed, as they had to reserve their strength for battle. Thus, responsibility for providing blood fell to the hospital staff.

"The staff of the hospital donated their own blood," explained Dai. *"I gave mine several times to patients...My donation was made only after, not before, an operation."* (A direct transfusion from donor to donee took place and, for that reason, never exceeded more than fifty to one hundred milliliters. Staff members were blood-typed prior to departing Hanoi so they knew to whom they could and could not give blood. In situations where the blood type of an unconscious soldier was unknown, Type O staff members provided blood as universal donors.)

A shortage of writing paper also posed special problems for the staff. Dai explained, *"We needed to write up patient records but lacked paper. At first, there was no paper at all. So, we carefully removed labels off of cans and used the blank side of the label."*

Each year, Dai recognized staff members for individual contributions, awarding them special certificates. But with writing paper so scarce, he used these certificates for patient records. When it was time for the award presentations, Dai became creative. *"I sliced bamboo lengthwise and used the inside surface to write the award certificate,"* he shared.

But the most constant and critical shortage for the hospital was food. Responsibility for food provision fell to a hospital staff already overburdened with the care and safety of a large patient population.

Dr. Dai described the shortage: *"We had almost no food supplies. The staff was responsible for providing its own food sources. For almost eight years, we constantly grew manioc. We received a very small amount of rice from the army. In addition to the rice, the army provided us with some salt and MSG. But we had to grow manioc for ourselves. Fortunately, the army provided rice for all the patients. So I had to organize a team of hunters and fishermen to do the hunting and fishing for the staff. For fishing, we were given nets; for hunting, we often used our AK-47s* (automatic rifle).

"We hunted wild pigs, deer and monkeys. The monkeys provided us with an ample food source. On one occasion, we actually ate a tiger. We hunted elephants—many, many elephants. The first year I was down south, our hunters killed eighteen elephants...One elephant provided several hundred kilograms of meat. But when you shoot an elephant, what meat you could not preserve you had to eat as fast as possible. Killing an elephant took care of our food shortage for about a month.

"The (elephant*) meat spoiled and started to smell within twenty-four hours, so we had to make provisions to preserve it. Sometimes we kept the meat in a stream where the cool water helped to preserve it longer. Sometimes we dried it. Other times we salted it, although there was a shortage of salt."*

Locating their prey was only part of the problem Dai's hunters faced. As they discovered immediately after their first elephant kill, other problems arose:

"The first time it was almost impossible to cut through the meat of the elephant due to its thick hide. So my surgeon suggested it might be best to cut the elephant's belly open, then step inside the belly and cut the meat from the inside out. My surgeon actually stood inside the elephant's belly, with blood up to his ankles, cutting away. It was terrible."

Some parts of the elephant were more preferable than others. *"One of the best parts of the elephant to eat,"* Dai shared for the benefit of elephant connoisseurs, *"was, first, the trunk and next the palms of the feet."*

It was impossible to remove all the meat from the animal's carcass. *"We could not always get all the meat from an elephant kill,"* said Dai. *"This was so for the meat found on the same side on which the elephant fell when it was shot. The meat on that side was very tightly compressed by the animal's bulk, so we could not cut through it."*

With the problem of carving up the elephant solved, a logistical problem still remained.

"We worked quickly to take as much meat as we could," explained Dai. *"Elephants were rarely killed near the field hospital—most of the time the kill took place fifty kilometers away so as not to give away the hospital's position to the enemy. But this meant the hunter had to return to the hospital to get staff people to go back to the kill site with him to help skin and carry the meat. Much time was lost in the transit—time in which the meat already started to spoil."*

As for taste, all the work involved hardly seemed worth the effort. *"Elephant meat—as well as tiger meat—was really not very good at all,"* confided Dai.

Little of any kill was wasted, however—even bones were put to use. Tiger and elephant bones were crushed and combined with a mixture to create a medicinal wine for rheumatism.

❋ ❋ ❋

One foray by a hunting party resulted in a grizzly discovery. While unable to remember the exact date (1970 or 1971), Dai recalled the incident occurred along Vietnam's border with Cambodia. The party stumbled across a helicopter crash site. Searching the wreckage for salvageable materials, they found the skeletal remains of six or seven occupants. Typically, these helicopters carried four or five South Vietnamese commandos and two Americans. They estimated from the jungle overgrowth and state of the remains that the helicopter crashed a year or two earlier. Teeth marks on some bones and the scattering of remains about the crash site suggested the bodies were long ago ravaged by wild animals. A Seiko watch was found hanging from the wrist bone of a skeleton inside the aircraft. It was engraved with a date and the words *"Buon Me Thuot,"* a locale in Dak Lak Province. Removing the watch from its skeletal caretaker, one member of the hunting party gently shook it. As he did so, it immediately began to tick—perhaps as a gentle reminder to those in the hunting party that time marches on for those of this life, long after the dead have departed for another.

❉ ❉ ❉

Hunting and fishing alone did not provide all essentials for the hospital staff's diet. They had to be farmers as well.

"We had a regulation," Dai said. *"Each unit was required to plant manioc. We had to plant up to one hundred hectares of it per year to get enough yield for our staff. Our manioc plantation was very, very primitive. First, we had to select the best location in the jungle, which was always a flat piece of land, near a stream. Usually there were many trees, so we cut them down and let them dry in place until March or April—until the approach of the rainy season. We then set fire to the field to clear it of the dead trees. Any trees remaining after the fire were removed. After that, we planted manioc, and rice. It was very difficult to plant rice. We used two sticks—one person was in front with the sticks, making two holes in the soil. Another person followed him, carrying seeds and placing them in each hole. We quickly buried the seeds or else the birds came and ate them. We then waited for the rainy season. Once the crops were sufficiently grown, we harvested them. This was done by hand—there was no possibility to use a tool, such as a scythe, because this kind of rice was very fragile. Also, we did not cut down plants for security reasons. While we harvested, aircraft were flying overhead. Leaving the plants in place provided concealment for the*

harvesters of the rice...All available staff personnel made the one day march to the fields to do the harvesting...They avoided attack by remaining concealed, squatting down to pick the rice off the plant and then putting it in a pack they carried on their back. In this manner, they were not discovered."

These plantations were twenty to thirty kilometers away from the hospital. Even if spotted by air during the burning process or as the rice paddies matured, usually they were left alone as pilots thought the fields belonged to the ethnics in the area. On those few occasions the Americans realized otherwise, Dai and his staff saw their hard work go for naught as fields were sprayed with chemical defoliants. In such cases, little could be done to salvage the rice, but harvesters moved quickly to salvage the manioc. Since the food source of the manioc is its underground root, Dai's men worked hard to retrieve it before the chemicals penetrated the soil.

❊ ❊ ❊

The Vietnamese soldiers living in this region often came into contact with ethnics whose roots went back thousands of years. Dai recalled one incident that occurred, involving a soldier and a beautiful, young ethnic girl. *"The ethnics are very simple people,"* he said. *"One day we stopped at a storehouse where the military was distributing rice to soldiers. I saw an ethnic girl standing nearby who appeared to be very angry. The ethnics are very good people but easy to anger. I approached her to find out what was bothering her. But she just kept repeating the same thing, 'One is one, two is also one.' She repeated it again and again, each time with growing disgust. I again tried to ask her what the problem was and what did she mean by 'One is one, two is also one.' She did not want to tell me but I insisted. Finally, she did.*

"A soldier apparently had convinced her, if he could touch her breast, he would give her a pin for her hair. She agreed and allowed him to do so. He proceeded to touch both her breasts—but only gave her one pin in return.

"'There were two touches,' she pleaded. 'So there should have been two pins.' When she finished, I asked her who it was that had touched her. I looked around and saw a young soldier who kept glancing at us

and looking away. I knew he was the one. I called out to him and asked why he had done that. He was very, very young, with a small moustache. I explained to him that it was not good to do what he did to this girl. And, I told him, now having done it; it was not fair to give her just the one pin. Looking very embarrassed, he informed me, 'I only had one pin to give her.'"

There were many occasions when necessities were obtained from the ethnics. To do so, one had to barter—a negotiating process at which the ethnics proved to be very good, as well as very informed, consumers. As Dai explained:

"They did not use money at all. In fact, they did not know how to use it, which did not matter since we, as soldiers, had no money anyway. So we made exchanges with the ethnics...If you wanted, for example, to buy a pig, you exchanged something of value for it. Once I gave my watch to an assistant with instructions to barter for a pig owned by an ethnic. But when my assistant returned, he said he was unable to do so. I asked why. He said because the ethnic informed him he could not swim with that watch on! The watch, I realized, was Russian-made and not waterproof. The ethnics often went into the water to fish and this ethnic was smart enough to realize the watch was not suitable for his needs."

Dai recalled another attempt to barter with an ethnic: *"One day I wanted to barter some shorts I had for a pig. I went to the nearby village. The ethnic who owned the pig told me he was willing to exchange it for my shorts. He only offered me a very small pig. I saw he had a larger pig and told him I wanted that one. He shouted he would give me the bigger pig if I gave him a bigger pair of shorts!"*

⁂ ⁂ ⁂

Some ethnics were brought back to Hanoi during the war to participate in a medical training program initiated by the Vietnamese. Dai remembered one ethnic in a Hanoi street market who found himself using money for the first time in his life, rather than bartering to buy what he wanted. As many denominations of Vietnamese currency bore the picture of the North

Vietnamese leader Ho Chi Minh, the process of using cash was somewhat confusing to him. Dai recounted the story: *"He was very confused over the use of money. He said, 'When I buy something, I give them paper money with Uncle Ho on it, but they return to me more money with Uncle Ho on it.'"*

✳   ✳   ✳

One incident involving an ethnic taught Dai what is illogical to one person may be very logical to another—as it simply is a matter of perspective. The ethnic was given a pin to wear bearing the likeness of Ho Chi Minh. But he insisted on wearing it upside down on his shirt pocket. When told he was wearing it improperly, he disagreed. He explained it was proper to wear it that way because, when he bent his head to look down at Uncle Ho, he saw him from the proper perspective—his head to Ho's head. If he wore it the other way, he explained, when gazing down at the pin he would see Uncle Ho upside down.

The ethnics observed some unusual traditions. One involved chiseling teeth down to the gums. It was their belief this practice, performed by the parents on their child at the age of twelve, ensured longevity and failure to do it meant an early death. Other ethnic traditions involved drawing body tattoos, particularly on the face, and ear piercing. (Richer families displayed a piece of ivory in the ear while poorer families adorned their ears with bamboo.)

As ethnics experienced city life in Hanoi, some began questioning their time-honored traditions. It was not long before they were getting teeth capped and stopped the practice of ear piercing.

When #211 Hospital first moved south, female ethnics commonly appeared bare-chested, Dai recalled. *"A family of ethnics was living near my hospital. One day I noticed the women started wearing bras. I realized then the women on my staff were bartering their bras for food."*

✳   ✳   ✳

At times, Dai performed his mission of mercy under very demanding conditions:

"Sometimes I spent all night in surgery, sleeping the next day. Many times bombs fell all around me. My operating room was above ground, but when it became too dangerous to operate there, we relocated to our underground bomb shelters...One afternoon in 1969; I started an operation in the above ground facility. I heard an approaching helicopter. The pilot must have seen us and reported our location as soon thereafter I heard jets overhead. This was about the time Sihanouk's regime was overthrown in Cambodia and the Americans started a campaign to bomb us along the border. As the American jets passed overhead, the helicopter I heard earlier dropped a smoke bomb to mark our location for them.

"A doctor was assisting me in the operation. As the attack began, we moved our patient to the underground shelter...IVs and other equipment were disconnected. The patient then was carried through a small tunnel and into the underground shelter. All the while, I kept my hands in my gloves and did not touch anything. Once inside the underground bunker, I continued the surgery. As I finished the operation, one jet fired rockets, destroying the facility where I had first started the operation."

⁂ ⁂ ⁂

During eight years of service in the south, Dai returned north on only one occasion. In October 1970, he was sent to Hanoi to participate in a meeting on surgical procedures for combat wounds. To provide better treatment for battlefield wounds, the conference was called to pool medical insights and surgical techniques of surgeons treating such wounds on a regular basis.

Seven other people accompanied Dai on his trip back up the Ho Chi Minh Trail.

"I walked the entire way," recalled Dai. *"It took me almost two months to make the trip north and a little more than two months to make the trip back. I spent an additional two months in Hanoi before returning south. There were many military stations along the Trail, so we would walk from one to another, shown the way by a local guide. After spending the*

night at a station, the next day a different guide provided escort services to the next station. Each station provided us with food—a fistful of rice—before our departure and water to fill our canteens. We just kept walking..."

The Trail Dai had transited on his way south in 1966 was quite different from the one he took north four years later. The route in 1970 was much more direct. As such, Dai did not feel compelled to cover the long distances each day he had to during his earlier trip. Also, the military stations were now much closer together allowing more frequent rest stops.

"We walked almost seven to eight hours between stations," said Dai. *"But later...the distance was shorter so we only had to walk four or five hours...I carried a very small chess set in my pack and when we stopped at a station I would play chess... But the pace of the horse going home is always faster than when it is leaving. As a result, some days going north we covered two sections of the Trail instead of just one...Every three or four days we stopped to wash, to rest some and then to continue on. After taking nearly two months to get to Quang Binh by foot, we were taken by truck to Hanoi."*

Just as Dai began his trip north, he experienced an ominous feeling. *"I had a premonition before I left—a sense that something bad was going to happen. During the trip, I constantly remembered a novel about World War II I once read entitled 'The Storm' by a Russian novelist. In that book, before something bad happened to the main character, he received a premonition...So I thought about the character in that novel.*

"Just as I departed for the trip, there was an air attack. I took shelter along the road and, although not wounded, kept thinking about the character in that novel. When I almost reached Hanoi, I encountered a group of people, which included some friends of mine, heading in the opposite direction. We were very happy to see each other. They handed me six or seven letters they had been carrying which were addressed to me. I went all night without reading the letters as we were having such a good time talking and catching up on things. Not until the next day, as my friends departed to continue their trip south, did I begin to read my letters.

"I was surprised there was no letter from my wife. I did not know why. But I had letters from several friends. I opened one. The first line read, 'We have received the bad news. I wanted to extend my condolences about your daughter.' Again, I was very surprised. I ran after my friends who were still within sight and asked them to tell me what happened to my daughter. They knew I did not know since I had not yet read the letters they delivered to me—and they were hoping they would not have to break the news to me. Then they told me she was involved in an accident. She fell off a building and died. When I finally saw my wife again, she told me and cried a lot about it."

The fourteen-year old girl Dai lost was his only child.

❖   ❖   ❖

It was not surprising such news would not have reached Dai. The postal system depended mostly on family and friends delivering letters to the front via travelers going south, or vice versa. It was a long, slow process—one continuously interrupted by aerial bombardments, the illness or death of the carrier, the tactical movements of the recipient's unit, etc.

"Letters took a very, very long time to reach us," explained Dai. *"It could take as long as six months or more. For example, my brother got married and sent me a letter to let me know. I sent a congratulatory letter back to him. He did not receive that letter until after he had his first child. Letters very easily got lost because they were being carried in this manner."*

The date a letter was written became very important to the recipient. Dr. Dai recalled a killed-in-action list released by Hanoi that identified a doctor with the same name as his who died in the south. *"My wife thought I had died. She cried for several months before receiving my letter"*—dated after the other Dr. Dai's reported death.

This somewhat unreliable mail system presented the enemy with an opportunity to conduct psychological operations against families in the north who did not know the status of their loved ones. *"I brought a letter from my friend, Mr. Minh, to his wife,"* said Dai. *"I gave it to her and she was very happy. I stayed in Hanoi for two months. During the second month, his wife came to me crying. She asked, 'Tell me the truth; is Minh still alive?' I told her, 'I am sure; I gave you the letter.' She said, 'But I received news he was taken prisoner by the enemy.'*

"*I could not believe this because the #211 Hospital, while near the fighting, was more in the rear. It did not make sense that it was attacked. But Minh's wife did not believe me. She told me a new group coming from the south had no letter from Minh for her. Again, I tried to explain but again she still did not believe me.*

"*I asked her, 'Why do you know Minh was taken prisoner?' She said, 'I heard it over the Saigon radio. They said Minh sent a message to the people in the north giving his address and names of others who also were surrendering.'*

"*After this I went to the military headquarters to inquire if my hospital was still safe. They said they just received a message from the hospital and there was no report of an attack or prisoners being taken. I went back to ask the man who brought mail from the south in the last group of arrivals whether anything happened to him during his transit. He told me he was attacked by a group of South Vietnamese commandos. To escape, he abandoned his mailbag, which the South Vietnamese captured.*

"*It became obvious to me what had happened,*" concluded Dai. "*The South Vietnamese had gone through the captured mail, extracting names and addresses to conduct psychological warfare against the intended recipients.*"

❖ ❖ ❖

As one in constant contact with the dying, wounded and ailing, Dai reported, in general, the health of the Vietnamese soldier was very poor.

"*In 1966 to 1968,*" he said, "*there was a very severe malaria problem in the south. Everyone who went to the Highlands came down with malaria for three to six months. We had no shortage of malaria cases.*"

One noted physician, an expert in the field, was sent south to assess the best way to treat the disease. Before he completed his study, he died, falling victim to malaria as well.

Diarrhea also was a serious medical problem.

"I was really surprised during the first three years we were in the south that there was such a high rate of diarrhea," related Dai. *"Many people died from acute diarrhea. Some became unconscious, with a high temperature. I performed autopsies on many of those who died and was astonished to find their intestines were thin as paper...Some of the victims had perforations of the gut from constant diarrhea...There was absolutely no control over it. It was terrible...In 1970, the rate decreased sharply.*

"There were also diseases caused by a lack of vitamins, such as Vitamins A and B," said Dai. *"A lack of Vitamin B can cause people to die from heart failure...A lack of Vitamin A can cause xerophalmia, creating blindness. Initially, we thought it was only due to the food shortage. But almost twenty years later, when I was working on the same issue, I was surprised to see it linked in a research paper to a shortage of Vitamin A...There were problems as well with diabetes and dysentery."*

There were also numerous cancer cases—the most prevalent being liver cancers. These victims could not be treated in the south and were sent to Hanoi. Many died while trying to return.

Dai proffered a possible cause for some of the maladies suffered by his fellow citizens while fighting in the south.

"It was only later," he explained, *"that I began to realize between 1966 and 1967 there was a very heavy spraying of Agent Orange. Exposure to it could have possibly caused damage to the immune system...I believe if one wanted to study the problem today one still could—simply by examining the bones of the people who died at that time. By doing so, one could measure the level of chemicals still within the bone marrow."*

✳ ✳ ✳

Other armies lurked in the jungles surrounding the #211 Hospital. Silently, they waited to ambush Dai and his unwary men. These were not armies of the two-legged kind but rather the multi-legged kind. In addition to the multitude of diseases making life miserable for the soldiers in the jungle, armies of insects gave no quarter to those who ventured into their domain.

"There were a lot of insects—terrible insects—in the jungle," Dai stated. *"Sometimes we came across millions of ticks. They bit and you pulled them off—but the head still remained in your skin. It was terrible...And there were many different kinds of ticks in the region. Some lived in the soil. When you walked along, they jumped onto your leg. There was also a kind of tick that lived on the leaves of trees that pounced on a victim passing by. These ticks even got into your nose. They were absolutely terrible.*

"Initially, I did not know about ticks. A patient came to see me who was bleeding from his nose. I did not know why. So I turned him over to an assistant on my staff who examined his nostrils. He discovered a tick...After latching on, it had grown bigger and bigger. It could live for months in your nose...Sometimes we saw the ticks in long columns moving through the jungle. They were all around. If you stopped for a short time to remove them, others started taking their place...So we moved very quickly through tick-infested areas ...We discovered that ticks did not like water. We went into the water and did not have to worry about them—once in the water, we only worried about leeches."

⁂   ⁂   ⁂

One thing not in short supply for the #211 Hospital was combat wounded. NVA soldiers fell victim to an awesome array of weapons in America's arsenal. Whether by aerial or artillery bombardment, by small arms fire or mines, combat casualties for the hospital staff were a regular occurrence. Dai shared insights on the nature of the wounds these combat casualties suffered.

"There were all kinds of wounds," he reported. *"There were wounds created by the CBUs (Cluster Bomb Units) which, at first, were difficult to locate and treat. If you ever saw a CBU explode, you wondered how it was possible for anybody to survive within a one hundred meter radius. As it exploded, hundreds of small pellets were released. For soldiers in their bunkers at the time of the attack, there was no problem. But for those in the open, it resulted in a terrible wound."*

Among the weapons instilling the most fear in soldiers were mines.

"There were many different kinds of weapons the Americans were using, including mines," explained Dai. *"Some were magnetic; there were also those that when stepped on, jumped up and exploded.* (This was an anti-personnel mine known as a "Bouncing Betty" which, when activated, released a spring loaded explosive device as the victim removed his foot. The device sprang into the air waist high, where it exploded.) *Our soldiers were taught if they ever stepped on such a mine to keep their foot on it. In doing so, while it might explode, their injury would be limited—perhaps the loss of a leg. But, if they failed to do so, the explosive was propelled into the air where a much more serious injury—or even death—might result.*

"There were also leaf mines, made very similar in size and appearance to an actual leaf. They were very difficult to locate. These too maimed and killed. Another type of mine dropped from aircraft would, after impact with the ground, shoot trip wires out in many different directions. You could not see these wires—they were very, very tiny. If you saw the mine and tried to run off in a different direction, you could very easily trip another wire, causing the mine to detonate."

❊   ❊   ❊

Surprisingly, the patient population of the #211 Hospital enjoyed a better survival rate than that of hospitals in Hanoi. Dai had his theory as to why this happened:

"The most severely wounded people died at the front before they could be evacuated to our field hospital. After the war, I calculated the death rate of patients who died from all different kinds of wounds at our hospital. That mortality rate overall was lower than the rate for those people wounded in Hanoi and taken to the hospital. The only way I can account for this was because our most severely wounded people never made it to our hospital."

Infection was a major problem for battlefield wounded who did make it to the hospital.

"*This,*" according to Dai, "*was a big problem. There was a group at the hospital responsible for developing procedures for treating wounds. We did not follow ordinary treatment procedures. For example, originally we closed all wounds—but later found if we did so in the field hospital, the wound tended to get infected. So we learned not to close a wound—we left it open. We also found the same was true in the case of an arterial wound. If we tried to sew the arterial wound and restore the artery, it most assuredly got infected. So we found the best treatment was to close both ends of the artery, on either side of the wound, leaving the wound open.*

"*We made a very interesting discovery about our people in doing this. We found because of all the walking they were doing on the Trail and through the jungles they, in many cases, developed new arteries* (known as "collaterals"), *which provided an ample blood supply through the effected limb. Because of this, when we closed a main artery, the blood vessels from the muscle and other places continued to supply blood to the limb...When operating on a leg under normal conditions and stopping circulation through the artery, there is a very high risk of infection if blood is not flowing to the lower part of the extremity. But we found in our soldiers, because they were getting so much exercise, these collaterals were performing the function of the arteries, providing the critical blood supply to the rest of the limb...We found ourselves using very simple procedures.*"

❋ ❋ ❋

Among the many casualties, Dai's hospital staff attempted to save were American POWs.

"*We treated two wounded American prisoners in my hospital sometime in 1968 or 1969. Wounded or sick POWs were brought to us since we were the largest hospital in the area. Unfortunately, both died.*

"*One died after one or two days, suffering a very severe wound to his backside in which his entire sacrum was lost. Although he was conscious when he arrived, neither I nor anyone else on my staff spoke English at that time, so I do not know what he said before he died. We could not communicate with him. We buried him near the hospital.*

"The second POW arrived about the same time with an abdominal wound. He died several days, maybe five days, later."

While the names of the POWs and their grave locations were recorded by Dai, those records, unfortunately, were later lost. The loss happened after the hospital's position was discovered by a reconnaissance aircraft. In a rush to move the hospital, Dai's staff inadvertently discarded the records—the locations and identities of the two Americans now known to no one but God.

❈   ❈   ❈

While #211 Hospital was able to maintain a relatively high survival rate for its patients, it lost an average of ten soldiers a month. The dead received simple burials. Burial teams wrapped the deceased in the nylon tent each soldier was issued, and then placed the body in a bamboo coffin. For security reasons and to deny the enemy intelligence on force losses, burial sites were scattered.

No grave markers were used. The initial practice was to mark the tree nearest the grave as a reference. But, it was found normal tree growth and weather exposure quickly took its toll, erasing the mark. Later, a policy of leaving no outside marker was adopted. Instead, a piece of paper with name, birth date and home province of the deceased was placed in an empty penicillin bottle, left inside the coffin. A written record was made of where the remains were buried. This same practice was followed for American POWs who died in captivity.

❈   ❈   ❈

Like many of his comrades, Dai experienced B-52 attacks. *"The B-52 bombings came very regularly, almost always at night, with the same time interval between each run. Thus, we were able to calculate, immediately after the second run, when to expect the third and subsequent runs. We then planned accordingly.*

"There were two rules to follow for these attacks: first, to build an A-shaped shelter; second, to put a shovel in each shelter. Often we knew the bombings were coming ahead of time. If we were surprised about anything, it was only the time interval between runs. Sometimes the

bombings went on all night long, but the intervals between runs were very constant—whether every thirty minutes, every fifty minutes, etc.

"After each bombing run, the procedure was for our people to call over to the next bunker to ensure everyone was safe. Our bunkers rarely received direct hits during the attacks. Most of the wounded received their wounds or injuries from the bomb's secondary effect—its concussion, which could collapse a shelter. We called out to the next bunker over to make sure everyone was all right after a bombing run. If there was no answer, we ran over to the bunker with our shovels to dig them out. While doing so, we looked at our watches to ensure we were back in our own shelters before the next run. If it was determined, the interval between runs was thirty minutes, after twenty-five minutes the signal was given for everyone to return to their shelters.

"In the bunker, we sat down and covered our ears, to protect against the concussion, and waited for the next run. During the attack, the proper position to sit in the shelter was not with one's back against the bunker's wall; rather, it was to sit in the center. There was a special way to sit: squatting, with hands over the ears, arms bent and parallel to the ground, legs and arms spread wide apart. The limbs were kept apart so if the soil collapsed, there was a greater likelihood for an air pocket to be formed.

"We did not sit with our backs against the wall so as to avoid injury from a bomb's concussion. A bomb could hit several meters away yet its blast or concussion still be felt reverberating through the bunker wall, causing injury.

"After one attack run, we used the interval of time before the next bombing to rescue our friends. Our A-shaped bunkers had bamboo ventilation tubes extending from the shelter to the ground to provide occupants with air. In removing the loose soil, the rescue teams left the ventilation tubes in place to maintain the air supply.

"If we were not rescuing people during the bombing interval, people used the time to relax. They smoked; they told funny stories; they caught a breath of fresh air outside their shelters. Then, once the five-minute warning signal was given, they went back underground and got into position. If a shelter collapsed after the first bombing, the rescuers were *at risk because we did not yet know what the bombing interval was. But after the two first bombings we knew the interval and relaxed in-between runs."*

In a final reflection on the war against America, Le Cao Dai clearly understood why Hanoi prevailed in its struggle. Victory went only to the side with the greatest motivation to win. That motivation existed for the North Vietnamese, Dr. Dai observed; it did not for the Americans. *"The motivating force in this war,"* he said, *"was the feeling of all Vietnamese people we had to reunify the country. Everybody felt this way. On the other hand, for the American people, as a nation, and especially for those who served in Vietnam, there never was a clear understanding of what exactly they were fighting for. There was never any doubt or hesitation on our side what we had to do—and would do. It was everybody's desire to have peace—but to have peace with reunification."*

Before his death on April 15, 2002, Dr. Dai had his own medical practice in Hanoi where he also served as a consultant on environmental protection issues and technology transfer. He worked on war-related environmental issues, such as Agent Orange contamination, which, for long after his death, will continue to plague his country.

HEALING THE WOUNDS OF WAR

Nguyen Huy Phan had many opportunities to bear witness to the devastating effects of battle wounds. As a surgeon in 1953, he participated in the war against the French; from 1964 to 1975, he fought against the Americans; and in 1979, he served in the border skirmish against the Chinese.

His experiences qualified him to speak with authority on the nature of wounds inflicted upon combatants from a vast arsenal of weapons. Over the years, he observed firsthand the increasing capability of weapons to kill and incapacitate—the result of technology and man's endless search for more effective ways to wage war. As such, technology evolved, the military surgeon's knowledge had to keep pace with how best to treat the special wounds these weapons inflicted.

Phan's responsibilities during the war involved not only mending soldiers' wounds to get them back on their feet and fighting again as quickly as possible, but also to analyze them to improve diagnostic and treatment times. Based on the constant introduction of new weapons technology by the U.S. onto the battlefield, this responsibility occupied much of Phan's time.

Phan organized and headed teams of medical personnel to study wound characteristics of new weapons to determine how best to diagnose and treat a particular wound. As a result, he acquired a rather unique perspective on dealing with combat wounds. It was a perspective, which, until his death in 1997, made him a world authority on one of the most unique, yet psychologically devastating, wounds a combatant could suffer. Phan became a pioneer in the field of male organ reconstructive surgery.

Experience is a great teacher. Unfortunately, for Vietnam's medical community, much of that experience was war related. The war with France impressed upon Hanoi the import of having trained medical personnel who physically moved with the combat troops. That war revealed many medical support shortcomings for the army, shortcomings addressed during the brief peace North Vietnam enjoyed prior to its conflict with America. Phan explained some of these and what remedies were applied:

"After 1954, there was a short period of peace—from 1954-1963. During that time, our government sent many young doctors to other countries—European countries—to improve their skills and knowledge. We had the opportunity to organize medical specialties within the army. So when war with the U.S. started, we already had specialists in many new areas. For example, during the war with France, we had no plastic surgery specialty; but during the war with America, we had enough specialists working in various fields, such as hematology, orthopedics, plastic surgery, and so on. These people were organized into specialized surgical teams with enough equipment to develop their specialty...We had a medical school not only in Hanoi, but in other big cities too. These schools continued to create additional specialties. During the war, these young specialists came to help from time to time. Those who worked regularly in the army's medical units were sent back to study at their medical schools for some months before returning to the military units. It was a kind of an assistance training that provided us with enough specialists to meet the army's needs.

"During the war with America, it was difficult for us to stay in one place. In order to follow the army, we organized mobile surgical teams. I served as chief of a mobile surgical hospital...At times, it was impossible to move the whole hospital so we organized mobile surgical teams of about 20-30 or 50-60 people, depending on specific needs...in order to put medical support on the battle line, closer to combat troops, where we could attend to the wounded.

"We had some experiences with these mobile units during the war with the French. But, by the time of the Vietnam war, we had more units, more teams, and many more specialists because we had almost ten years more of specialist training in countries friendly to us, such as the former Soviet Union, Hungary, and Bulgaria. We sent many specialists to study in places like Berlin, Czechoslovakia, Cuba and other locations—a practice we continued during the American war. After specialization, they returned to Vietnam to serve in the army. So we had enough specialists.

"We did not distinguish a difference between the military and the civilian sectors at that time. The army cooperated with the civilian sector and the military surgeons also served the civilian people if they needed our help. Our soldiers and officers were treated by civilian

doctors, when it was possible to do so. When military units were having difficulties, they shared duties with the civilian medical community. There was full cooperation and a good understanding between the two sectors, which was very helpful. Without full cooperation, it would have been difficult. During the war, I can say the best medical specialists were serving in the army.

"All our units were provided with comparatively good medical care because they received very strong logistical support from friendly countries such as the former Soviet Union, China, etc. They provided us with the means to do our work—the equipment, the instruments, the medicines, the pharmaceuticals—but not with personnel as our specialists were all our own. Personnel from other countries were offered, but we refused their services. It was an issue of self-determination, of responsibility for the people...and our independence in all our activities. So we refused all such offers. On the enemy's side, the Saigon government relied on America's help. Even other foreign troops participated in the war with the Americans. But on our side, we were alone.

"The mobile surgical hospital had 200 medical corps personnel assigned to it...Twenty-five percent were doctors. Sometimes it received as many as 500 wounded soldiers in a short period. So we operated day and night. At times, we performed surgeries 24 hours a day for as long as two or three straight days. And we had to do so occasionally under abnormal conditions—sometimes even in trenches or in bunkers."

Phan and his highly motivated medical colleagues pooled their knowledge and expertise when new types of weapons took their toll on the battlefield. This technique was very helpful after the introduction of a particularly devastating bomb used by the U.S. known as a "CBU" or Cluster Bomb. The CBU contained about 300 iron pellets, each no more than 5.5 millimeters in diameter. When the bomb exploded, it propelled the pellets in various directions. For the unfortunate victim caught within the blast area and not immediately killed, these mini-missiles either passed all the way through the body or remained embedded within it.

The pellet left an almost indiscernible entry/exit wound on the victim's body, posing a serious medical problem. Without a clearly visible wound, it was very difficult for the treating surgeon to make a diagnosis—a fact that obviously affected his ability to treat the wound. Such a diagnostic delay increased the likelihood of the patient dying.

Cranial wounds compounded the diagnostic problem. In many cases, the pellet pierced only one side of the cranium.

"The intra-cranial wound was so special," explained Phan, *"because it was just like a billiard ball."* The force of the pellet's momentum caused it to ricochet repeatedly within the cranial cavity before finally coming to rest inside.

"The pellet entered into the cranium, through the brain, and ricocheted down and back," continued Phan. *"It had a zigzag trajectory...We had a lot of cranial and facial wounds with the CBUs. Sometimes we had many wounds from only one bomb—wounds extending from head to foot. The army medical corps focused from the beginning on these wounds and organized a special group of doctors, surgeons and other specialists to specifically study this problem. I was one of the people in charge of finding a solution for CBU wounds.*

"I studied this problem with the help of different organizations within our army, including the engineering corps. We spent three or four months on a solution—and finally found one.

"We wrote many papers on this problem, as well as others. Sometime between 1968-1970, these papers were brought to other countries to share our experiences with their surgeons. I was General Secretary of this doctor group. The papers dealt with how to diagnose and surgically treat various wounds. Through our experiences, our allies were able to lower their casualties on the battlefield.

"Before our study, it was so difficult, so complicated to treat people. But afterwards, we became experienced in these matters; we knew how to diagnose and treat wounds in the best way. We re-wrote all the guidebooks for army surgeons. The best specialists, the leaders in

different specialties, shared their experiences, providing solutions in each specialty. We had guidelines for each young surgeon which had to be followed in the treatment of their cases."

❊   ❊   ❊

As to the ultimate diagnostic solution to the CBU problem, Phan continued, *"Before the use of CBUs, such cranial wounds were unknown...But with CBUs, the entry hole was so small you could not see it. Since the pellet was so small, it left a very small skin puncture. What we learned to do to diagnose this type of wound was very simple—we took the victim's skin and squeezed it to see if blood...or air...came out. In this way, one could immediately recognize where the entry hole was...Repeatedly we grabbed segments of skin on a part of the body and squeezed it. This solved the problem quite easily."*

Ultimately, Phan's group also discovered there was no need to remove all the pellets imbedded in a wound.

"We discovered the pellets were not very contaminated," he explained. *"So we let them remain in the wound for a long time, especially since they were small. In the beginning, many doctors tried to get all the pellets out, creating other problems. So after discovering we did not have to take all the pellets out, we only focused on treating the wound."*

Although CBU wounds created their own special problem and solution, other types of wounds required extensive treatment and recovery time. Most notable were napalm wounds.

"The burn areas were very severe—third or fourth degree burns which were very deep and very serious...The wounded remained hospitalized for long periods of time, for long and expensive treatments. Afterward, it was so difficult to restore the function of the affected area due to the severity and deepness of the burn. We had great difficulty with napalm. There was also a very high risk of infection because the patient stayed in the hospital for so long...Doctors devoted much time to taking care of these burns. They were painful..."

Having treated wounded in both the French and American wars, Dr. Phan noted a major shift between the two in the prevalence of the types of wounds soldiers experienced on the battlefield. *"During the war with France, the wounds were mainly from small arms; but against America, most came from rockets and bombs...from aviation and, to some extent, heavy artillery. There were much fewer cases of wounds from small arms."*

While shortages of medical supplies, equipment, care, etc. were more of a problem for North Vietnamese forces fighting in the south, there were times when even Hanoi felt the pinch. However, alleged Phan, this never created a problem in treating American POWs.

"I remember in 1969 to 1970, I had the occasion to operate on two pilots who had been shot down in North Vietnam. I cannot remember their names—the reason for this was at the time each one received a special Vietnamese name." (Typically, jailers used Vietnamese nicknames for POWs as they had difficulty pronouncing American names.)

"The pilots were brought to us by medical units from the front. These were difficult cases, sometimes requiring specially qualified medical care. I remember they both had legs broken from jumping out of their planes...One was probably shot down in a suburb of Hanoi while the other was brought in from farther out. But they had not been shot down in Hanoi itself as they had received emergency care before coming to us. When they reached us, their broken legs had already been fixed but they needed specialized care. I was serving as a surgeon generalist at the time—one of two chiefs in the surgical field at the central city military hospital. I was a lieutenant colonel. I met with them and asked how they were injured and about the care, they had received. I sent them for an x-ray examination, after which we performed surgery. Very soon afterward, they were taken to Hoa Lo Prison, better known as the 'Hanoi Hilton.' They stayed there and, if they needed care later, other doctors went to the jail to care for them. If their doctors had difficulties, they consulted us...We did not follow up on these cases—but other specialists did. It was their duty—a special duty for staff people."

The more extreme shortages experienced by North Vietnamese soldiers fighting in the south sometimes necessitated the use of field expedients. One critical shortage was saline solution. Coconut milk, mixed with other ingredients was an expedient field replacement.

As to medical conditions in the field, Phan reported, *"We had some problems with infection, but they were not severe as we had a great deal of experience with war wounds. We knew the best way to treat combat wounds was to leave them open and not suture them.* (This is a procedure now followed by many American doctors as well.)...*We operated carefully to prevent infections. Occasionally we made mistakes, but we regularly organized meetings among doctors, surgeons, and nurses to limit such occurrences. After a mistake, we immediately organized a small group to chart the problem, to recognize what had been done well and what had not. We invited good specialists from other units to meet with us too. During the war, we held meetings regularly, sometimes very close to the battlefield."*

The explosive power of U.S. weaponry and the shower of shrapnel it generated caused many male victims to suffer a rather unique war wound—a severed penis. While not life threatening, it was a wound that imposed immense psychological pain and trauma upon its victims. Such suffering motivated Phan to study the best way to reconstruct the organ. He explained:

"During the war, I developed a significant specialty in this area because there were so many cases in which the penis had been severed...I spent many months studying the matter. After doing so, I surgically reconstructed the victim's penis and other parts of the genital organs. This included not only cosmetic, but also functional, restoration as well, so later the victim could have children normally. Afterwards, these patients got married and enjoyed sex like normal people. I shared my experiences with my colleagues in other countries. For example, in 1979 I presented a paper in Paris, at the 24th Congress of the Plastic Reconstructive Surgery of France. By that time, I had performed twenty-five surgeries—all total reconstructions of the penis...on which I reported at the Congress. Since then, I have performed ten surgeries using more sophisticated techniques such as microsurgery."

After the war, microsurgery made reconstructive surgery of this organ much easier—for both doctor and patient. Comparing the reconstruction process today to his first case in 1968, Phan explained:

"Instead of six reconstructive operations requiring six to seven months of hospitalization, now only one operation is necessary using the micro-

technique—and the patient need stay in the hospital for just three weeks...Sometimes the war provided us with the opportunity to improve our skills in certain areas and to study new techniques. So, in a way, it contributed to the progress of our medical science...

"We rebuilt the penis by taking matter from the abdominal wall. We transferred nerves from the arm. The abdominal material and nerves were then transplanted to the pubic area...We implanted cartilage into it—to restore not only the form but also the function. The result was the patient could void his bladder while standing; he could enjoy a normal sex life. This became especially so with the evolution of this new technique. Now, not only can the penis be restored but the erotic sensation as well by the use of the nerve from the forearm—something known as the forearm flap or so-called Chinese forearm flap...we implant the cartilage, restore the urethra...everything concerning the reconstruction is done in one stage."

Dr. Phan's expertise in reconstructive and plastic surgery was well recognized as he was tasked during the Vietnam war with altering the physical appearance of a very important secret agent, Tu Mau (pictured below, before and after), whose identity was discovered by the South Vietnamese in Saigon, where he was an operative for the Hanoi government. Tu Mau successfully escaped but was considered so critical to Hanoi's operations in the south that it was decided he would return to Saigon—after his appearance was surgically changed by Dr. Phan so Tu Mau could not be recognized. (Phan reported he had to perform the surgery twice on Tu Mau, as his commander was still able to identify him after the first operation.)

＊　＊　＊

Two generations of Dr. Phan's family experienced the tragedy of war.

During the French struggle, Phan's father was living in Hanoi as a teacher. Recognizing a need for a school in the province of Bac Tai, he went there to establish one. He was well known within the village as a man who did much for the community.

One day in 1950, as Phan's father was teaching school, a French infantry company entered the village. In the process of trying to escape with the children, Phan's father was fired on by French warplanes. He and two children were instantly killed. Only after the French left the village, were the villagers able to recover the bodies at night and bury them.

At the time of his father's death, Phan was living elsewhere and was unable to return to the village. Of four brothers, only Phan's youngest brother, Duong, then 16, was living at home with his mother. The death of their father prompted Duong to volunteer for the army to fight the French. Denied this due to his young age, Duong then chose to go to China to study. Sixteen years later, Duong volunteered for the army again—this time to fight the Americans. At 32, age was no longer a problem. The father of a two-year old girl and a newborn son, Duong went off to war. He never saw his children again. One year later, in 1967, he was killed in action.

The tragedy of Phan's younger brother's death was compounded by the fact the family had no information as to the location of his remains. In the Vietnamese culture, it is important a family be able to honor their dead by visiting the gravesite of a departed loved one. It is also an important aspect of the life cycle: the remains are buried in the village of birth; those remains then nurture crops grown on the land; those crops then feed surviving family members. If Duong's remains were not found, Phan and his brother's family would be unable to share in this cultural tradition.

Phan embarked upon a 17-year search for his brother's remains. With the help of some of his brother's fellow servicemen, that search ended in 1984 in an empty field near Danang.

"Many people gave us information about my brother," explained Phan. *"One of the problems we encountered was that, since the war, with new construction or land being prepared for cultivation, remains of war dead were constantly being relocated. My brother's remains were relocated three different times before we found them. There was a metal marker on the gravesite that had his name and date of his death. The gravesite was located about 50 to 60 meters off the provincial road. Other bodies were nearby. While I am not a forensic specialist, I identified his remains as I recognized his teeth. The body was brought back to Hanoi. His wife and children were very happy about its recovery and continue to visit the gravesite each year. Both they and my dead brother,"* concluded Phan, *"are now at peace."*

DOCTOR PAIN

Vo Hoang Le bears the scars of a combat warrior. He was wounded six times in his 43-year military career—twice during the war against the French and four times against the Americans.

The latter wounds provide an appreciation for the range of weaponry available within the U.S. arsenal. For Le, 1967 was not a good year: from an air attack, he bears the scars of napalm on his right elbow; from a ground attack later in the year, he shows the marks of shrapnel from an M-79 grenade on his upper left arm; from an artillery attack, he displays the healed wounds on his back from a round that exploded too closely. But Le's most devastating wound was suffered the following year. A round from an M-60 machine gun struck his hand, exploding on impact, severing part of the hand and little finger. As he sought medical assistance, a nurse hesitated to amputate the lower portion of his hand as it dangled lifelessly. So, Le pulled out his knife and, without anesthesia, cut off the now useless appendage.

You might assume Le was a front line infantry soldier. In fact, his primary mission was not to take life—but, as a surgeon, to preserve it. Stationed in the tunnels of Cu Chi, a massive tunnel system just outside of Saigon, Le was involved in the daily struggle for survival—for himself as well as his patients. His wounds were a brutal testimony to the intensive fighting that took place at Cu Chi.

Le, affected by the loss of his hand and unable to perform surgeries, limited himself to a supervisory role—one he performed until the war's end.

Le's military service was not untypical for many of those who served in the army. He joined in 1947, quickly gaining his *"baptism by fire."* Only fourteen at the time, he felt compelled to join the fight for liberation against the French. Assigned to the medical corps, he trained first as a nurse and later as a doctor. Acquiring most of his skills by field training, Le developed expertise as a brain surgeon. When the war against the French ended, he went north to sharpen that skill further. In 1960, as the struggle with Saigon intensified, he was again sent south. The battlefields of South Vietnam became home to Le for the next fifteen years.

The fighting against the French and, later, the Americans, took a heavy toll on Le's family. By the fall of Saigon in 1975, seven family members had lost their lives.

Le's father was a village chief. When the French captured the village, they arrested Le's father and put him in prison, where he died in 1947. His body was never returned to the family and, to this day, Le has been unable to locate the remains.

Le's mother did not fare much better. Arrested by the Diem regime, she was imprisoned and tortured. Released shortly thereafter, she died in 1961. Of his four siblings—three brothers and one sister—none survived the war. All joined the army and died fighting the Americans. The remains of one brother are still missing.

While the loss of parents and all siblings was a high price for any individual to pay for victory, a final pound of flesh was extracted from Le in 1969. His wife, Nguyen Thi Than, two years his senior, was also a doctor. A captain in the same unit as Le, she joined him in the south, serving in Binh Duong (what is now Song Be Province). Normally, adequate warning of an impending B-52 attack was received. However, on this particular day in 1969, the attack came suddenly and unannounced. *"The attack came so quickly, we hurried to hide ourselves in our shelters. Everyone was assigned to a numbered shelter. My wife and I were in different shelters. Just as I got into mine, there was a tremendous explosion nearby. It was so close part of my shelter was destroyed. The concussion left me so I could not hear anything. When the bombing finally stopped, we crawled outside. We went to those shelters that had been destroyed to help the occupants. Many bombs had fallen. Unfortunately, one shelter suffered what was almost a direct hit. I knew my wife was in it. Many people rushed to look for survivors. It took an hour to reach the occupants of the collapsed shelter. I tried to dig but was pulled back by others. Three people were brought out—including my wife. Examining the victims, you could see the effects of the bombing and its concussion—blood flowed from their mouths and noses. They were given urgent treatment and CPR, but all three died. My wife was only thirty-eight years old."*

Of the fifteen years Le served in the south, the majority was spent in Cu Chi. Heavy defoliation of the area by the U.S. forced his hospital underground.

"We fought above ground and when the enemy advanced, we then went underground," Le explained. *"During the period 1960-1968, it was very difficult for us because there was much enemy activity. We constructed an entire hospital underground—complete with operating room, lab, pharmacy, recovery rooms, etc. We carved these rooms out from the surface to a depth of three to four meters. We erected support beams and a ceiling, the latter normally made from metal apron sheets the Americans used for their airstrips. We then covered everything with soil and vegetation.*

Entrance to an underground hospital complex

"The different parts of the hospital were connected by tunnels. Inside, we also dug water wells. Empty cartridge boxes were used for toilets. At night, we took these up to the surface to clean. Our rooms were no bigger than 2.5 meters by 3 meters. We found it dangerous to have rooms any larger as they might collapse or easily be discovered.

"The operating room was sufficient to accommodate a doctor, assistant, equipment operator, anesthesiologist and nurse. Sometimes, for major surgeries such as stomach operations, we had two assistants involved so six people were in the room. Generators provided lighting but when we feared the noise of the generator might give away our position, we used flashlights attached to our helmets during surgeries.

"At times, many times, we had no anesthesia. In such cases, we used Novocain for small operations; for major operations, Novocain on the spine or vein of the spinal cord was used. The patient was awake but could not feel anything. Even Novocain was in short supply, however, and we had to water it down. When this happened, I informed the patient that, while we had enough Novocain to deaden his internal organs to pain, we did not have enough to inject into the skin to deaden the pain of the initial incision. We conducted stomach operations in this way.

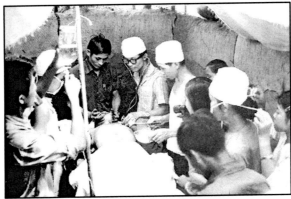

Surgical Bunker

"In many cases, we lacked both anesthesia and Novocain but, due to the seriousness of the patient's wounds, could not delay surgery. A soldier might have a wound so badly infected with gangrene it would smell and a limb had to be amputated immediately without anything to deaden the pain of surgery. After informing him there was no anesthesia, he was told, alternatively, if we failed to operate immediately, the infection would spread and he would die. It was a very difficult thing to do—for both doctor and patient. But there was no choice—we had to do it."

"If an arm was to be amputated, we tied a tourniquet above the point of amputation. A knife was used to cut through the meat of the arm. When we reached the bone, we used a saw. We tried to complete the amputation in fifteen minutes. During surgery, the patient screamed and, due to intense pain, lost consciousness. Although there were times a patient initially refused surgery without anesthesia, after reflection, he

knew there was no choice. He knew it was a struggle between life and death—and in the end he always chose life."

Le noted the contrast in medical service available to his patients as opposed to the Americans: *"My patients suffered greatly during these operations. Here we were, isolated by the enemy in these tunnels, just outside of Saigon where medical facilities were readily available to alleviate pain and suffering for the enemy wounded. It was terrible seeing our soldiers in pain, knowing relief was available—but not accessible—nearby. While our soldiers suffered, enemy wounded enjoyed much greater comfort."*

The terrible medical conditions endured by the guerrillas in some situations were, perhaps, best illustrated by Le's explanation of how brain surgeries were conducted: *"On occasion, we performed brain surgery without anesthesia or Novocain. The need for this kind of operation arose to save a victim's life; for example, a bullet lodged in a soldier's brain had to be removed. If a limited amount of Novocain was available, we injected it into the scalp after shaving the patient's head. After cutting through the scalp, the problem was trying to cut through the skull to operate on the brain.*

"To do this, several holes first were drilled into the skull. Normally, a special surgical drill was used as it limits penetration by the drill bit so as not to puncture the brain accidentally. We had none so were forced to use a regular hand drill, thus running the constant risk of damaging the brain during surgery.

"We put antiseptic on the drill before beginning. The skull has two layers—one white in color, the other pink. The surgeon had to know how deep to drill. We had to rely on our experience and knowledge of layer thickness of the skull to determine exactly how far to drill. If I were to write a book about this, readers would never believe me—but it is true. After drilling a series of holes in a circular pattern, we used a special tool—a pincher—to grab a hold of the skull bone between the holes to either pull chips of skull bone away or enlarge the holes we drilled. Sometimes dental pliers were used.

"Instead of pinchers, another technique involved using coarse wire as a saw, inserting it down into one hole and up out of the next, then

grabbing the two ends and pulling it back and forth to slice through the bone in between. This procedure was repeated between each set of holes as pieces of the skull bone were chipped away, exposing the brain underneath.

"By the end of surgery, there was rarely a large enough piece of skull bone to fit back into the skull as the missing section of bone came out in many small pieces. We had to leave the hole in the skull and just sew the scalp flap back over it. After doing so, one could see the scalp over the open part of the skull bone 'palpitating'—much like a heart beating. Such patients required additional surgery later to insert a metal plate over the hole to protect the still exposed brain (protected only by the thin layer of scalp).

"We constantly were forced to come up with creative ways to treat the wounded. It was much like treatments by the Egyptians thousands of years earlier. One technique they applied was for an amputee to briefly place his bleeding stump into boiling oil. This caused veins in the stump to shrink and, as a result, reduced bleeding. In our case, to reduce bleeding, we tied line around the stump—not medical thread but usually parachute threads provided by the Americans."

"We came up with various innovative treatments. We applied turmeric or honey to a wounded area as an antiseptic solution. When we performed tracheotomies, we often lacked the normal medical tube to insert into the patient's windpipe, so we used young shoots of bamboo. To operate on broken bones, we searched airplane wrecks for small screws to use to keep the bone in place. These screws worked very well. We also used coconut shells as IV bottles. The exhaust pipe from a downed helicopter or aircraft was good, when cut in half, to use as a brace for a broken bone."

Le's hospital was faced with its greatest number of casualties during the Tet offensive of 1968.

"Our hospital was just a transitory facility. The wounded received immediate care from us but we had to send them out to permanent hospitals for specialized care. If our treatment was sufficient, the patient was sent back to the front. We could adequately handle about sixty to seventy patients at a time. During Tet, we received a thousand

wounded soldiers. We treated them before distributing them to other hospitals where they were safer. We waited for a break in the fighting and then quickly moved them."

There was little alternative to the hardship Le's patients endured. Limited medical supplies, combined with a constant influx of wounded whose lives teetered on the brink of life or death, did not afford Le the luxury of delaying treatment for a more ideal time. Medical conditions were nightmarish but he said, *"it was a price we paid for victory."*

THE FIGHT ENDS BUT THE REAL BATTLE BEGINS

Having fought in the south for more than a year, Lieutenant Nguyen Van Khanh was an experienced combat veteran. Commanding an infantry platoon of Division 312 in 1967, he was preparing a surprise reception for U.S. Marines soon to be landing on a hilltop at Khe Sanh.

Khe Sanh, like the Ho Chi Minh Trail, represented a test of wills between the U.S. and North Vietnam. A combat base had been established by the Americans at Khe Sanh primarily for operations by which the Ho Chi Minh Trail could be interdicted and to bait NVA commander General Giap into massing his forces to attack the somewhat isolated base camp. (In a September, 1994 meeting with General Giap, I asked him whether his strategy at Khe Sanh was intended to be a repeat of Dien Bien Phu where he had laid siege against the French army, forcing their surrender. He said he knew that U.S. air reinforcement capability made another Dien Bien Phu at Khe Sanh unlikely—so at Khe Sanh he only sought to inflict casualties on U.S. forces in order to lower American morale.)

The presence of a unit the size of Division 312 suggested to the Americans their bait might be working.

Khanh arrived at Khe Sanh in March 1967, in response to the U.S. build-up. It was here his contribution to the war effort was cut short— Khe Sanh would be his last battle against the Americans.

One morning, Division 312 observers noticed a U.S. reconnaissance aircraft, an OV-10 Bronco, circling overhead. They chose not to fire upon it, instead remaining concealed, as they saw an opportunity to lure the Americans into an ambush.

The Division 312 commander was familiar with U.S. doctrine; he knew the OV-10's presence probably meant landing sites were being reconnoitered to insert U.S. forces. As the OV-10 circled two hills within the heart of the division's positions, the Division 312 commander did not want the Americans to know his troops were there until he was ready to spring the ambush. His plan was to allow the Americans to land before hitting them hard with a division-size attack. Division 312's objective was not to take the enemy positions, but rather to inflict significant losses upon the heavily outnumbered Americans.

As anticipated, Marines were soon flown in by helicopter to the two hills. From atop a third hill 400 meters away, Khanh and his concealed platoon waited. Two-thirds of his 22-man platoon consisted of new recruits, only 17-18 years old; but Khanh knew he could depend on them.

The Marines arrived in several waves that morning. To Khanh's amazement, however, they failed to immediately dig in or establish defensive positions. As the last helicopter departed, the Division 312 commander gave the order to attack.

Within minutes, all hell broke loose for the Marines on top of those hills. Armed with AK-47s as well as with B40 and B41 rocket launchers (pictured at right and below)—and supported with artillery—Division 312 caught the Marines by surprise. Scrambling for cover, the Marines organized a hasty defense and returned fire in what was the start of a six-hour battle.

As Khanh directed his troops in the attack, the Marines called in artillery fire and close air support on the NVA positions. The intensity of this fire forced Khanh's platoon to shift positions repeatedly during the fight.

Four hours into the battle, Khanh continued to direct his platoon's attack on the Marines as he lay on the ground. An artillery round exploded five meters away. Shrapnel tore into his left leg, which began bleeding profusely. Several men rushed to his side, but Khanh directed them to assist two other soldiers seriously wounded by the explosion. Knowing he would soon lose consciousness, he tore off his shirtsleeve to make a tourniquet to tie around his leg. Oblivious to the full extent of his wound, he rejoined the battle.

By the time the fighting stopped, Khanh was exhausted. He felt consciousness slipping away and, for the first time, the intense pain of his wound. His tourniquet temporarily slowed but did not stop the loss of blood. From the gaping hole in his leg, he saw a severely broken bone.

With the battle over, Division 312 began the arduous work of transporting its wounded to the first aid station. Two of Khanh's men alternated carrying him on their backs. While the distance to the aid station was only two kilometers, the vegetation and hills made the task onerous. It took almost three hours to make the journey.

One doctor and three nurses met the wounded at the aid station. Upon examining Khanh, the doctor knew nothing more could be done there for him. His leg required immediate surgery—an operation for which the aid station lacked the necessary facilities. Khanh had to be transferred to the main field hospital. With no motor transportation available, he faced a life-threatening fifteen- day journey by stretcher. The doctor knew the risks to Khanh of such a trip were significant—but there was no alternative. Surgery was his only hope. Bandaging the wound and administering morphine, the doctor immediately sent Khanh and his transporters on their way.

In a stark contrast of capabilities, as Khanh started his transit by stretcher, Marines wounded in the same battle already were receiving medical attention, having been medevaced hours earlier from the battlefield.

As the journey by stretcher wore on, Khanh faded in and out of consciousness. In brief moments of the former, his transporters fed him. But he rarely ate, usually just taking water. His weight dropped drastically—from 58 to 36 kilograms. More worrisome was the discoloration of his leg—gangrene was setting in. Khanh knew if medical attention did not come quickly, the infection would spread to the rest of his body. At best, his leg would have to be amputated; at worst, the loss would not matter. He was in a race against time.

When the group arrived at the field hospital, Khanh was fading fast. The treating physician rushed him into surgery, where he amputated the decaying limb. Regaining consciousness after surgery, Khanh gazed at the empty space under the blanket left by his missing leg. The sight of the stump did not alarm him.

"I just felt grateful to be alive," he reported. *"I knew when I joined the army; there was substantial risk of death. But I was one of the lucky ones—I survived. And after all,"* he reasoned, *"I only lost one leg—I still had another left."*

Seven days after his surgery, Khanh was shipped back north. Once again, he traversed the Ho Chi Minh Trail, which he had traveled several years earlier by foot. *"At least this time,"* Khanh said, *"I did not have to walk as I traveled by the comfort of truck."*

A hammock was set up in the bed of the truck, and Khanh headed north. Moving only at night, his convoy made good time, averaging one hundred kilometers between dusk and dawn.

"There was one advantage to my situation," Khanh mused. *"Since the trucks were carrying wounded soldiers, they had priority over all other traffic moving north. I thought to myself, 'See how fortunate I am.'"* The trip took roughly three weeks.

The transit was not without the normal problems associated with traveling the Trail—for the convoy was attacked by U.S. aircraft three times. In each case, warnings came down via the Trail's listening posts that American planes were on their way. Warning times were sufficient for convoy personnel to dismount, move the wounded into shelters along the road and hide their trucks.

Khanh's trip north ended at a hospital in Thanh Hoa Province, 150 kilometers south of Hanoi. There he convalesced for one and a half months. For five years, he walked with a cane, until he received his first artificial leg. In 1989, he received a new, very versatile prosthetic leg— one made by the country that claimed his real one.

Today, Khanh still considers himself a lucky man—for he, unlike many of his comrades, had cheated death at Khe Sanh and lived to talk about it.

Section 2:

Survivor's Luck

In the Vietnam war, every day was a fight for survival.

In combat, many variables played a role in determining whether such a fight eventually proved successful or not. Knowing some elements in the survival equation were constants, the soldier realized others might come into play as well. Thus, survival also became a matter of luck. Sometimes luck did not work in favor of the soldier; sometimes it did— as the following accounts suggest:

A Run for Life 67

Buried Alive! 69

Freedom Flight 71

A Near Fatal Mistake 74

A RUN FOR LIFE

Le Minh Dao considered himself lucky. While the Vietnam war extracted a heavy toll from the majority of families supporting Hanoi during the conflict, Dao's family managed to emerge intact. His father, his father-in-law, his two brothers—all proudly served and survived. But Dao came very close one day to becoming the family's only casualty. For a brief moment in time, he and an American soldier shared a common focus—Dao's life.

In June 1968, Dao's regiment was operating in Dong Khoi, Ben Tre Province—an area left barren by Agent Orange spraying. Unbeknownst to Dao's unit, the Americans also dropped listening devices into the area. The devices served their purpose, picking up Dao's regiment as it moved through the area.

As Dao and his men stopped to rest, a U.S. reconnaissance aircraft approached. Circling, the pilot must have radioed in Dao's position as, minutes later, attack aircraft swarmed in overhead. Bombs, rockets and machine gun fire pounded the area. Running for cover, Dao and the others sought to escape the barrage.

Dao and another soldier suddenly stumbled out into an open area. Like an eagle sighting its prey, a helicopter swooped down on top of them. The aircraft was so low, Dao could see in through its side door as it approached. His heart pounding as he continued to run, Dao's eyes briefly locked with those of an American standing in the doorway of the aircraft.

"I saw a young soldier, his face flushed with excitement," recalled Dao. *"I watched him as he raised an M-79 grenade launcher which he held in his hands, placing the butt of the weapon in his shoulder as he prepared to fire."*

Terror gripped Dao as the American pointed the M-79 directly at him. A tree line stood a hundred meters away; Dao knew he would never reach it in time.

The sound of his heart racing faded as Dao heard the hollow "thud" of a round being fired from the M-79 launcher. He could only watch helplessly as the round hit just two meters in front of him, in between

Dao and his scrambling comrade. As Dao braced for the inevitable explosion, it never came! He watched in disbelief as the shell fell lifelessly to the ground. Fortunately, for Dao, it turned out to be a dud— his life had been spared!

There was little time for Dao to reflect on his good fortune, however, for the helicopter was turning to make another run at him. Dao and his comrade continued to race for cover. Before the helicopter could complete its turn, the two men were able to reach the safety of the jungle.

As the aircraft passed overhead, Dao managed a smile. He knew the frustration the young American gunner in the helicopter must have felt, being denied his prize. Fate had spared Dao to fight another day—and, by doing so, kept his family's survival record intact.

BURIED ALIVE!

Pham Tan Thanh, born in 1932, joined the fight against the French at the age of fifteen. His first combat experience against the Americans came at age 34, in January 1966, as the U.S. Army launched Operation Crimp. The mission of Operation Crimp was to trap guerrillas believed operating in the Cu Chi area. The experience proved to be a most memorable one for Thanh.

A captain serving with the NLF at the Cu Chi tunnels, Thanh had thirty men in his command. As U.S. forces approached, Thanh's unit fired at the Americans, moving from one position to another in an effort to confuse them.

As U.S. Army tank units pressed forward, Thanh's men fell back to bunkers tied into the tunnel system in Cu Chi. They held these positions as long as possible, until the superior firepower of the tanks drove them into the tunnels. Along with four of his men, Thanh withdrew into a connecting tunnel just as the bunker they occupied was destroyed by an exploding round from a tank's gun. The explosion immediately sealed off the tunnel entry point, removing Thanh and his men from the fight.

With one end shut off, the group made its way through the tunnel to another exit, where they hoped to outflank advancing U.S. forces. They felt the rumble of tanks overhead. Weakened from earlier bombardments, a portion of the tunnel in front of Thanh suddenly collapsed under the weight of the tanks. Thanh and his men were now cut off from their only remaining access to the surface. They were entombed within a 100-meter stretch of the tunnel, with a limited supply of air.

Thanh's combat experience against the French had taught him to remain cool under pressure. Cut off from his parent unit, he knew his main priority was to initiate action to rejoin the fight. Committed to locating a way out, he was also prepared to accept the consequences of failing to do so.

Lacking tools to dig, Thanh used the nozzle of his AK-47 rifle as a pick to cut away at the hardened earth overhead. The men alternated digging in this manner. It was a painstakingly slow process. As one man dug away at the earth, others collected the loose dirt falling to the tunnel floor, pushing it behind them.

Thanh was proud—despite their situation, his men did not panic. Sealed off from the rest of the world in an underground tomb, working in the dark with a limited air supply, could arouse panic and fear among the toughest of men. Yet, in spite of their youth, they remained calm. Thanh was not surprised. He knew his men well and always felt they would work well together in times such as these.

The air inside the tunnel grew stale. With no lighting, it was difficult to monitor how much progress was made in digging their way out. They kept tunneling upward, however, knowing there was but one direction for them to go.

An hour passed since the collapse. It was Thanh's turn to dig. He relieved one of the other men but soon stopped. Listening intently, he realized he was now only centimeters away from breaking through to the surface. Uncertain, however, if American troops were still in the area, he waited and listened for several minutes. Hearing nothing, he was unsure exactly what the silence meant. Were the Americans waiting quietly for Thanh and his men to emerge from their tomb—or had they departed the area? With one last thrust of his rifle, he broke through to fresh air—and an abandoned battlefield.

Undaunted by their temporary setback, the five men immediately scrambled through the opening, gathered themselves up and, in accordance with regulations, concerning units separated during battle, set off to continue the fight.

FREEDOM FLIGHT

Ever since completing his journey down the Ho Chi Minh Trail in 1964, Lieutenant Colonel Phan Loung Truc operated in Military District 8, east of Saigon. There, he became intimately familiar with the Cu Chi tunnel system, using it to freely move around the district. He frequently conducted reconnaissance missions, making use of the tunnels to approach his objectives. One excursion in late 1968, however, almost proved fatal.

While most activities outside the tunnels were conducted at night, on occasion a daytime sortie was required. Truc and another soldier were sent to collect intelligence on U.S. activity. Utilizing an unlit portion of the underground network they knew would bring them out in close proximity to the objective area; they followed a main tunnel to where it intersected with a feeder (or secondary) tunnel.

A little taller than most Vietnamese, Truc traversed these long passageways with knees bent and upper torso at almost a ninety degree angle. Not particularly comfortable, he knew it beat the alternative of traveling above ground, where his chances of detection increased while trying to get close to his objective.

Although the tunnel was unlit, Truc required no lighting. Four years of living underground had made him a skilled traveler, capable of navigating his way through them in total darkness.

Reaching the feeder tunnel, the two men followed it. Truc knew its entry/exit point lay but a few hundred meters further on. Once he sensed he had gone far enough, Truc lifted his hands above his head and began feeling around in the darkness for the wooden hatch separating the light of the outside world from the darkness of his subterranean one. As his fingers touched the hatch directly overhead, Truc felt pleased about his navigational skills. He slowly stood up, partially opening the hatch to scan the horizon for enemy troops in the area before exiting from the tunnel. But as Truc stood there, basking in the sunlight that temporarily poured into the darkness below, he was startled to hear a commotion from within the bowels of the tunnel. There was a tremendous squawking noise, followed by the sound of wings flapping frantically.

Among the activities conducted underground in the tunnels of Cu Chi for daily survival was the raising of pigs and chickens. Apparently, a chicken escaped its underground coup, making its way down the main and into the feeder tunnel. Drawn to the burst of sunlight as Truc held the hatch open, the excited chicken sought to make good on the final leg of its escape!

Startled by the squawking noise, Truc threw the hatch wide open, giving the bird a momentary, but clear, path to freedom. Wasting no time, the bird flew towards the sunlight and open air, its wings brushing against Truc as it did so. Recovering, Truc was worried, not over the loss of a meal, but over another familiar sound, he heard and instantly recognized as an incoming helicopter! Bad timing had resulted in the chicken making good its escape just as an American helicopter was approaching.

Originally, the tunnel hatch amidst ample vegetation was sufficiently concealed above ground for those entering or exiting the tunnel. However, in subsequent years, chemical defoliants stripped away much of the natural vegetation. While the hatch itself remained well camouflaged on the surface, those emerging from it immediately found themselves in the open, forced to dash several hundred meters to the nearest jungle concealment.

Thus, the bird's escape was made in the open, clearly visible to the incoming helicopter pilot. Slamming the hatch back down, Truc returned to his world of darkness and waited.

Attracted by the chicken's startled flight, the pilot circled overhead to investigate. After what seemed an eternity, the sound of the rotor blades faded off in the distance. Truc still waited a few more minutes to make sure the helicopter was not returning. Satisfied it had departed, he slowly opened the hatch a second time. His secret hideout had not been compromised by the incident and he and his companion exited the tunnel, quickly disappearing into the nearby jungle.

Within the safety of the jungle's concealment, Truc looked at his watch. Almost ten minutes had elapsed since the helicopter's departure. In the wake of the continuing silence, he grew more confident he had successfully avoided detection. As he and his companion prepared to set out for their objective, Truc heard yet another sound with which he was all too familiar.

As the whistle of an incoming 175 mm artillery round grew louder, Truc realized his earlier confidence had been misplaced—his position had, in fact, been compromised by the fleeing fowl. The two men raced back to the tunnel hatch as the ground shook from the explosions of the 175 mm rounds raining down on top of them. Truc's companion was first to reach the hatch. He quickly squeezed through the small opening. Truc, however, was less fortunate. Awaiting his turn to enter, a round exploded nearby. Severely wounded, Truc fell to the ground, his upper body, legs and feet ripped by shrapnel. He immediately lost consciousness. As 175 mm rounds continued to rock the ground around Truc, a hand reached out through the open hatch and pulled him down into the safety of the tunnel. Dragging Truc's limp body, his companion made his way back to the safety of the main tunnel and on to the underground hospital.

Following a month convalescence, Truc returned to the tunnels. As far as he knows, the chicken did not.

A NEAR FATAL MISTAKE

The U.S. actively encouraged defections among members of the NLF through an amnesty program known as “Chieu Hoi” or “Open Arms.”

On May 17, 1970, that program almost succeeded in effecting the capture of a senior level official within the Viet Cong hierarchy, Colonel Nguyen Van Si (pictured at left in black), commander of Region #2. (Operationally, Hanoi divided South Vietnam into three military zones and six military regions. Region #2 included most of Long An province. As a regional commander, Si reported directly to commander of the Viet Cong forces, General Tran Van Tra.)

* * *

On April 29, 1970, American forces expanded operations outside of Vietnam, into Cambodia. Thirteen major ground operations were launched to clear North Vietnamese sanctuaries located within 19 miles of the South Vietnamese border.

Colonel Nguyen Van Si transited back and forth between Cambodia and Vietnam to coordinate Viet Cong activities in the region. During these trips, he was always escorted by a two-man security team.

Policy dictated Si, as a senior level commander, not operate in any area longer than two or three days to avoid the risk of his location being compromised. Upon entering a new area, his security detail immediately identified a secure hiding place for him in the event of an emergency. Normally, such a hiding place merely consisted of a concealed hole dug in the ground, the location of which was known only to Si and his team. Though a visit to a particular area by Si might last no more than 48 hours, the digging of the hiding location was always to be the first thing done—even if its construction might take a good portion of that period.

A few weeks after the U.S. incursion into Cambodia, Si was operating out of Svay Rieng, in Cambodia. He and his team successfully avoided detection by ARVN troops positioned only five kilometers away.

Having arrived at Svay Rieng three days earlier, Si made a near fatal mistake. Contrary to command doctrine, he decided to remain in the same operational area beyond the 48-72 hour time guideline.

On the morning of May 17, Si was engaged in rather lengthy planning discussions with his executive officer, lasting until 1:00 A.M. Exhausted, the two men departed their meeting to get some sleep. Policy dictated the two senior level officers never remain together, other than for operational purposes. Thus, they both left for different locations in which to spend the night. This was a practice designed to avoid the risk of losing the command's two senior members at the same time. Arriving at his separate accommodations and still guarded by his security team, Si soon fell asleep. He awoke at 6:00 A.M. the next morning.

Following breakfast, Si and his security team relocated to a position 300 meters outside the village. Here, they had easy access to their hiding locations while his security detail, awake all night guarding Si, finally got a chance to get some sleep.

As his security people slept, Si maintained a watchful eye. He heard a plane overhead. As it approached, he saw it was an American spotter aircraft. Si's suspicions were aroused as the plane immediately went into a circular search pattern. He awoke his security team, ordering them to police the immediate area to remove any signs of their presence. All three men then climbed into their hiding locations and waited.

Within a half hour, American troops were everywhere. Although Si quickly realized he and his men were in the middle of a large, sweep operation through the village by the Americans, he did not realize that the specific purpose was to search for him.

From their hiding positions, Si and his men were unable to observe enemy activity; they could only listen in silence. Soldiers were heard yelling back and forth, along with the constant rumbling of armored vehicles traversing the area. The three men dared not lift their heads out of their concealed positions, fearing the Americans were too close. Despite the severe discomfort of waiting in a crouched position inside their holes, they remained there, motionless.

This continued for many hours. Si's biggest fear was the Americans might have search dogs with them to sniff out their prey. (To throw dogs off their scent, the Viet Cong employed a tactic of rubbing soap over their bodies—but as Si and his security team had received no warning of the Americans' arrival, they had been unable to do so.) At one point, Si had to relieve himself. Doing so, he feared the dogs might pick up his scent.

Soon, the voices of the American soldiers got closer. Si pulled out his pistol and pointed it at his head. He was prepared to shoot himself rather than fall into enemy hands.

Around 6:00 P.M., the noise subsided. All seemed quiet again. However, the three men remained in their holes, uncertain if all the Americans had gone or whether a small force had been left behind to watch for any activity after the main body's departure. Finally, one of Si's security guards emerged from his hole. Carefully searching the area, he determined all the Americans had departed. He returned to notify Si. Relieved, they quickly left the area.

As they withdrew, Si feared for the safety of his executive officer. He was unsure if he too had escaped the search by the Americans. Two days later, Si learned of his fate.

Early in the morning of May 17, his executive officer had made his way to ARVN lines and surrendered under the Chieu Hoi program. With a senior NLF staff officer in their custody, the ARVNs immediately notified the Americans, positioned 30 kilometers away from Svay Rieng, of their catch. A U.S. helicopter was dispatched to pick the executive officer up for further interrogation. He then informed his Americans interrogators he had met with Si in the Svay Rieng area just a few hours earlier. Realizing Si might still be in the area and the importance of his capture, the Americans reacted swiftly, initiating a lightning sweep and search operation to catch him.

Si said he never picked up any sense that his executive officer intended to betray him that morning. What Si did not know was his executive officer had just recently relocated his wife from My Tho to Saigon, obviously in preparation for his defection—a defection Si attributed to a failure in the officer's philosophical training.

❖ ❖ ❖

While questions remain about the effectiveness of the Chieu Hoi program, perhaps its greatest strength for the U.S. side was the fear it instilled on the guerrillas' side. As Si observed, it posed a constant threat to their cause, as they never really knew whose philosophical training might be lacking.

Section 3:

The Civilian Toll

Long gone are the days when armies engage each other on battlefields far removed from civilian populations. The boundaries of 20th and 21st century battlefields have proven to be without limit; the lines marking them blurred and "collateral damage" a clear and present danger.

In this conflict, war encompassed all of Vietnam—from the ground fighting in the south to the bombings in the north. When the boundaries of war have no limits, an unavoidable consequence arises—the inability to limit its effects to the combatant alone. Until "smart" weapons prove capable of discerning between combatants and non-combatants, civilians will always be casualties of war. Vietnam—a war in which the civilian casualty toll reached two million people—was no exception—and is, perhaps, an egregious example.

What follows are the personal stories of Vietnamese civilians—parents, siblings, children—who suffered losses and disruption to their lives wrought by the war which engulfed their nation for so long.

The Reunion Not to Be 79

Child of the Jungle 88

Digging Deep for Higher Education 100

Hanoi's Christmas Nightmare 105

THE REUNION NOT TO BE

A strikingly handsome woman even in her mid-seventies, Bui Thi Me's gentle face and features betray the tragedy still weighing heavy upon her heart. Only the medal she proudly displays on her native aodai (dress), given her by a grateful nation in recognition of her extreme personal sacrifice, suggests she has a tragic story to tell.

Me and her husband, Nguyen Van Nhon, were teachers. Between 1942 and 1957, they became proud parents of four older boys—Sanh, Tai, Dai and Dao—and two younger girls. For many years, they ran a school for children in Cho Lon, a suburb of Saigon. But soon after the birth of their last child, Nguyen Thi Binh, the Saigon government forced them to close it down.

Following World War II, as the French made clear their intention to re-colonize Vietnam, Me and Nhon joined the revolutionary movement to drive the French out. They were disappointed when their country's victory over the French at Dien Bien Phu in 1954 failed to reunify Vietnam. Continuing to run their school, they became determined to do what they could to achieve reunification. It was a decision that quickly brought them into disfavor with the Saigon regime.

Upon closing their school, the family moved to Saigon to live with relatives. Denied a license to operate a school there, they began tutoring children in their home. Learning an arrest by Saigon authorities for their anti-government activities was pending, in 1960 Me and Nhon made plans to leave the city. They feared leaving their sons, then aged twelve to eighteen, behind as the Saigon police might arrest the boys later to lure the parents back. Thus, they decided to take their sons with them, leaving their two daughters, aged nine and three, with their aunt. They departed for the Mekong Delta.

Taking up residence in the Delta, Me and her husband established a school in Tra Vinh Province as a front for their anti-Saigon government activities. As educators, they made special efforts to ensure their own children received the best possible education. Because of this, the boys were much better educated than most of their peers. This provided an unexpected dividend for the family as the older boys quickly obtained jobs as teachers. Eventually all four boys turned to teaching to be able to contribute to the family income. The sons' financial assistance enabled Me and Nguyen to devote more time to furthering the goals of the NLF movement through their new "school."

In 1964, as the tempo of the war in the south increased, Me and her husband decided to leave the Delta and join the NLF headquarters  command. The headquarters was hidden deep in the jungles outside Saigon, far from areas regularly patrolled by government forces. Known as "R Base," it was situated in Tay Ninh Province ("R-Base" headquarters meeting pictured at left).

They took their eldest boy, Sanh, with them, leaving the other boys behind to continue their teaching careers.

While the parents entrenched themselves in NLF activities at R Base and efforts to recruit others to the cause, Sanh made a career change. Talented as a singer and dancer, he began performing for audiences at R Base, where he became very popular. But in 1967, he volunteered for military service to participate in the upcoming Tet offensive.

Soon after Sanh departed to begin his military service, Me and Nhon received news of another decision. As revolutionary activists who opposed the Saigon regime, they could not say the news surprised them. A letter arrived from son Tai. He tenderly explained to his parents what they, in their hearts, knew was inevitable. Having observed firsthand the commitment of their parents to NLF, the remaining three sons announced they had all decided to join the fight against the Saigon government as well.

Tai, as perhaps the most sensitive and articulate of the male siblings, felt compelled to explain to his parents why he decided to join his brothers in the country's fight against America. The letter, in its entirety, reads as follows:

"May 25, 1967

Our Beloved Parents:

"I am writing to inform you that in early April 1967, I volunteered to enlist in the armed forces and was approved for service. In doing so, I was to inform you before enlisting, but due to the distance and time factor, I could only let you know once I settled in the service.

"Our beloved parents, I knew that when my younger brother, and then I, enlisted you would be worried; particularly you, mother. This is because you are a Vietnamese mother, worried about her sons confronting enemy troops and involved in heavy fighting at all times.

"I also know you will be proud and satisfied with my decision.

"Being away for these few years, I will always be thinking about you. And the more I think about you, the more I realize I must contribute to the revolution so you will be proud and satisfied that your children were willing to sacrifice--without hesitation--their young lives for this fight. I have chosen the military career to bare arms to fight the forces of aggression, not only because I believe this is a serious situation, but also because the cause is a most glorious one. This is the only sensible way I can demonstrate what I believe in.

"I do not join the military only to fight the U.S., although that fight will be a long one. I must pursue a military career. Because I am young, I can make a major contribution as I have my whole life ahead of me. That is why, starting now, I will train hard to develop my skills and serve my country in this glorious moment to have a promising future. In such a challenge, the best place to develop one's skills is on the fierce battlefield that puts my strength against that of an enemy with stronger firepower. I will use my physical and mental toughness to gain victory!

"During the fighting, if an unfortunate thing happens to me, I will gladly accept it. For I believe my loved ones will grieve over me and be *proud of my service. I would rather die fighting than die a coward child or a shameless brother. I never felt more confident and fervent before in my life than I do now.*

"Parents, please have faith in me. I promise you that in my next letter I will not only report my well-being, my thoughts and my sentiments, but also my unit's and my combat accomplishments.

"For myself, my current energy level is high, well enough to fight for many years! I have been assigned to one company in Regiment #3.

"Brother Sanh is currently with an artillery battalion of Regiment #3. He did write to me with prayers and high spirits. Brother Dao is still operating in Vinh Long. He seems uneasy about his responsibilities but I wrote to him boosting his morale.

"Our beloved parents, I am writing to you while our forces take the initiative to mount a major offensive against the enemy and I believe I will fight my first battle.

"I pray I will make you happy by doing what you raised and taught us to do and that we prove worthy of the education and training given to a determined revolutionary soldier.

"I send you all my love and best wishes from a child who is far away. Also, I send my best regards to all our relatives, our aunts, our uncles,--good health and great success in their work.

> *Your son,*
>
> *Nguyen Huynh Tai"*

Me received the letter with mixed emotions. While proud her sons were so moved by Ho Chi Minh's call for all young people to do their duty to fight for their beliefs and while accepting of her sons' decision to join the military, nonetheless, she was sick with worry. She knew they had received limited combat training for what lay ahead.

In late 1967, the feeling was the south could be liberated. As preparations for the 1968 Tet offensive mounted, Me knew her sons would be involved in much of that fighting.

She took some comfort in knowing not all four boys were serving in the same unit. Heavy fighting by one son's unit would not necessarily expose her other sons' units to the same battle.

As promised, Tai continued to correspond with his mother to keep her advised of his and his siblings' experiences. Periodically the brothers encountered each other in the field—the others always tasking Tai with responsibility to write their mother for them. Me anxiously awaited the letters, which often took months to reach her.

Knowing her sons were seeing much combat, Me tried to keep her mind focused on her work.

In late February 1968, Me was working in an isolated part of R Base with a small group of co-workers. She remembered it was a beautiful day as she sat at a table in her thatched hut office. Her superior walked in and, somewhat hesitantly, approached her.

"I have bad news," he began. *"I was just notified that Tai and Sanh have fallen in battle!"* Tai, aged 24, died in December in Can Tho Province, but it took two months for the news to reach Me. It was a tragic coincidence that word of Tai's death arrived simultaneously with news of the death of her oldest son, Sanh, aged 26. Sanh was killed at An Lac in Binh Chanh District, during the Tet offensive several days earlier.

Me was shaken. *"When I received the news, I thought at first it was a terrible mistake. How could I lose two sons at once? As I realized it was not a mistake, I felt I was in a place without gravity. I returned to my shelter and cried. Tears fell like water. I felt like someone cut away my insides piece by piece. My husband, working nearby, came to console me."*

Me had mentally prepared for the possible loss of one son; she was totally unprepared to lose two sons at once. Nor was she prepared for what came next.

The following week, Me returned to work, trying to cope with her loss. She sensed, however, something was wrong. Her colleagues looked at her and quickly turned away. She went to her superior and implored him, *"Please tell me now if something else is wrong! Do not hold back! I need to know!"* Sitting her down, he told Me, shortly after news of the deaths of her two sons was received, notice arrived of more bad news: her third son, Dai, aged 22, was killed in Vin Long while her fourth son, Dao, aged 20, was severely wounded. Many of Me's colleagues rushed to console her, crying over the additional tragic news she had just received. However, Me was unable to shed a tear—she felt only numbness.

Her son, Dao, survived his wounds. Not wishing for Me and Nguyen to lose a fourth son by leaving their only surviving male child in harm's way, Dao's commander ordered him to join his parents at R Base. His commander knew such an order did not necessarily guarantee Dao's safe return—for R Base was regularly subjected to air attack. But he knew Dao's parents would rest easier having Dao there with them. Traveling by himself, Dao set out for Tay Ninh Province and R Base.

The journey to R Base took several weeks. It almost did end up costing Me her fourth son as Dao narrowly survived an artillery bombardment while trying to make his way to the camp.

A month after receiving news of her third son's death, Me was surprised to walk out of her office at R Base and see Dao rushing up to greet her. The tears that failed to come earlier now flowed freely. Those tears, and a mother's love for her son, blinded Me to Dao's physical appearance as she held him tight, oblivious to the battle wounds that left his face disfigured. An exploding M-79 grenade left several pieces of shrapnel imbedded in Dao's face and one eye.

As Me embraced her sole surviving son, she reflected on how the four brothers vowed when they joined the military to hold a reunion after the war. It was a reunion Me now knew would never take place.

For her losses, Me was presented with the War Medal for Mothers, honoring those who suffered substantial family losses—the death of all sons or of three or more sons.

"As a mother," Me explains, *"I have a universal understanding of what it is like to have children at risk in war, to have those children fall in battle and to be unable to put a child to his final rest. To this day,"* Me shares with tears in her eyes, *"I have been unable to recover the body of one of my sons and know I never will."*

Me's extraordinary loss of three sons and the disfigurement of a fourth, remarkably, did not leave her embittered towards the Americans responsible for her personal tragedy. While most mothers might feel anger, Me is unique. In her heart, she feels compassion for those American mothers unable to recover, and put to rest, the remains of a fallen son on a battlefield in a far off land.

She, perhaps better than any mother, can well understand their grief.

※ ※ ※

Me's story is just one of many. An exhibit at the Army Museum in Hanoi contains the names of Vietnamese mothers who suffered significant family losses. Not all-inclusive, it lists dozens of mothers, bonded together by feelings of mutual suffering and of outliving a generation of children who, in the normal progression of life, should have outlived them. There are many other Vietnamese mothers who suffered such losses. Nguyen Thi Diem lost a husband and two sons; Tran Thi Trang—a husband and five sons while a sixth son was wounded; Huynh Thi Tan—five sons. A post-war report indicated, in Saigon alone, over 1,400 mothers lost three or more sons.

 While the loss of a child is a great personal loss for a mother, obviously those hardest hit by the war were those mothers who saw an entire generation of their children fall on Vietnam's battlefields.  Whether the loss was a mother's only son or all of her sons, the impact was just as devastating. If tragedy is a measure of sheer numbers, two mothers stand out above the others in their losses: Nguyen Thi Thu (pictured at right and her bust above), who saw the war claim nine children, a son-in-law and one grandchild; and Nguyen Thi Ranh,

who lost eight sons and two grandchildren. The devastation of such horrific losses by these mothers never lessened their resolve to see the war through to victory. That message was clear in a letter sent by one mother, Nguyen Thi Loan, in January 1968. Having lost a younger son, Le Viet Dung, she pleaded with authorities to allow her only remaining son, Le Viet Hung, to join the fight to avenge his brother's death.

The stoicism demonstrated by Vietnamese mothers who lost their sons in the war was extraordinary. It reminded me of the story told of a French mother awaiting the return of her son from a battle in another war of an earlier century. Her only son—all she had in the world— fought in a great battle of the Franco-Prussian War. Soundly beaten in the fight, demoralized French deserters streamed through her village. For hours, she stood on the village street, searching out the face of every soldier returning home. When, at long last, darkness fell on an empty road and the last deserter had passed her by, she exclaimed, *"Thank God! He did not run away."*

❊ ❊ ❊

The burden one family can suffer, as the result of siblings serving together in wartime was made clear to Americans during World War II. At Pearl Harbor, twenty sets of brothers died during the surprise attack by the Japanese. Less than a year later, tragedy visited a family by the name of Sullivan as five sons perished when the ship on which they all served was torpedoed and sunk with most of its crew by a Japanese submarine.

Primarily as a result of the Sullivan incident, the U.S. Government implemented regulations that allowed but did not require the discharging of a sole surviving son from service if a sibling had been lost in combat. This was general policy during the Vietnam war. However, such a policy for Hanoi was impractical—if not impossible— in view of the severe manpower shortages it experienced during the conflict. As a result, many families who supported Hanoi—such as Me's—did so at a very high price. (It is the bond between a mother and the son she brought into the world that bridges the divide between cultures. As I listened to Me recount her loss, the lament of another mother over the loss of her son in our own American Civil War came to mind. Louisa Meigs, wife of a U.S. Army general, after losing her son in 1864, wrote:

"When I remember that I have seen the grass growing green already over his young head, my heart overflows with sorrow and I am only another Rachael weeping for her child and refusing to be comforted because, he is not.")

CHILD OF THE JUNGLE

Nguyen Thi Binh was the younger daughter of Bui Thi Me and Nguyen Van Nhon (parents of the three sons killed in "The Reunion Not to Be"). Three years after her birth in 1957, Binh was separated from her parents and brothers and placed, along with her sister, in the care of an aunt.

In 1964, the aunt feared the Saigon government might try holding the two girls, then thirteen and seven, as hostages to bait their parents into returning. Through an elaborate communications system utilizing a network of volunteer couriers, the aunt relayed her concerns to the parents at R Base. It was decided the girls would join them at the base as soon as possible.

On the designated day, a volunteer messenger appeared at the aunt's house and escorted both girls to the local bus stop. The three boarded a bus for Tay Ninh Province where their father, Nhon, eagerly awaited them. Upon their arrival, no time was wasted with personal greetings. Quickly setting out on foot, Nhon led them deep into the jungle, into a world hidden from sunlight—and aerial observation—by a thick roof of forest vegetation.

It was a full day's journey to R Base. The trip was difficult, but Binh was happy to see her father and looked forward to seeing her mother again. Nhon led them along several narrow dirt roadways, created over the years by natives pulling their oxcarts through the jungle. The existence of most of these roads was known to only a few outsiders. Nhon and his daughters reached the camp by nightfall.

R Base was designed and organized to provide NLF headquarters with sufficient facilities to do staff planning, co-ordination and implementation of overall strategy for the war. It contained not only command and control, but all support facilities to perform this function as well. Not wishing to risk the loss of its entire command structure, these facilities were carefully spread out over a very large area. Included among them was a school for children. Along with fifty to sixty other students, the school became Binh's home for the next half of her childhood. Her hopes for spending time with her parents were quickly dashed as she was led off to her new school—and new home.

The school included grades one through six. Seven years old at the time of her arrival, she was placed in first grade; her thirteen-year old sister, too old for school, was assigned elsewhere at R Base as a nurse. Binh found herself separated from not only parents but her sister too.

The children lived together at the school as a single family. Because the parents' activities at R Base took up so much of their time and due to the long distances between the school and the parents' working and living area, mothers and fathers rarely were able to spend time with their children—even for short visits.

Binh saw her parents every three months or so—due more to unscheduled, than scheduled events. Increased air and artillery attacks against R Base or the enemy's initiation of new ground operations in the area often resulted in a temporary suspension of classes. At such times, children were returned to parents or bundled into groups of three, and distributed around R Base for safekeeping, under the supervision of other adults. The purpose of such a distribution plan was to prevent a single catastrophic loss of the children in the event the school was hit during an attack on the camp. Before she left R Base, Binh came to fully appreciate the wisdom of this plan—and the tragic consequences of failing to follow it. She came to dearly value the unscheduled visits she had with her parents.

The first few months at R Base were the most difficult.

"When I first arrived," she explained, *"I was afraid of everything— both real and imagined: ghosts, wild animals, insects, snakes—and the bombs. When I first heard the bombs, I covered my head with my blanket and was shaking. But after a few months, I got used to it and eventually was not afraid of anything."*

Binh entered R Base a frightened little seven-year old; she departed seven years later, a fearless young teenager, confident of her ability to overcome any adversity.

But life in the jungle was by no means easy.

Five teachers were assigned to the school. Additionally, twelve other adults assisted in caring for the children, showing them how to survive in the jungle.

"We were constantly subjected to air attacks at the base," explained Binh. *"So the first thing they showed us was how to dig tunnels and shelters. While they did the work initially, over time we were expected to do it for ourselves. This was a constant task for us as the school was moved quite regularly."*

Food gathering was also a regular task for the children. Binh described how food requirements were met:

"We collected our own food. We were only supplied with rice. Sometimes there was not enough so we went out and got our own food. We ate only two meals a day, usually eating no breakfast. If we felt hungry, we went into the jungle to look for fruit. We were taught what we could and could not eat. We could eat many kinds of leaves. Sometimes we even received books, written for the benefit of American soldiers, which explained exactly which kinds of mushrooms we could and could not eat. We were also taught how to make traps to catch small animals. We ate snakes—and scorpions. We learned about two kinds of scorpions in the

jungle. One was poisonous. It was smaller, with a brownish color. The other was quite big, about four inches long, and black. These were edible and, fortunately, moved slower. Known as mountain scorpions, we were able to catch them quite easily. We always found them crawling around our shelters. There was a little meat in their claws, enough to fill half a spoon; it tasted like shrimp. The claws were the only edible part. The first time I saw one, I was scared but I quickly learned to control my fears. There were young boys in the class who, if they knew the girls were  *scared, used that fear against us. But we were always taught to be brave for we had to do things for ourselves. Many times, though, the boys taught the girls how to catch food."*

Because the teachers lacked adequate training aids, the subjects taught in school were quite limited. *"We learned only mathematics and literature,"* continued Binh. *"There were not enough teachers to teach anything more and there were no books."*

During bombing attacks, the new arrivals at the school were always worried about their parents. Most were lucky and did not have to suffer the loss of a parent. But some were not so fortunate. *"Usually,"* said Binh, *"the rest of the school children discovered a child lost a parent before the child knew, but we kept silent. We could tell because the adults were particularly attentive to that child's needs before the child was told about the death. After the child was informed, we tried not to remind the child about the loss. We were usually so busy anyway with all we had to do daily to survive that we had no time to think about anything else—even personal tragedies. But we tried to care for the child and ease their situation. We were all very close and acted like one big family. We did what we thought we should do."*

While Binh did not suffer the loss of a parent at R Base, she did not escape personal tragedy. In late February 1968, she was the one who received special attention from teachers and friends normally reserved for those who had lost a loved one. She knew something was wrong but did not know what. Believing one of her parents had been killed or wounded, she was relieved, at first, to learn she was going over to visit her parents.

"I sensed something was wrong, but was never informed about the deaths of my three brothers. I was sent to live with my parents for a while. One night I was almost asleep on their bed when their friends came over to talk. My parents thought I was asleep. I remained silent so I could listen to them. I heard the friends give their condolences and start talking about the deaths of my brothers. I knew then what had happened. I cried silently but never spoke to my parents about the deaths. I was with them for a week to ten days."

Although R Base was bombed regularly, the school was never targeted. But in early 1971, some parents' worst fears became a reality. Binh was spared the horrifying experience; but many classmates were not.

"I had malaria and was sent to the hospital," she explained. *"My parents had malaria too, so we were all there together. We were in an underground bomb shelter built for the patients. An air attack started without warning. The school was holding classes in a bunker with an A-shaped roof made of wood and covered with about twenty centimeters of earth—but the school had no bomb shelter. We were moving every month and there was no time to dig one...The school was hit. It was the first time it was ever bombed. Thirteen children and two adults were killed. I knew all the victims...As the bombings continued at R Base, the decision was made to send us (the children) north."*

For the trip north up the Ho Chi Minh Trail, children were split up into groups of sixteen to eighteen, escorted by three adults. The youngest and least healthy children were evenly distributed. A number was assigned to a group and a schedule posted, listing an individual departure date by the assigned group number. The dates were staggered, with a 10-15 day interval between each. The deaths of the thirteen children earlier in the year underscored the importance of spreading the risk of loss among the various groups. Such a tragedy, it was decreed, would not be repeated on the trip north.

"We knew about one month ahead of time when we would be leaving," said Binh. *"Prior to our departure, we were allowed to spend two weeks with our parents. It was not hard for us to leave them behind as,*

by this time, we had adapted to living away from them. The departure was more difficult for the parents, however. My father did not want to send me north as I was experiencing constant bouts of malaria and he feared I would not survive the trip. It was a very difficult time for him."

Her father's concern over Binh's impending trip was understandable. Traversing the Trail had claimed the lives of soldiers in far better health and condition than she was in. Undoubtedly, he felt with the loss of half his children and the disfiguring wound suffered by another, that the war had already cost him dearly.

Before departing, the children received instructions on what to take and how to pack.

"We had to bring a hammock, mosquito netting, a thin blanket and other items with us. Everything was placed in a rucksack, made by folding material in half and sowing three sides shut. To give it form, a small rock or other hard object was placed in the two bottom corners and tied off with line. A shoulder strap was tied to the corners of the rucksack. A large plastic bag was placed inside as a liner so the interior would not get wet. We carried extra plastic bags as well."

After spending time with her parents, Binh rejoined the classmates assigned to her group. They assembled at 5:00 AM on May 19, 1971 to begin their journey to a new home.

"Our departure did not make us nervous or anxious," said Binh. *"We were used to change. But I do remember being homesick—not necessarily for my parents but for our 'home' in the jungle...For after so long, we learned to enjoy life there...We all felt we would miss the south."*

As her group set out on its journey, Binh immediately savored the beauty of the jungle. Many flowers were in full bloom, adding to its scenic beauty.

"We reached one binh tram each day of the trip," she explained. *"Sometimes we completed the trip in half a day; sometimes it took longer. It depended on people's health. Strangely, during the entire trip I never experienced a recurrence of my malaria, although back at R Base I was getting a fever every week. Perhaps I was growing up and*

getting more energy. Others, who never had malaria, became ill along the way. For them, what should have been a three-month trip took four to five months to complete. In such cases, the sick person was left behind by the group at the next binh tram."

An ill child remained at the binh tram until healthy enough to continue, simply awaiting the arrival of another group that was heading north. The ranks of some of our groups were totally depleted by various health problems the children had.

"One group reached the north with only four people," related Binh. *"There was a friend of mine in our group who ultimately reached the north with a different group."*

Upon arrival at a binh tram, the group rested, ate and slept, departing early the next morning. A guide, or "giao lien," from one binh tram led the group half way to the next binh tram. At that point, a giao lien from the next northerly binh tram met the group to lead them to their camp.

Mornings at the binh trams, prior to departure, became fairly routine.

"Giao Liens"

"There was a supply of rice for us," said Binh. *"The cooked rice was placed inside pieces of cloth cut from American parachutes. We rolled the rice into a small ball and pressed it hard to make it very compact. This way it did not spoil so quickly."*

Binh's father had prepared some dried fish meat for Binh to take with her, which she added to her rice. As binh trams only provided the children with rice, the group collected bamboo shoots along the Trail to supplement their rice rations. But thousands of troops traversing the Trail had, by this time, left little else available. Long stretches were stripped of anything edible. *"The cassava leaf is edible but is dangerous to eat in excess,"* added Binh. *"Since we could not find food, we used cassava leaves to make soup with salt and water. On rare occasions, we arrived at a binh tram and they had canned fruit. They put it into a very large pan, known as a 'chao dung,' and cooked it for us."*

Wild animals were not an available food source to the group. *"We saw no wild animals during the entire trip,"* Binh pointed out. *"It seemed that none had survived the daily bombings on the Trail."*

Binh was impressed with the "giao liens" (guides), who constantly listened for reconnaissance aircraft. If one was heard (they could not be observed usually due to the heavy vegetation), the giao lien determined the extent of the reconnoitered area, and then avoided it. It was wise to do so as such areas usually became the target of an immediate air attack. The guide either delayed the group for a while, until the danger passed, or increased its pace to pass through the area quickly.

"There were no bomb shelters on the parts of the Trail we traveled," shared Binh, *"so we sought cover near a big tree or rock. We were bombed almost every day. The Americans bombed us because they knew the Trail was there, not because they knew we were on it. Some children in other groups were lost—but not many. The guides understood the behavior of the American air force and implemented a good plan for guiding us through...They simply looked for the best route available—which sometimes meant heading off in a direction where there was no trail at all."*

The guides rarely allowed the group to rest—they constantly pushed their wards to move forward. *"We kept going...they never waited for us. The children ran a lot to keep up. Sometimes adults in the group could not keep up with the children. On occasion, part of a group arrived at the next binh tram hours before the rest of the group did, but nobody ever got lost...We always slept at the binh tram, never on the Trail. If you slept on the Trail, it was because you were lost."*

Two weeks into her journey, Binh recalled her first encounter with an enemy soldier:

"A South Vietnamese special forces soldier was captured. He joined our group and was escorted, with hands tied behind him, by the guide to be transferred north. I was very curious about him, walking directly behind him the whole way...Nobody spoke to him, not even the guide...I never met an enemy soldier before so I was very curious."

This was not Binh's only encounter with South Vietnamese Special Forces. She provided the following account about a commando group she once observed being inserted by helicopter into the jungle:

"Enemy special forces were brought in by helicopter sometimes to try and locate the Trail. I remember watching two commandos, immediately after being dropped off, write a large sign by which they made known their desire to surrender. Then they just hid and waited for our soldiers from the binh tram who, after hearing the helicopter, came out looking for them. The binh tram soldiers came out and captured them. They had a lot of food with them, which our soldiers took away and gave to us."

(The U.S. Central Intelligence Agency in 1961 initiated a covert plan to insert South Vietnamese commando teams into North Vietnam to conduct guerrilla operations. The effort, taken over by the Pentagon in 1964, was—by 1968—a failure as approximately 500 commandos had been killed, captured or turned into double agents. Both former Secretary of Defense Robert S. McNamara and former commander of U.S. forces in Vietnam, General William C. Westmoreland were highly critical of the plan. This program is documented in a book by Sedgwick Tourison entitled **SECRET ARMY, SECRET WAR: WASHINGTON'S TRAGIC SPY OPERATION IN NORTH VIETNAM**. Binh's observation may explain why some of these South Vietnamese commandos failed to return.)

For much of the journey, guides followed stream banks where it was cooler to travel. It provided the additional benefit of allowing the children to stop and bathe regularly.

But traveling along the banks also presented occasional dangers as well.

"The most difficult part," explained Binh *"was when the rain came. Flash floods roared down the streambed. There was no time to prepare for it. You simply heard it, and then it was there. We tried to get on top of a high rock. Although it was the dry season, sometimes we still got heavy rains. I encountered these flash floods two or three times. Many of us did not know how to swim so it was very dangerous for us. After the flash flood, the stream was much wider and more difficult to cross. So an adult tied a line to a tree, taking the other end of the line across the river, tying it to another tree on the far bank. The children held on to this line as they crossed holding their rucksack in their other hand. The rucksack was wrapped in an extra plastic bag, which served as a life preserver. We were very well trained and very adaptable to any situation, so we crossed these rivers without problem. If you were afraid, you had a problem. If you were never afraid, you could overcome any problem."*

Three months and one week after leaving R Base, Binh's group completed their odyssey. They arrived at Binh Tram #5 in Ha Tin District, Ha Dong Province, on August 27, 1971. The trip to Binh Tram #5 was the last made on foot. For the rest of the journey, they enjoyed the relative luxury of truck transport.

When on foot, the children traveled during daylight hours; but on the trucks, they traveled only at night. They were taken to Quang Binh Province. Once they reached the Gianh River, they boarded boats, making their way to Vinh; from there they took a train to Thuong Tin.

Upon their arrival at Thuong Tin, the children in Binh's group were sent to a special camp for three months. Here, they rejoined classmates who departed R Base before them and awaited the arrival of those who departed later. The first night in the camp, they enjoyed a special treat for dinner—meat. While not a large portion, it was satisfying nonetheless. They also received physical examinations and were tested for malaria.

Once all the children arrived, they were put into a school specially oriented for arrivals from the south. As their studies in the south were limited and sporadic, it was felt they were not ready to join their northern peers who were attending school regularly.

Binh and her fellow students stayed together at the same dormitory. Here they received instruction in courses they were not given earlier— geography, biology, history, etc. All their food and clothing requirements were now met by the government. Additionally, they received some pocket money for personal items. It was here Binh remained for the duration of the war. As the children arrived safely in the north, Hanoi notified their parents in the south. Due to the unreliability of the mail system, Binh waited nine months before receiving confirmation from her parents they knew of her safe arrival.

In spite of the good treatment they received from the government, the children could not help but feel homesick. They longed to return south where their roots were. And the timing of their arrival in the north raised concerns over whether they were any safer in Hanoi than they were at R Base. For they now were subjected to two major threats: B-52 attacks and flooding. As the B-52 attacks in the north increased in tempo, the children again were separated into small groups and distributed among local families.

In 1974, Binh was pleased to receive unexpected visitors—her parents. America's withdrawal from the conflict by this time greatly enhanced travel times and conditions along the Trail. With the threat of air attack no longer real, her parents made the transit in relative luxury compared to the very harsh conditions young Binh endured.

Their visit to Hanoi was prompted by a medical problem her father was experiencing with his eye. From Hanoi, he continued on to the Soviet Union for eye surgery, where it was estimated he needed at least six months recuperation. When he departed for Moscow, Binh's mother, Me, came to stay with her. Her father, however, returned to Hanoi only two weeks after the surgery. He was eager to return to R Base as he realized victory in the south was close at hand. Binh was grateful for the month she was able to spend with her parents before they departed.

With the fall of Saigon in April 1975, Binh and her classmates were excited about returning south. But they were disappointed to learn they would not return until their schooling was completed. The boys became particularly disruptive in an effort to convince their teachers they should return to their homes, even going so far as to set fire to their dormitory.

Finally, in August 1975, the school relented and the students were taken to Haiphong for transport by ship to Saigon. Binh was joined by her sister, who had come north in 1974. Four years earlier, it had taken her three months to complete the trip by foot along the Trail, free of illness; now it took only a few short days by sea to complete a transit during which time she suffered from a serious bout of seasickness.

The ship stopped first in Vung Tau, south of Saigon, arriving the next day at Ba Son shipyard in Saigon. There she and her sister were met by their parents. Binh's family spent their first night together in a Saigon hotel.

The next day, a family badly decimated by their protracted struggle to reunify their country returned to reoccupy the home they were forced to abandon fifteen years earlier. It was a time of mixed emotions for Binh. While the return to their home was an occasion for joy, it was also one of somber reflection, as she knew that never again would three of her brother's pass through the doorway.

DIGGING DEEP FOR HIGHER EDUCATION

America has a fortunate history. Since gaining her independence, her civilian population, in times of war, has been spared—with one exception through the end of the 20th century—the devastation wrought by a foreign occupation force. That exception was the War of 1812, when British troops landed on American soil, setting fire to the White House and other public buildings.

The combination of geography, the relatively slow advance of long range weapons technology for much of our history, and an increased capability by the U.S. to defend itself thousands of miles from its shores have enabled America to shield her civilian population from the hardship and suffering of warfare other countries have long had to endure. Perhaps this good fortune caused us to forget just how devastating war can be when visited upon a civilian population that finds itself within the battlefield's boundaries.

While Americans followed the Vietnam war in the news media, the Vietnamese lived it as part of their daily existence. While American children rode buses to well-lit, climate-controlled classrooms, Vietnamese children walked to school, wearing camouflage, to attend school in underground classrooms. While American girls were taught to be homemakers, Vietnamese girls were taught to treat combat wounds

(as pictured at left, even those of American pilots). While American children enjoyed leisure time with families at home, Vietnamese children in the south were separated from natural parents to live with adoptive ones in the north—some of whom were never reunited with their families. While American children awoke to occasional nightmares that were not real, Vietnamese children regularly experienced nightmares that were.

With no foreign invaders since 1812, the American people have become de-sensitized to the suffering such an invader can impose. Few Americans, undoubtedly, have given pause to reflect upon the hardship the war imposed upon the Vietnamese population. But it was a war in which a generation of children found themselves being educated under conditions unimaginable to their American counterparts.

As a teacher, Nguyen Thi Phuc Hoa knew these hardships well. Born in 1945, she taught secondary and high school students in Quang Binh Province for most of the war (1964-1972)—a province targeted by U.S. bombers on numerous occasions. She saw her students graduate from high school year after year, only to go off and fight a war from which many never returned.

Classes were held in bunkers dug two meters deep, large enough to accommodate the 30-35 students Hoa normally taught each year. From ground level, all that was visible was the classroom's thatched roof. Underneath it was a ceiling, made from a mixture of dried rice plants and soft clay. Applied to the ceiling framework, the mixture dried in place, creating a fire retardant barrier between the thatched roof and the students underneath.

In a far corner of the structure was the entrance to a long tunnel, meandering for several hundred meters away from the classroom. The children constantly drilled on how to evacuate through the tunnel to safety in the event of an attack. A bomb shelter, much smaller than the classroom, constructed nearby, was often dug jointly by teachers and parents.

The secondary students started class at 6:00 A.M. each day, studying for three hours before returning home to their parents. They walked to and from school, with camouflage on their backs. The camouflage consisted of a specially designed device into which plant stalks were inserted.

Wearing this device (pictured above), children were taught, whenever an aircraft approached, to lie face down on the ground. By doing so, the plant stalks stood straight up, disguising the child while giving the appearance, from the air, of being a natural plant. (Hoa confided, while she never believed American pilots intentionally fired upon schoolchildren, she felt *"they tended to shoot at anything that moved in the mistaken belief it might be the enemy."*)

High school students attended class from 6:00 A.M. to 10:00 A.M. They lived at the school with their teachers in a communal environment rather than at home with their parents. After class, they participated in activities necessary to maintain the commune's self-sufficiency, such as farming. After three years of high school, they graduated. The boys, now young men, joined the military to fulfill their patriotic responsibilities.

Due to a lack of medical services in her village, Hoa taught children first aid. She incorporated into her training many medical problems that were realities of daily life including, for example, treating abdominal wounds by clamping a bowl firmly against the wound to prevent the patient's intestines from spilling out. To stop bleeding, children were taught to press leaves against a wound; for a broken bone, to use bamboo as a splint.

"Occasionally," reported Hoa, *"American airplanes dropped packages of toys and other things such as pens. We collected these and kept them. But one day we were* (falsely) *told the Americans put certain chemicals into these items and if we kept them, we might die. So we burned everything."*

As concern mounted in villages over the children's safety when bombing activity increased, a safety re-location program was initiated by the village elders. Such a program started in Vinh Linh in 1968. Authorities there worked with elders from the northern villages to identify parents willing to serve as foster parents for children from Vinh Linh.

In addition to the hardship of sending their children away, Vinh Linh parents were never given the names of foster parents—they were only told the name of the village to which their child was sent. The natural parents occasionally received progress reports on their children based on input provided to the elders by the foster parents.

It was several years before many of these families were reunited. In some cases, they never were as children died or records of their locations were destroyed or lost. Although her school was never directly targeted by U.S. aircraft, Hoa estimated she still lost seven to ten students between 1966-1970. These were the true *"innocents"* of war, she said sadly, who happened to find themselves in the wrong place at the wrong time.

HANOI'S CHRISTMAS NIGHTMARE

To residents of Hanoi during the war, "Kham Thien" has special meaning. It is a name symbolic of the terrible suffering and tragedy visited upon the civilian population during the Christmas bombings of 1972.

On December 13, 1972, the Paris peace talks had stalled. Washington determined Hanoi was only using the bombing halt, called as a result of the scheduled talks, to continue infiltrating troops into the south. President Nixon wanted to send Hanoi a strong message—one designed to bring the Vietnamese back to the negotiating table. On December 18, 1972, Nixon authorized Operation Linebacker II, or what came to be known as the "Christmas Bombing" of Hanoi and Haiphong. Conducted by the U.S. Air Force, the operation continued through December 29.

Linebacker II resulted in the assembly of the largest air armada in history up to that point in time. Using a rotation system for pilots that allowed the same aircraft to continuously be flown throughout the operation, the U.S. Air Force conducted both day and night attacks. Daytime attacks were conducted by tactical strike aircraft; night attacks by B-52s and F-111s. Military targets such as airfields, antiaircraft batteries, surface-to-air missile sites, railroads, and storage facilities were hit repeatedly during the eleven-day period.

The actual damage inflicted upon Hanoi and Haiphong during this bombing period was not limited to just military targets. An unfortunate consequence of war is that collateral damage—i.e., damage inflicted upon targets not intended to be hit—always occurs. On the evening of December 26, U.S. aircraft inflicted extensive collateral damage upon the residents of Hanoi as thirty-nine bombs fell on Kham Thien Street.

❉   ❉   ❉

Although the order for residents to evacuate the city was given, Phung Thi Tiem, then 50, stayed behind, as she was responsible for providing security along Kham Thien Street.

"All the people evacuated the city in accordance with the government's order. It was the day after Christmas, however, and many believed the U.S. would not bomb on this occasion. So several residents returned to Hanoi to get food and other items before returning to the evacuation site." That was why many people were in Kham Thien at the time of the bombing." (The above picture is of part of Kham Thien Street after the bombing.)

"We were told by the government ever since 5:00 P.M. that U.S. war planes would come later that day. Other people working in the factories in Hanoi could not leave due to the importance of their jobs."

"When we heard the sirens, we immediately went to our underground shelters. The sirens started around 10:15 P.M., while I was at home. I immediately ran out and shouted to people to go to their shelters. I rushed out with my husband and (seventeen-year old) son. My husband and I climbed into a two-man shelter on the street while my son found another one. Some people built shelters in their homes; others depended on those along the street provided by the government."

(Three kinds of shelters were constructed in Hanoi during the war:

[1] Most were small, circular two-man shelters made simply by inserting a concrete drainpipe upright into a hole in the ground (pictured at left and on the following page). The open end was flush with the surface. After entering the shelter, occupants slid a five to six-centimeter thick cement lid into position to seal themselves in. The handle of the lid consisted of two elongated holes used to slide the lid overhead. These holes served the additional purpose of providing ventilation. The shelters were located along both sides of Hanoi's

streets about ten meters apart.

[2] The second type was a rectangular shaped shelter dug a meter deep into the ground. Most shelters dug in other parts of the country were much deeper but the soil in the Hanoi area retained water at fairly shallow depths. The deeper a person dug, the greater danger wet  shelter walls might collapse. Shallow, open-air shelters were dug, which were then covered by an A-frame roof constructed of bamboo and dried mud. A few of these shelters were built along each street, accommodating up to ten people. Obviously, such a shelter afforded occupants little protection against a direct or near-direct hit, although it protected against shrapnel from bombs exploding several meters away.

[3] The third type of shelter was a zigzag-shaped trench line about the same depth as the rectangular shelter. This too had a bamboo and mud construction roof. These shelters accommodated the largest number of people—up to as many as thirty.)

"There were no pre-assigned shelters. People just jumped into the nearest available shelter during an attack.

"The bombs began to fall about 10:45 P.M that evening . . . As they did, I tried to envision where they were falling . . . They got closer and closer. One of the last ones fell about twenty to thirty meters away from our shelter, blowing the top off. When that happened, I stood up. There was dust in the air (from collapsed buildings)*...After the bombing stopped, we went to any place where a house had been destroyed or we heard voices...I immediately would assist the injured get into an ambulance. We heard the voice of an old couple but could not help as a four-story building had collapsed on top of them. We attempted to get them out but the debris was too heavy. The voices soon stopped. The next day we found their bodies after a crane was brought in to assist. There were many instances of people being buried under rubble and cranes having to be used to get them out.*

"It was not until three hours later I saw my son and knew he was all right." As to the scene of destruction that day, Tiem observed, *"We*

could not cry. The tears had dried from our bodies. If I had seen an American pilot that day, I would have killed him."

❖ ❖ ❖

Colonel Le Kim (pictured at left), a veteran of the war with the French and a journalist, was in Hanoi on the day of the Kham Thien bombing.

"I worked at the newspaper," he related. *"My house was located two kilometers from my office, on the other side of Kham Thien Street. Today the street is completely different from what it was. During the war, it was a poor and heavily populated area with only a few multi-level buildings.*

"The order was given earlier in the morning and later at noon to evacuate the street. People were sent at noon to ensure residents complied with the earlier order. I wondered at the time why there was such a special order. It was only after the war I learned Ho Chi Minh predicted the B-52s would drop bombs on Hanoi as a last effort to end the war. Ho Chi Minh even suggested to General Giap that he bring all the antiaircraft batteries and missiles from the DMZ (to Hanoi) to attack the B-52s—but Giap did not want to leave his troops unprotected.

"My wife was a teacher. She and my two children departed for the evacuation site while I stayed behind to work in my office...returning to my house later that day. Only my nephew and I stayed there. At night, the B-52s dropped bombs in Hanoi and, although there was no military target there, also on Dong Anh, located thirteen kilometers away from Hanoi, where my wife and children had gone.

"The attacks went on for several days. On the first night, a B-52 was shot down and the pilot captured. On the following day, I met that pilot. When I asked him his name, he said it was Richard Johnson. We took him along the streets damaged by the B-52s. He said he was just doing what he was ordered to do. I smiled and told him not to worry because the ones who committed the crime were Richard Nixon and Lyndon

Johnson. I told him it was ironic his name was a combination of the names of both those presidents.

"But for the next few days the situation got worse. As a journalist, I found it more difficult to fight with a pen than with a rifle. My pen could not shoot at the B-52s—but my rifle could. I was working at the newspaper until midnight as we had a 3:00 A.M. deadline. While on my way home on my bicycle, the B-52s came again. Bunkers were built along the streets of Hanoi every several meters so whenever the planes came, people immediately looked for an empty one.

"On the first days, many houses were destroyed but with few casualties. The biggest loss came on December 26, 1972. The rumor circulated that, since U.S. pilots loved Jesus Christ, they would not bomb Hanoi at Christmas time. Believing this, many people returned to Kham Thien Street. When they were advised over the loudspeakers to evacuate the streets, they just nodded and continued to go about their business.

"That night, there was a blackout in Hanoi as the sirens were sounded and information was broadcasted that the American bombers were 80 kilometers away, soon followed by an announcement they were only 50 kilometers away. Everybody immediately went to their shelters. The next broadcast reported the planes were 30 kilometers away, nobody was to be outside and all militias were to be ready."

(Militia members were required to take their weapons with them and occupy open-air shelters so they could shoot at low-flying aircraft.)

"After the last broadcast, we faintly heard antiaircraft fire off in the distance—followed, a few minutes later, by the first bombs being dropped. Even though some of the bombs fell as far as 30 kilometers away, we still felt the concussion in Hanoi...

"Soon the sounds of the bombs falling were drowned out by the nearby sounds of our antiaircraft batteries firing...One B-52 was on fire and lit up the sky over Hanoi (pictured above). Hearing about this, some

children immediately left their shelters and clapped their hands. They were so excited they came out of the shelters while our anti-air batteries were still firing.

"Later I heard but could not believe that Kham Thien street was bombed. I rode over on my bicycle with a friend to see for myself. The street was destroyed so we could not get in there. One side of the street had mass destruction—much more so than the other side. The air was full of smoke. The next day the smell was even worse, continuing for four days due to decaying bodies.

Bach Mai Hospital after the bombing

"Carpet bombing took place, from Bach Mai Hospital to Kham Thien. It was a terrible bombardment...Kham Thien was the most crowded street in Hanoi. As it was far from any military target, the residents thought it was safe...but we took our heaviest losses there...

"A lot of planes were shot down and pilots captured. The last pilot I met was a Harry Ewell who was shot down by a gunner named Bham Tuan. (Colonel Kim was unsure of the spelling of the pilot's last name. I was unable to find a POW by the name of "Ewell.") *I witnessed a discussion between Harry Ewell and Bham Tuan after Ewell's capture. The two men represented quite a contrast—Bham Tuan was young and single; Harry Ewell was older and married with seven children. Despite the circumstances, the meeting between the two men was not spiteful...Harry Ewell's name reminded me of another president, Harry*

Truman, who dropped the nuclear bomb on Japan. Because of the coincidence of the name similarities to all these American presidents, I was able to remember the names of those pilots."

꙰ ꙰ ꙰

Nguyen Van Tung, 46, was the proud father of six sons and two daughters. His eldest son, Nguyen Van Giang, 26, spent four years in the army, serving at Khe Sanh and driving supply trucks along the Ho Chi Minh Trail. Giang was released from the army in 1971 as he had contracted some sort of ailment, which caused his body to swell. He was sent back to Hanoi to live with his parents and recuperate. Soon after his return to Hanoi, Giang married Cao Thi Duc, 23.

As his physical condition improved, Giang returned to driving trucks down the Ho Chi Minh Trail, as a civilian volunteer rather than a soldier. He spent Christmas Day, 1972, and part of the next packing his truck for his transit late that night. As fate would have it, Giang's truck would make the trip down the Ho Chi Minh Trail—but Giang would not.

With tears in his eyes, Giang's father, Tung, provided the details of his son's last hours.

"My son came home to sleep (in preparation for his trip)," he explained. *"My wife, two daughters and two of my sons were taken to the evacuation site earlier."*

Tung, Giang's wife and three of Tung's other sons were together in the house with Giang as he slept. Awakened by the sirens, Giang immediately rushed outside with the others to find shelter. Tung watched to make sure Giang and his wife, as well as his other three sons, were safe before he climbed into a shelter. Having seen the three boys scramble into one shelter and Giang with his wife jump into a zigzag trench, Tung found his own shelter.

"I was in a two-man bomb shelter by myself," he related. *"During the bombing, it was violently knocked sideways, causing it to partially collapse. I was covered by mud and debris. When the bombing stopped, I was unable to remove the top of the shelter to get out. But I knew there*

were specialized teams that went around the city after the bombings looking for people to dig out. About 3:00 A.M. the next morning, a team member stuck a pole inside my shelter to see if anyone was alive inside. I grabbed the stick to let him know I was. They opened the lid and had to twist my body to get me out. It took them fifteen minutes to remove me from the shelter."

When Tung was pulled out, he was immediately greeted by three of his sons. Giang and his wife, his other sons informed him, had not yet been found. Tung looked over at the shelter he had seen Giang and his wife enter. To his horror, it was totally destroyed.

"There were two bomb craters, one right on top of their shelter. My three sons and I began to look for some sign of the occupants. There were none to be found."

Tung and his sons searched outside the shelter as well, soon making a macabre discovery. *"I found a body about one hundred meters from Giang's shelter,"* said Tung. *"While the face on the body was indiscernible, I could tell from the watch and physical build it was my son.*

"We brought his body back to our house. We placed him inside a coffin provided to us by the government, and took him to the cemetery."

The remains of his daughter-in-law were never found—as was the case with most other occupants of the shelter—the force of the two explosions having vaporized their bodies. It was believed the shelter held as many as twenty-seven people at the time it was destroyed.

What made the event even more painful for Tung was the fact his daughter-in-law was six months pregnant with what was to be his first grandchild.

❉ ❉ ❉

In late December 1972, Dang Ngoc Long, 26, stood at the front door of her home on Hang Ngang Street in the Hoan Kien District in central Hanoi, silently observing the activity along her street.

"I saw droves of people leaving due to the bombing of Hanoi. The city was becoming a ghost town as 80 percent of the population departed. This was a significant increase over previous times when, at most, 30 percent of the people evacuated. It was a very cold day. It was sad to see everyone go. Vietnamese are very family-oriented, traditionally remaining in the same area where they were born. It ran against this tradition to pack up our belongings and leave our homes. I felt sad—but I also felt proud. For I knew they were leaving to survive—in order to propagate the next generation. It was difficult too because, upon leaving the city, the families were split up to spread the risk of loss."

Even when her area was not bombed, Long's concern was constantly for friends and relatives who were in those areas that fell under attack. *"My brothers, sisters and parents lived in different parts of the city and surrounding area,"* Long explained. *"If I heard a bombing in progress 30 kilometers away, I always turned in the direction where they were living and worried about their safety."*

The government advised all nonessential inhabitants to vacate the city. Only those people whose assistance was necessary to continue running city services and to defend Hanoi were instructed to remain.

The exodus of residents was constant. As Long gazed down the street, she saw evacuees, their belongings packed onto bicycles, hurriedly making their way out of the city.

Long and her husband, while nonessential residents, made the decision to remain behind. They had been enduring bombings in the city ever since they had first started.

"The first time the bombers came, we were very afraid," recalled Long. *"But then we became used to it. Some people became so used to it over time they did not even bother going to the shelters. We constantly heard the sirens. The number of bombings we experienced each day varied. Some days there were several; others there were just one; sometimes it was a false alarm and there was no bombing at all.*

"In 1970-1971, two and three man circular bomb shelters were dug all along the streets of Hanoi," Long shared. *"These shelters influenced the preparation of our food. Often there were insufficient rice supplies*

to feed our students. So wet flour was used to make cakes to feed them. These were baked in the same shape as our bomb shelters."

City residents remaining behind in Hanoi were under orders to go to individual shelters once the sirens sounded. Perhaps it was the only way to demonstrate their defiance against the Americans, but during the entire war, Long and her husband never once sought the safety of a shelter. They remained at home, waiting for fate to run its course.

The tradition of remaining close to one's birthplace was followed by Long and her husband—a tradition they hoped to pass on to their children. The couple was married on Christmas Day, 1971. By the time the Christmas Bombing campaign got underway, Long was nine months pregnant with her first child.

However, not even Long's advanced pregnancy prompted her to seek shelter during air attacks. As Christmas Day, 1972, arrived, a lull in the bombings created a false sense of security among many of the civilians. Residents, who evacuated earlier, returned to the city in large numbers following President Nixon's announcement the bombings would be halted in observance of Christmas Day. The residents of Hanoi assumed the halt would carry over to the next day. It was an assumption that cost many of them their lives.

Most of those who returned on December 26 were younger evacuees. The trip back into the city was too burdensome for the very old and very young. So the more robust evacuees took on the responsibility of returning to Hanoi to retrieve food for the others and to check on homes.

"I cannot describe everything we endured, every sacrifice we made," related Long. *"How could we bear such hardship during that time? Because we respected ourselves, we had to scratch out a living. We endured shortages of food, a lack of electricity and many other needs that people require. And it was even tougher for those in the countryside for we had more facilities in Hanoi than they had. We lived with fear, worry, a longing for loved ones. We had not only material wants but emotional ones as well. The young evacuees who periodically returned to the city traveled a hundred kilometers. And when they got there, the*

streets were in bad shape; it was difficult to get around. People banded together, however, to survive."

Earlier in the day on December 26, Long began feeling contractions. By 5:00 P.M., she realized the birth of her child was imminent. Her husband helped her onto the back seat of his bicycle. As he pedaled feverishly, Long tried to keep her balance, her contractions increasing in frequency.

Long's husband took her to Ngo Quyen Station. This was not the main hospital. It was a makeshift facility built specifically for maternity patients. Due to air attacks, it was decided to detach those medical facilities that were more self-contained from the main hospital to reduce the risk of losing an entire hospital staff. These facilities were then positioned at different locations around the city.

Ngo Quyen Station consisted of a single level, above ground facility, with a delivery room and patient ward. A specially designed maternity treatment area was dug underground—one with which Long would become intimately familiar before her discharge.

Long's husband was not permitted to remain with his wife, so he returned home to await the birth of his child, leaving Long in the care of the center's doctor and two nurses. Long was initially placed in a room with five other women—and an equal number of babies. The equal number of babies to mothers suggested to Long that all the other patients were recovering from their deliveries and were simply waiting to return home with their newborn children.

As she lay in the aboveground portion of the facility, Long felt her contractions become more severe. In her pain and discomfort, she was grateful the babies were mercifully quiet. Having just completed another contraction, she glanced over at the clock. It was 8:00 P.M.

As Long awaited her next contraction, the relative quiet was shattered. Air raid sirens began to wail. Electricity to Ngo Quyen Station—and the entire city—was immediately cut off. As the nurses lit kerosene lamps, Long felt the tiny life within her womb struggling to get out. By 8:15 P.M., she gave birth to a healthy, 3.1-kilo baby boy.

The birth was a rough one for both mother and baby. It tore Long's vagina, resulting in severe bleeding.

A nurse explained the tear had to be sutured, but no anesthesia was available. Additionally, due to a shortage of surgical needles and self-dissolving thread, the procedure was to be performed with ordinary sewing needle and thread.

As the two nurses set about their task, Long reflected on what a stark contrast they represented. One, very young, appeared to lack adequate training; the other, in her mid-50s, wore thick glasses but appeared to be more experienced.

As the surgery progressed, Long became somewhat discomforted by the older nurse's obviously bad eyesight, especially as the woman's vision had been further encumbered by the limited lighting provided by the single kerosene lamp in the room. Long felt conditions were ripe for disaster. Unfortunately, her fears were well founded.

The older nurse, straining to see what she was doing, inserted the needle and pulled the thread through. After one or two more insertions of the needle, however, she realized there was insufficient lighting to observe what she was doing. Needing a pair of younger eyes, she called the other nurse over to assist.

"Although I never cried out during the entire time of my delivery," shared Long, *"whenever I felt the needle pass through me, I shrieked in pain. The entire room heard my screams. The other patients became very nervous and anxious. I felt the needle pass through me again and again, followed by the pulling of the thread behind it. After twenty minutes of this, during which time the needle was inserted a total of ten times, the nurses told me the suturing was done improperly and needed to be redone."*

The surgery involved sewing the labia majorum (an outer layer of skin on either side of the vagina) together with the labia minorum (an inner layer similarly situated), on both the left and right sides. In the limited lighting, however, the nurse inadvertently sewed an outer layer on the left side with an inner layer on the right of the vagina. Consequently, the thread had to be pulled back out through the skin, resulting in additional bleeding by the patient. After removing the suturing thread, the two nurses began to repeat the surgical process.

Conditions were far from ideal for surgery. The absence of anesthesia, the lack of lighting, the cold, the intermittent drone of air raid sirens and constant blaring of loudspeakers announcing the closing distance between the bombers and the city—all served to complicate a rather simple surgical procedure.

As the procedure commenced a second time, Long again screamed out in pain. After twenty more insertions of the needle, the nurse finally informed the operation had been successfully completed. Additional complications quickly arose, however. Considerable swelling developed in the area of the original tear. Concerned about infection, the nurse applied a handkerchief she had dipped into boiling water. It was so hot tongs had to be used to extract the handkerchief from the water. The nurse repeatedly applied the steaming hot handkerchief to the swollen area of the vagina. Each application was met with yet another scream from the patient.

"This procedure," Long said, *"proved even more painful than the actual surgery itself."*

At the end of the operation, she was moved to a small table to rest.

"Exhausted at this point, I thought I would be able to stay there for a while. But then the sirens started again and I was moved to the underground shelter. In a normal situation, I would have been left to rest upstairs—but the pending attack denied me that simple luxury."

An underground level to the maternity hospital had been excavated for situations such as this. Access was made through a hole dug in the floor, located in a corner of the aboveground facility. There, a narrow stairway, carved into the earth below, led down into total darkness. Only one person could walk down the stairs at a time. Guided by a faint light emanating from the room above her, Long made the descent alone. Still suffering from her surgical process, each step was excruciatingly painful.

"To avoid rubbing my thighs together as much as possible, I walked like a bear," she recalled.

The steps in the floor descended to a depth of about 1.5 meters. At the bottom, Long found she stood in a small open area known as a "frog shelter." Standing in the center, she saw four very short horizontal tunnels extending in each direction—hardly long enough for one person to lie down in. Each tunnel opening was eighty centimeters wide and dug into the earth about knee-high. It was clear the purpose of each of these tunnels was to serve as a delivery chamber during an air raid. Their design allowed an expectant mother, lying on her back, to slide into the tunnel chamber with legs extended out. From the nurse's station in the center of the frog shelter, the nurse had 360-degree access to care for any one of four expectant mothers at once.

While the design of this frog shelter was one seeking to enhance delivery of a new life into the world under difficult conditions, Long could not help but view the shelter much differently.

"It was cold," she said. "There was a lack of oxygen in the shelter. The four chambers reminded me more of death than of life. Each looked like a coffin rather than a birthing chamber."

As Long crawled into her chamber, she saw two of the three remaining chambers were occupied. Another recuperating mother, who gave birth earlier in the day, was in one; four newborns, bundled together in a single container and covered with blankets, slept in the third. Among these was her own child. By 9:45 P.M. that evening, Long was lying in her chamber, gazing up at the earthen roof only centimeters above her face.

"I just lay there and listened," she reported. "I heard bombs fall and felt the earth shake. Dirt and small stones fell on my face. I feared the earth would collapse around my baby and me. I was suffocating and very uncomfortable. My back hurt; my vulva hurt; my legs were numbed by the cold and the hard earth upon which I lay, cushioned only by a single sheet under me. It was wet. I could not sleep. I felt dazed. Periodically a nurse came down to check on us. My son began screaming like a siren. The air attack that night was the most terrible to which Hanoi was ever subjected. It was clearly the most terrible night of my entire life."

Although the bombing stopped around 11:30 P.M, Long was not allowed to leave the chamber. She remained until 7:00 A.M. the next morning, fading in and out of sleep. After dawn, she was returned to the aboveground facility and placed in a bed. Still in much pain from her surgery, she remained in the hospital for two more days and nights.

During her hospitalization, the air raid sirens continued to sound on occasion. When they did, Long immediately gathered her son up and, having mastered her bear walk, took him to a nearby shelter. Hospital regulations required a mother in Long's condition remain at the facility for at least four days. But unable to endure the situation there after the first two days, Long signed a release agreeing to accept personal responsibility for her condition. She then called her husband to come pick her up.

While Long's husband had been able to transport his pregnant wife to the hospital on his own bicycle before the delivery, the overnight increase in size of his family now required a different mode of transportation. He arrived at the hospital in a "cyclo." (Pictured at right, a cyclo is a common means of transportation for hire in Vietnam. A hybrid between a bicycle and a rickshaw, it has a rickshaw-like seat, with wheels on both sides in front and the rear half of a bicycle behind the rickshaw seat. The driver  sits on a bicycle seat, directly behind the rickshaw seat, from where he pedals and steers.)

The events of that night left its scars on Long and her son. It was six years before Long was able to put the pain, fear and anxiety she experienced that December night behind her, thus giving her the courage to have a second child.

For her son, Quan, the problems were more enduring. The harsh realities of a nation at war were visited upon him at the moment of his birth. His screams that evening and during the subsequent nights of the Christmas Bombing, with sirens wailing in the background, resulted in Quan being given the nickname "coe"—Vietnamese for "siren." Into his late teens and early twenties, Quan experienced problems with sleep walking, insomnia, and anxiety. Sudden, loud noises would spook him, leaving him anxious and on edge. To this day, he still fears cold, dark places.

⚜ ⚜ ⚜

Perhaps those who suffer most in war are the children exposed to its full fury.

Tran Cong Tan, a war correspondent for Hanoi, had the opportunity to see much during the Vietnam conflict.

But to Tan, the worst aspect of the fighting was witnessing the impact war had on the children. *"It forces a child to grow up too quickly,"* he observed. *"It causes a child, much too early, to learn the realities of life and death."*

"In December, 1972, Hanoi—and in particular Kham Thien in the central part of the city—had suffered through twelve days of bombings. Children were sheltered underground in the care of attendants. At one point, a bombing lull occurred and a group of attendants, fearful the attacks were getting too close to their shelter, decided to transfer the children to a safer location.

Rescue & Recovery Efforts

"An assistant, emerging from the shelter with a one-year old baby girl, set her down for a moment to render help to an injured victim. A few feet away, several bodies—all victims of the most recent bombing attack—were laid out, to be picked up later by a disposal team. "The child crawled over to the bodies. Perhaps thinking the dead were merely sleeping, she placed both hands upon a body as if attempting to wake the person up. Unable to do so, the child pulled her hands away— only to find them covered with blood. The assistant, now realizing her charge had wandered off, rushed over to pick the girl up. As she did so, the child held her upturned hands towards the attendant. Still of too tender an age to speak, the quizzical look on the child's face said it all. "Had the child been able to understand, how could it be explained to her?" inquired Tan.

✻ ✻ ✻

According to Hanoi's records, the bombing at Kham Thien claimed 283 civilian lives, 55 of whom were children. Another 266 civilians were wounded, including 31 children. A total of 178 children were orphaned. The loss of many of these young lives is documented in photographs and film footage in Hanoi's archives. One of the saddest testimonials to such a loss was reflected in film footage taken immediately after the Kham Tien bombing.

Part of Kham Thien Street after the bombing

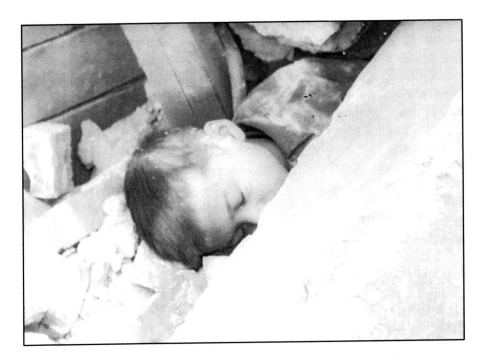

The film clearly reflects the utter devastation of the air attack. Along Kham Thien Street, few homes and buildings can be seen still standing. Mounds of rubble stand where buildings used to be. As the camera pans the devastation, the observer's eye is caught by a particularly tragic scene. Protruding from amidst the rubble is the upper torso of a child—a young boy, perhaps nine years of age—crushed by the heavy debris scattered about his lifeless body.

His arms lay outstretched, as if he were carrying something in his hands at the time of his death. As the camera continues to pan the scene; the final focus of the child's attention in the last moments of his brief life becomes apparent. On the ground, a half meter away from the boy's hands, lays a partially crushed birdcage. While the falling blocks of concrete claimed the life of the young boy, they spared the lives of two small canaries, still fluttering about within what space remained in the cage.

The last act of this boy's life was one of love—to save his cherished canaries.

In addition to the human toll, there was a heavy loss of property. Records indicate 533 houses were totally destroyed with 1200 more seriously damaged.

Residents of Kham Thien contend nothing of military significance lay in the area at the time of its destruction—the closest possible target was a railroad station more than 200 meters away. But even that, they pointed out, was destroyed five days earlier in another attack.

In spite of the grief over their losses, many Kham Thien survivors forgive the American pilots who bombed them. They do not believe their tragedy was the result of intentional acts by their attackers but rather, as one victim simply described it, *"an unfortunate accident of an unfortunate war."*

Section 4:

Patience

To the American fighting man in Vietnam, time meant everything; to his Vietnamese counterpart, it meant nothing. While the American soldier regularly kept count of the number of days he had left to serve "in-country," the Vietnamese soldier never knew how long his tour would be. For some, death or the loss of a limb would cut short their service; but for most, it was commonplace to serve five years or more at the front. Dates and time lost significance to the Vietnamese. All that mattered was one's survival today so he could fight again tomorrow. This taught the Vietnamese soldier patience. He learned if opportunity did not come today, to wait; and, when opportunity did arrive, to remain patient in the conduct of the attack to ensure ultimate success.

The following accounts provide some insight as to how the Vietnamese viewed patience as a weapon to be used against their enemy and how they effectively employed it to ensure the success of their attacks.

By the Dawn's Early Light 126

Hello, Dolly! 133

BY THE DAWN'S EARLY LIGHT

No single group generated more concern among U.S. and South Vietnamese forces than the North Vietnamese Special Forces.

These commandos earned the respect of those they faced on the battlefield. They presented a multiple offensive threat to American forces, the most formidable of which was their incredible ability to silently penetrate even the most secure positions. In some instances, the commando took days to enter and exit a facility without the defender's knowledge. Always working in teams, with the number of teams determined by the mission, an argument can be made that, pound-for-pound, these men probably inflicted more damage on the American war effort than did any other single combat unit.

In 1972, Colonel Tong Viet Duong commanded Special Force Regiment #113—over a thousand men strong—specially trained in the art of unconventional warfare. He dispatched a squad of his commandos to conduct an attack against the enemy's largest ammunition storage depot, located at Long Binh (pictured above) near Ben Hoa.

The facility at Long Binh was large, covering an area of almost fifty square kilometers. Various types of munitions were stored here, from small arms ammunition to artillery rounds to aircraft armament—all for later distribution to bases throughout the South. Recognizing such a munitions depot posed a tempting target, U.S. and South Vietnamese defenders strove to make Long Binh impenetrable. They thought they had.

A series of nine wire mesh fences, standing two meters high and topped with barbed wire, encircled the facility. The distance between the first (or most exterior) fence and the ninth fence was several hundred meters. Small hills and streams permeated the area. The interval between the first and second fence was much greater than the interval between all the remaining fences. Guard towers were situated at regular intervals, between 200 to 500 meters, just inside the exterior perimeter fence. They were arranged to allow defenders a fairly effective crossfire against intruders. The towers were manned twenty-four hours a day. For nighttime observation and security, searchlights were mounted on the guard towers, continuously sweeping the area in front and behind the first perimeter fence after sunset. Tin cans were tied to interior fences to alert defenders of an inattentive intruder who brushed against them. Anti-personnel mines were buried in between fences. The defenders periodically relocated these to keep intruders guessing as to exact locations of the mines at any given time. Trip wire flares were set. When accidentally triggered, a flare was fired several hundred meters into the air, deploying a small parachute and providing several minutes of illumination for the defenders as the flare floated back down to earth. The storage facilities within the Long Binh compound were widely dispersed so as to prevent an explosion at one from causing a sympathetic detonation of another. Motorized sentries regularly patrolled the area, usually at five-minute intervals. Foot patrols, some with guard dogs, supplemented the motorized patrols.

While minefields within the perimeter fences seemingly provided defenders with a sense of security, indirectly they worked to the benefit of the intruder. Due to the presence of mines in between the fences, the grass there could not be cut—so it was allowed to grow freely. The tall grass provided ideal concealment by which an intruder could penetrate the facility. Complacent, the defenders allowed this grass to grow all the way up to the exterior fence, making it possible for an intruder to conceal his entire approach. This avenue of approach did not go unnoticed by Colonel Duong.

It is important to recognize attacks such as the one planned on Long Binh were seldom the result of a quick decision; rather, they usually took place only after months—or even years—of planning. During the planning phase, extensive intelligence was gathered on a potential target. In the case of Long Binh, the facility was only one of several possible targets considered and was selected only after a two year collection effort had been completed.

"If we focused just on Long Binh," explained Duong, *"we effectively put all our eggs in one basket."* Time was spent assessing intelligence collected on a number of possible targets to determine which one was to be given top priority. Long Binh, Duong explained, was ultimately selected for two reasons, *"It was the most easily accessible target and, due to its size, we could inflict the greatest damage on the enemy's weapons storage system."*

Duong compared the use of intelligence collected on a target to the collection of rice: *"When one collects rice in the field, one cannot immediately eat it all. If one does, he will starve in the future. Intelligence, like rice, has to be collected and saved, to be used at the right time.*

"We were constantly sending intelligence people out during daylight hours into the facility to get information—and they were constantly given access," said Duong. *"Sometimes we were able to sneak personnel onto the base. This was done a number of ways. We might send someone, ostensibly to meet a friend or relative on the base, but really to observe and record pertinent information such as distances and locations of various storage areas. Or, sometimes, a South Vietnamese officer loyal to us was scheduled to go to Long Binh to pick up a delivery and took one of our intelligence officers with him. Or, on occasion, our people might accompany local workers on base, such as off loaders and drivers, who were loyal to us. These workers also volunteered information as to where they felt the weaknesses in the base defenses were. And, sometimes, personnel loyal to the Saigon government unintentionally provided us with information."*

Taking the needed time to develop it, all intelligence collection on Long Binh had been completed and the facility was given priority status as a target for Regiment #113.

Several days prior to the actual attack, a "dry run" was planned and conducted. This was standard procedure for important targets. Undertaken by a single two-man reconnaissance team, so as not to risk the entire commando squad, it had numerous objectives including: testing the facility's defensive perimeter and security, establishing entry/exit routes into/out of the depot and determining the actual time to reach the pre-determined targets located inside the facility to set explosive charges.

All the activities of the commando squad to be carried out on the actual day of the attack were carried out by the reconnaissance team with one very important exception—no explosive charges were carried with them. When the actual attack was launched a few days later, it would be this reconnaissance team that would lead the commando squad into the facility.

After nightfall, a two-man reconnaissance team began its dry run on Long Binh depot. Inching its way on the ground towards the exterior fence, the team's approach was easily hidden by the tall grass. Upon reaching the first fence, they did not cut the wire—that was only to be done during the actual attack. Instead, the fence was spread, to let the team to pass through, and then carefully returned to its original form. To cut the fence would leave a sign that a penetration of the facility had occurred, eliminating the element of surprise for the actual attack.

After penetrating the exterior fence, the reconnaissance team slowly threaded its way through minefields while avoiding detection by guard tower personnel. Mines and trip wires were located and then deactivated by inserting a pin into each device. As the team successfully dealt with each device, it inched its way forward to its objective—the next interior fence. Reaching that, the team repeated the procedure of locating and disarming mines and flares in between the next successive set of fences as it progressively cut an access path through the facility's perimeter defenses.

The reconnaissance team's dry run began at 8:00 PM that evening; its objective was to get half way between the fifth and sixth fences by 11:00 PM. That timetable was met. While several hours of darkness remained, the team did not want to risk getting too close to the base interior by sunrise. Still concealed by the tall grass, both team members dug a hole into the ground, crawled in, and waited.

As dawn broke, the daily routine commenced inside the Long Binh facility—its defenders unaware intruders lurked nearby. The reconnaissance team quietly rested in their hiding places, remaining there throughout the day, only meters away from enemy soldiers.

After darkness descended, the team continued its progress in penetrating the remaining fences. Just after midnight, they crawled through the last interior fence and into the depot itself. Once inside, they wasted no time, marking off distances to the pre-determined targets and noting times required to reach each. Its mission completed, the team withdrew just as silently as it had entered, retrograding its way back out through the nine fences the same way it had come in.

By dawn, the team was safely back at its regiment, briefing the commando squad responsible for making the actual attack on Long Binh.

As the reconnaissance team withdrew from Long Binh, an observer was posted in a concealed position, a safe distance from the facility, where constant surveillance could be maintained over the facility and the reconnaissance team's marked approach route. This was to ensure the defenders did nothing to impact the route before the actual attack.

To meet its timetable, the squad set out in the evening two days before the attack, at 8:00 PM. The same reconnaissance team commenced a reentry into the Long Binh facility. This time, it was followed by five other commando teams—each armed with explosives and timing devices.

Twenty men were involved in the operation. Each team consisted of either three or four men, depending upon their assigned target within the compound. The larger a target, the more explosives required, thus necessitating the assignment of another man to carry additional explosives.

As the reconnaissance team led the way through the exterior fence, this time a hole was cut through the wire mesh, large enough for one man to pass at a time. The last man to pass through reconnected the wire mesh to conceal the squad's penetration. The lead team continued to advance along the same route it took a few days earlier, still checking every inch of ground to ensure no new mines had been planted or overlooked on their previous penetration.

Once the teams departed for Long Binh, Colonel Duong had no further contact with them. The squad members communicated amongst themselves silently through the use of hand signals. As the lead team reached the halfway point again between the fifth and sixth fences, the squad held up its advance and dug in for the night. As dawn broke, the teams were still well concealed within their hiding places. They remained there throughout the day, quietly waiting for nightfall to return. Soon after dusk, they continued to move forward.

By midnight, the squad had breached the last fence. Each team immediately proceeded to its individually assigned target, carefully avoiding the mobile sentries within the facility. Explosives were set using an MI-8 timing device. No bigger than a man's finger, this device allowed for detonation to be delayed several hours so teams could safely evacuate the facility. Using a three-hour delay on the devices, the teams began their withdrawal.

The teams were to reassemble on the outside of the last interior fence before commencing their withdrawal together as a squad. A five-minute leeway was allowed—no longer. If a team failed to show within that time, the others withdrew without it.

The operation went well—each team completed its assigned mission and rendezvoused on schedule. The withdrawal commenced with each squad member following in trace of the man in front of him, along the same route used to enter the facility: where one man set his foot or hand print, nineteen other sets of hands and feet followed. With the access route having been cleared several times now, the squad was able to withdraw much more quickly than it had advanced. Once outside the exterior fence, the commandos made their way to regimental headquarters. There, the squad leader reported to Duong that their mission had been successfully completed.

❉ ❉ ❉

As dawn approached that morning, Colonel Duong stood with his division commander on the high ground overlooking the Long Binh facility. Both men repeatedly checked their watches. The silence was soon broken. One tremendous explosion after another was heard as each of the detonating devices went off in quick succession—followed by numerous secondary explosions as stacks of ammunition throughout the facility were sympathetically detonated. Dawn came early that morning as 30,000 tons of exploding munitions lit up the sky. The ground beneath the two men shook with each explosion. The concussion was so great tremors were felt thirty kilometers away.

When daylight finally arrived, Duong saw a huge cloud of smoke billowing from the Long Binh facility. Satisfied with the results, he and his commander quietly slipped back into the cover of the jungle. Though neither man spoke, the continuing chain of explosions spoke for them. Two years of planning had met with great success. The enemy had been dealt a serious blow and, to Duong's further satisfaction, without the loss of a single commando.

HELLO DOLLY!

In war, success or failure on the battlefield often turns on the quality of intelligence collected about one's enemy. During the Vietnam conflict, both sides gathered intelligence from whatever sources were available. Information was constantly collected, assessed and evaluated to determine its value. The ultimate goal was to learn as much as possible about every aspect of the enemy's fighting capabilities—his strengths, his weaknesses, his strategy and planning, his morale, etc.

Sometimes what was obtained by either side was very accurate; at other times, it was not. When accurate, it provided the user with a significant opportunity to exploit the other side; when inaccurate, it often spelled disaster for the side relying on it. But it was all part of the game to learn as much as possible about one's enemy and to apply that knowledge to the user's advantage.

The story of Colonel Tran Van Sang is of interest for three reasons. First, it occurred in the early stages of the war as Hanoi attempted to assess the fighting capabilities of the American soldier. Second, it involved one of the most bizarre pieces of information to be gathered on a battlefield and relied upon for its intelligence value. Third, it involved an assessment, which enabled the North Vietnamese to assess, inadvertently yet, in the long run, accurately, a weak link in the American fighting soldier's armor. At the time this information was obtained, the North Vietnamese were desperately searching for an American "Achilles heel" to exploit. They found it, renewing confidence in their ability to defeat a superior fighting force.

* * *

In late 1965, Colonel Sang's force engaged one of the U.S. Army's best fighting units, the 101st Airborne Division, at Plei Me. After the battle and withdrawal of the 101st from the area, Sang's men immediately searched the battlefield. This was a common practice—to locate any items of possible intelligence value the enemy may have discarded.

The search resulted in a rather bizarre find—an inflatable doll, which became a life-sized, anatomically correct female!

At first blush, such a discovery appeared to have no significant intelligence value. However, a Vietnamese intelligence officer thought otherwise. In his assessment, the inflatable doll provided, for the first time, valuable insight into the mindset of soldiers from one of America's most elite fighting units—specifically, their staying power to fight a protracted war.

For Sang's entire life, the Vietnamese people had known nothing but war. Such a history resulted in immense hardship for the Vietnamese fighting soldier. Occupying armies in Vietnam—whether the Chinese, the Japanese, the French or the Americans—robbed many a Vietnamese soldier not only of his youth but also of his opportunity to raise a family. Even for those who were married, long separations from home and family were an expected way of life. But these were all sacrifices the Vietnamese soldier was willing to make—for no price was too high to pay for reunification. Such separations were to be endured for as long as necessary to achieve the final victory.

It was this Vietnamese intelligence officer's assessment that the presence of the inflatable doll on the battlefield was indicative of an inability on the part of the American fighting soldier to make the same sacrifices his Vietnamese counterpart was willing to make. Unlike the Vietnamese soldier who left loved ones behind to fight as long as necessary to gain victory, American soldiers, whose service in Vietnam was normally for a single year, were incapable of making a similar commitment. To the intelligence officer, the inflatable doll was evidence of weakness—for the American soldier was unable to serve his one-year tour without an "artificial" wife or girlfriend to accompany him. Thoughts of the American soldier centered on home and family rather than war and victory. This was to be exploited—and, to do so, all the Vietnamese needed to do so was exercise patience. As the war dragged on, Americans would lose their will to fight.

The Vietnamese came to believe, locked deep within the American psyche, was a lack of resolve to see the war through—it just needed to be tapped. The inflatable doll, the cigarette lighters adorned with naked women that were popular with American GIs, all this suggested Americans were too focused on what they had left behind—and not on what lay ahead. While American soldiers thought only of leaving Vietnam, Vietnamese soldiers thought only of driving them out. From the Vietnamese perspective, these two mindsets fit well together if Hanoi was to prevail.

No longer did Sang and his men perceive the Americans as invincible warriors who had never lost a war. Instead, they saw Americans as vulnerable young men, longing for home and loved ones left behind—thoughts that impaired their ability to perform the mission that lay before them.

For the first time, Sang realized the Americans could be defeated.

Section 5:

Ingenuity

The Vietnamese recognized, before ever first engaging U.S. troops, that success on the battlefield turned on Hanoi's ability to counter the enemy's superior technology and firepower—a tall order for a country with comparatively limited resources. But what they lacked in material resources, the Vietnamese were able to compensate for with creativity. They demonstrated amazing ingenuity on the battlefield, drawing on it time and time again, to offset US battlefield advantages.

On the ground, this called for a strategy known as *"holding on to the belt of the enemy."* Literally translated, it meant: Engage the enemy yet remain so close to him he is denied his superior air and artillery support out of fear its use will endanger his own troops.

In the air, it resulted in adopting combat tactics and a strategy that enabled the Vietnamese to accomplish extraordinary feats against vastly superior air forces.

In the accounts that follow, the focus is on the air war. They provide a sense of how—in a war in which, technologically, the deck was heavily stacked in favor of America—the Vietnamese were able to play their ingenuity card quite effectively

Flying the Unfriendly Skies 138

Shoot Out over Noi Bai 150

Unknown U.S. soldier, pilot or airman, escorted by a diminutive Vietnamese captor. This picture is almost a visual metaphor for the difference in pure military might that the Vietnamese faced fighting the U.S

FLYING THE UNFRIENDLY SKIES

As America sought to maintain air superiority in the skies over North Vietnam, Hanoi wanted to make those skies as unfriendly as possible for U.S. pilots to fly. The Vietnamese accomplished this through the ever-increasing efficiency of a rather unique air defense system.

Evolution of this air defense system began with a simple premise: While it is a big sky, if you fill it with enough lead, something will fall out of it. And, in one extraordinary incident shared, not even a bullet was required to bring an aircraft down.

The U.S. bombing of North Vietnam began August 5, 1964.

"We used everything to shoot at American planes," explained Colonel Nguyen Van, an air defense soldier who, at that time, was in his first

year of army service. *"We used small arms. Then we employed antiaircraft guns such as the 57mm. Later, we began receiving surface-to-air missiles, which were very effectively incorporated into our air defense system. We were generally organized in such a manner, though, that everyone—soldiers, militia, anyone who could fire a rifle—was involved in trying to shoot down an enemy plane flying overhead. People from other countries found it hard to imagine we actually used our rifles to shoot at these planes. But we first started doing that against French aircraft in 1947. As we had some success with the practice, we continued it against the Americans."*

The air defense system was established in sectors, horizontally and vertically. In tandem, both attempted to create a virtual wall of fire through which an aircraft had to pass. Horizontally, three to four guns worked in coordination. Vertically, various weapons concentrated their fire at different altitudes depending on their effective ranges: small arms fire, such as the AK-47, up to an altitude of 300 meters, machine guns from 300 meters to 1000 meters. Antiaircraft guns and surface-to-air missiles both covered elevations above 1000 meters.

"The positioning of missile batteries was driven by the mission in a particular area," Van added, *"but, usually, if it was an area in which we had very few militia forces, we established a battery to compensate."*

Van recalled his first battle against U.S. aircraft.

"During a soldier's combat career," explained Van, *"there are some things he will always remember. His first combat experience is one of those. It always makes a heavy impression on him. My experience occurred April 3, 1965."*

At the time, Van commanded an antiaircraft gun battery defending Ham Rong Bridge (pictured at left). Ham Rong, crossing the Ma River in Thanh Hoa province in North Vietnam, was a very difficult bridge to build, requiring special engineering skills. It was completed in 1964 with some assistance from the Chinese.

The attack was conducted by thirty A-1 and A-4 aircraft, supported by twenty F-4 and F-8 aircraft, all from carriers USS HANCOCK (CVA-19) and USS CORAL SEA (CVA-43). Although the bridge was destroyed (pictured at right), it was not without cost to U.S. air forces. Two planes from HANCOCK were lost, an A-1H and an A-4C.

"During the war, we always remained close to the battery site," continued Van. *"We were never more than fifteen meters away. We ate at the site; we kept bookshelves near the site with reading materials. We virtually lived there to always be ready for an air attack.*

"A power station, rice mill and chemical fertilizer factory were located near the bridge. Their presence

obviously meant a civilian population was located there too. Because of the civilian presence, many people did not believe the area would be attacked. We were told otherwise as these facilities appeared on the Americans' target list. Since U.S. planes also recently attacked a similar area in Quang Binh Province, we were ready for them.

"The air attack came. It was not a single combat action, for the fighting lasted two days, April 3rd and 4th. Everyone shot at the airplanes as they approached and dropped their bombs. Parts of the rice mill and power station were destroyed. Since this was my first combat experience, I felt great trepidation over my battery's performance. That soon faded in the heat of battle.

"There were 43 American planes shot down over the two-day period. I do not know how many of those my battery shot down because everybody was shooting at all the planes." (Obviously U.S. records do not support the claim 43 planes were lost in this action. Significant discrepancies existed during the war between the number of aircraft Hanoi claimed were shot down and the number Washington actually reported as lost. Losses were not always acknowledged right away by Washington as, in some cases, recovery operations for a downed pilot were still ongoing. Only after all downed pilots were recovered or determined to be MIA was the actual number of aircraft losses acknowledged by Washington. Even to this day, U.S. and Vietnamese totals do not agree.

While U.S. numbers are undoubtedly correct, there may be a logical explanation for Hanoi's claims. A certain number of reported kills may well be the result of overeager propagandists rather than due to the accuracy of Hanoi's air defense system. But the majority of kills reported may well have been made in good faith. For Hanoi, there was

really no way accurately to determine how many enemy aircraft were shot down in any given action. With so many people shooting at a plane, when one was hit, everyone took credit for it.

If ten batteries shot at one aircraft that was then hit, one kill was reported as ten. And if an aircraft was hit and broke apart in the air, debris was scattered over a very large area—with every debris site discovered on the ground often being reported as a single crash site (a C-47 breaking up pictured at right). Thus, several purported kills may well have just been multiple debris sites for a single plane. {Even the Party

leadership sometimes doubted the accuracy of the reports. As General Giap stood before them to report, for the first time, a B-52 had been shot down over Hanoi, he was instructed to personally go to the crash site and physically inspect it to verify the kill really had, in fact, been made.})

Whether missiles or anti-aircraft batteries were employed against a specific target was dictated by the daily situation. *"We never considered missiles to be any more or any less important than the anti-aircraft guns,"* reported Van. *"The number of remaining SA-2 missiles never influenced our decision on whether or not to use this weapon. For even if we were down to our last missile, but that day's tactics required its use, we employed it. Usually, though, we estimated how many missiles we needed at the start of a campaign and planned accordingly."*

SA-2

In a war, which was a continuing chess match of moves and counter-moves, air defense proved to be no exception. That match was elevated to a new high on July 24, 1965, when North Vietnam introduced the first surface-to-air missiles, the SA-2, into their air defense system. No one was more surprised by their employment than the American pilots on the receiving end.

Van explained, *"This was the first time we ever used the SA-2. And we experienced great success with it. It undoubtedly came as a surprise to the American pilots who attacked us. We fired at a group of F-4s about 40 miles west of Hanoi. We succeeded in shooting down three of the planes. We immediately broadcast our success over the radio. Today, the date of July 24 is traditionally celebrated each year by our anti-air defense forces in recognition of the great victory achieved that day."*

The attack of July 24, 1965 was followed the next day by a second air attack.

"The Americans attacked the same place again the following day in revenge for our missile attack of the previous day," opined Van. *"But this time we did not use the missiles. We used only our anti-aircraft guns. We planned on using just the guns as we anticipated the planes would return, this time flying in at lower altitudes—so low we could not use the missiles. We shot down five aircraft. After these attacks, we knew the Americans would now be looking for our missile sites. Therefore, we began building fake sites, made out of bamboo. We even positioned forces around them in order to give them the appearance of being real missile sites."*

The confusion generated by the fake sites was acknowledged a few years later by the Deputy Commander of MACV (Military Advisory Command Vietnam) for Air, General William W. Maimer. He stated:

"The number of SAM sites remained fairly constant throughout the campaign, at about one hundred seventy-five to two hundred. I never considered these numbers a significant indication of the threat since a

site could be occupied one day and vacant the next. Regardless of how intense our reconnaissance, it became very difficult to determine how many sites were occupied."

The SA-2s arrived in Hanoi several months before they were employed that July, accompanied by Soviet trainers and technicians. The Soviets advised the Vietnamese that at least one year of training was required to become proficient in the operation of the missile. However, the first group of Soviet-trained Vietnamese operators established proficiency much sooner than expected. They then went on to become the core trainers for a future generation of missile operators.

"The Soviets told us we needed one year of training," said Van. *"But as the training started, we discovered these missiles were not very difficult to operate. We anticipated only needing four months to develop our expertise. It took only three."*

Although the Soviets taught the Vietnamese how to operate the missiles, the Russians never manned the batteries during attacks.

"While there were Soviet advisors present during combat operations," said Van, *"they always stayed away from the site. They assisted with any technical problems that arose during an action. There really was no reason for them to be physically present at the site. They were very helpful to us."*

The introduction of the SA-2 into the war made life much more dangerous for American pilots. An early estimate of the missile's accuracy calculated a loss rate of 61 aircraft per 100 SA-2s fired. (Such a kill ratio, again, is at odds with what the U.S. reported during the war.)

Van described the selection process for the SA-2 operator candidates: *"Whenever we were ready to assemble another group of operators for training, we selected soldiers from many other units—a soldier may have previously been a driver, or another may have been an artilleryman, etc. They were recruited from all different specialties."* This stemmed from the belief every soldier was part of the air defense system team, regardless of specialty, and thus came equipped with some knowledge of U.S. combat air tactics.

It was a challenge for North Vietnamese trainers to keep up with U.S. air capabilities and tactics. *"The United States had several different aircraft and employed many different tactics,"* said Van. *"As they modified these tactics periodically to confuse us, we adjusted in a similar manner. Sometimes the modification might involve an altitude change; sometimes it might involve the way in which they approached a target. But, whatever change the Americans made, we made a corresponding change in our tactics as well. In some instances, the Americans made no changes because their tactics were proving to be quite effective. For example, we shot at the SR71 but were never able to bring one down."* (The SR71 was a U.S. reconnaissance aircraft used for several decades as a very effective spy plane. It flew at such high altitudes it was impossible to shoot down with the limited air defense arsenal available to Hanoi during the war.)

In the air defense chess match both sides played, various measures and counter-measures were constantly implemented to tilt the game in favor of one side.

One counter-measure implemented worked off the ground radar emission used in support of the SA-2 batteries. After an SA-2 was fired, it was guided to its target by ground radar. This radar emitted a beam that the missile effectively "rode" all the way up to its target. While providing the missile with great accuracy, there was a drawback to this system. Since the ground radar had to radiate to guide a missile to the target, American pilots developed an effective counter-measure. Special electronic equipment onboard the aircraft enabled the pilot to detect the beam as soon as it was radiated from the ground, so it could then track the beam back to its radar source. Even though the missile may have been launched by this time, if the pilot destroyed the ground radar before the missile reached its target, he effectively "blinded" the incoming SA-2—converting what was a guided missile into an unguided one. As the radar site and SA-2 battery were normally co-located, the pilot was able to destroy both. In a reversal of roles, the hunter—the missile battery—became the hunted.

Following the loss of several SA-2 batteries, the Vietnamese began to realize what counter-measure tactic was being employed against them by the Americans. This prompted them to employ their own counter counter-measure to defeat it.

With the emission of their own radar beam being used against them, the Vietnamese realized any counter counter-measure they developed, to be successful, had to deny the Americans this advantage. But, without the beam, the missile was effectively blind. How then could they deny the Americans this advantage yet still guide their SA-2s to their targets?

It was decided, rather than emit a beam simultaneously with missile launch, which would maximize the pilot's response time to locate and attack the radar site; the operator would first launch the missile and allow it to gain altitude without emitting a beam—i.e., sending it skyward in an unguided mode. Only after the SA-2 gained a certain altitude would the operator then turn the radar on, emitting a beam, thus converting an unguided missile into a guided one. Only for the last leg of its flight would the operator actual guide the SA-2 directly to the target. While such a counter-counter-measure did not provide the missile with guidance during the initial leg of its flight, it did during the most crucial leg—the approach to the target. In doing so, it minimized the American pilot's response time to locate the beam and destroy the radar emission source.

Other counter counter-measures were adopted by the Vietnamese.

"Many times," Van reported, *"the Americans also tried to jam our missile radars. When they did that, we opted not to use the SA-2 radar but others, such as our artillery gun radar. We knew the Americans did not have the capability to jam all our different radars at the same time. It was a constant battle for us to develop our tactics to overcome their technology. In the end, even the Soviets learned these tactics from us. On a technical level, the Soviets were our teachers; but on a tactical level, we were theirs."*

✴ ✴ ✴

The Vietnamese knew the success of their air defense effort turned on first mastering the tactics employed by American pilots.

"One tactic in particular was often used by the Americans," said Van. *"Taking off from their ships at sea, they flew parallel to the coastline to reach a major waterway, and then navigated along that waterway at a very low altitude to make the inland penetration to their target. We*

positioned our air defense units so they could shoot directly into this area over the waterway as the low-flying aircraft attempted to make its approach. Our air defense units were co-located with the local population, normally on both sides of a waterway. These locals, using their own rifles, participated in the effort to shoot down the planes as they flew overhead. In one year, one air defense platoon was successful in shooting down two planes."

Even the civilian population studied U.S. air tactics. Colonel Le Thanh Chon (pictured at left), a North Vietnamese pilot who trained other pilots on American tactics, commented, *"We developed many different methods to fight the Americans. Sometimes we established an air defense system in a tree or on a rooftop. When the Americans were using a lot of F-111s in their attacks, civilians monitored their tactics and studied the flight paths they used. When approaching aircraft were reported, they positioned themselves on the high ground underneath the known flight path to be able to defend against the planes. This resulted on one occasion in civilians shooting down an F-111 with small arms fire."*

One man intimately familiar with Hanoi's air defense system was General Vo Nguyen Giap. *"We fought the air defense war with determination, intelligence and creativeness,"* explained the General. These qualities, he believed, were well represented in their efforts to shoot down the high flying B-52s.

"How could we fight these B-52s," he queried. *"Again, it was determination, intelligence and creativeness...It was a challenge. For example, these planes were equipped with devices for disturbing our frequencies, hindering our ability to defend against them. But our commanders dealt with that. Sometimes, it took eleven missiles to bring down a single plane; other times we accomplished it with only two missiles. It was courage and intelligence—the kind of intelligence emanating from the highest command as well as from units on the battlefields—and sometimes even from just one person. So we say the war was a war of the entire people."*

The B-52 bombings of Hanoi forced the evacuation of many of its citizens. Among these was Giap's son. The General shared how his son who, evacuated outside the city for his safety, found himself in the path of a plummeting B-52. Sifting through the crash debris, Giap's son located some items he later took to his father in Hanoi.

"He brought two documents back to me," said Giap. *"One was very thick, from the U.S. Department of Defense, on the cover of which was printed 'For Internal Use Only, Not To Be Taken Out Of The Department of Defense.' When I received the document, I immediately wrote underneath this, 'Except The Defense Ministry of Vietnam.' The second document was very long and included orders from the Air Force Command. The order given was to attack anti-aircraft positions, both real and camouflaged, as well as other targets in and around Hanoi. Once the mission was completed, the order instructed the pilots to return in good order with their plane intact. But, I noted, the pilots did not return in that manner—instead they went to the Hanoi Hilton."*

The General's reference that *"just one person"* was capable of bringing down an aircraft was evidenced by the following story he related:

"In the early attacks against the North, the U.S. air force used low-flying tactics. We had problems at the beginning with this. I once went near the 17th parallel and met with some people who were successful in shooting down planes with rifles or machine guns. In the group was an eighteen-year-old schoolgirl. She told me she observed the planes daily. She saw when they reached a spot between two mountain peaks; they lowered their altitude at a certain point. So she went to that point and waited for a plane to fly lower—and then shot it down. She said it was a simple rule. I told her she was truly a philosopher—for philosophers know rules. I later shared her story with President Ho Chi Minh."

✶ ✶ ✶

But Colonel Chon went on to report one of the most remarkable downing's of a U.S. aircraft to take place during the war—one that did not even require firing a single shot.

"We also developed a tactic of incorporating air balloons into our air defense system," said Chon. Made of heavy rubber and filled with a

lighter-than-air gas, the balloons ranged from two to four meters in diameter. The tactic specifically involved putting thousands of these balloons aloft at certain locations, staggered at various altitudes, ranging from 180 to 200 meters, and tethered to the ground on long lines.

The locations selected for placement of these balloons were either where American pilots had already fallen into a predictable operational pattern or, alternatively, where the defenders sought to direct pilots into taking certain approaches.

In the latter situation, the balloons were deployed for daylight use. They were configured to force an aircraft to make a low-altitude approach from a different flight path than what the pilot intended. The pilot encountered more balloons as he entered the area than he could shoot down as he made his pass to his target. He was forced to maneuver his plane through the only clear flight corridor left open for him—one carefully studied ahead of time by the defenders. This flight corridor led the pilot directly into the line of fire of awaiting anti-aircraft gun and missile battery crews.

Balloons were employed too where American pilots were known regularly to make low level approaches to specific targets. Again, many airborne balloons were positioned to block the aircraft's approach. Used at night, the balloons sought to place an aerial hazard directly within the flight path of a fast-moving aircraft. If an unsuspecting pilot flew close enough, a balloon might be sucked into the plane's jet engine intake, forcing it down. According to Colonel Chon, this tactic proved successful on at least one occasion, in 1967, over Phu Ly city in Ha Nam province, just south of Hanoi in the Red river delta.

"The balloons were deployed in such a pattern so as to create a valley stretching for a rather long distance," described Chon. *"Each night the balloons were raised into the air and each morning were brought back down. The highest balloon was positioned at 200 meters altitude, the lowest at 50 meters. There was not more than 20 meters between each balloon. One night an American A-6 entered into this valley, resulting in a balloon being sucked up into its engine. The airplane crashed. This tactic was only successful once as the pilots quickly learned to approach the area at a higher altitude*

As to the status of the pilot, Chon reported the aircraft was flying so low, it crashed before he could safely eject.

"We used every tactic possible against the Americans," explained Chon. *"In this case, because we used this same tactic repeatedly, the Americans stopped falling for it."*

In researching the use of air balloons in this manner, it was learned initial planning was to arm the balloons with directional explosive devices. However, it was never implemented.

This tactic of using air balloons was eventually abandoned, with help from an unexpected source.

"A soldier responsible for raising the balloons at night and taking them down the next morning eventually became frustrated with this job," related Chon. *"He felt he was doing all this work yet saw no results for his efforts. One day he decided to use the balloons for target practice, shooting most of them down. So we stopped using them."*

Van took great pride in what his country, despite its lack of technology, achieved against a world superpower in its conduct of the air defense war.

"The history of warfare involving the Vietnamese people has been a long one," he related. *"So, we have many memories. To have fought for several dozen years against the Japanese, and the French, and then the Americans was natural for us. How we accomplished what we did is clearly something outsiders cannot understand."*

SHOOT OUT OVER NOI BAI

Le Thanh Chon displays a discernible air of confidence. But then, having survived wars against both the French and Americans, perhaps he has a right to do so.

Born in 1937, he joined the Viet Minh at the age of fifteen. The savagery exhibited against his people by the French instilled in Chon a determination to expel them from his country forever.

Part of a reconnaissance team, Chon recalled his firsthand experience in witnessing their brutality but being unable to assist for fear of revealing his team's position: *"One time, a French Legionnaire tied a Vietnamese woman up and proceeded to disembowel her by cutting out her liver. On another occasion, I observed a French soldier repeatedly kick a helpless, pregnant woman."*

With the defeat of the French, Chon moved to Hanoi, leaving an older brother, younger sister and parents in the South. It was a move resulting, much like the American Civil War, in family division several years later as his siblings fought for the South while Chon fought for the North. *"Many families had siblings on both sides during the war,"* explained Chon. *"The difference was in the North we fought because we believed in what we were doing while in the South it was because they were forced to join."*

In 1958, Chon attended the Air Force Academy at Cat Bi in Haiphong, training on both the YAK-18 (pilots in training pictured at left) and MIG-17. In early 1962, he was sent to China for flight control and advanced combat training, remaining there for three years. To Chon, it was time wasted. *"In reality, upon my return to Vietnam I could not use the Chinese techniques against the Americans,"* he recalled. *"Chinese air combat training was based on China's experience against the U.S. in the Korean war. However, the sophisticated U.S. aircraft technology used in the Vietnam war did not even exist during the Korean war."* Another shortcoming observed by Chon was that the air war in Korea primarily involved encounters by air forces of relatively equal numbers, while in the Vietnam war; NVA air forces were heavily outnumbered by the Americans.

Chon was critical of Soviet pilots as well. When attacks by U.S. aircraft on Hanoi were imminent, he reported Soviet advisors, there to monitor air battles, were very nervous. Such nervousness, for pilots not in combat, surprised Chon as he always thought the Soviets would have been better trained than that. If they were this nervous as observers, he wondered how effective they were as combat pilots.

Despite the training provided by its allies to its pilots, North Vietnam developed its own tactics to fight the Americans. Chon, then an Air Force major, spent much of his time studying U.S. tactics and developing counter-measures. He believed the key factor in successfully engaging the Americans was to do so *only when we wanted* rather than allowing the Americans to dictate the terms of engagement. He became a combat tactics flight instructor. (Dogfight pictured above with a MIG-17 having the altitude advantage).

Chon acknowledged heavy losses by the North Vietnamese in the early years of the war *due to the way we were trained by the Chinese; but then we began to use our own techniques and strategy.*

Accepting both America's air superiority and its rapid reinforcement capability, North Vietnamese pilots focused on employing tactics that

proved successful in fighting the Americans on the ground—"hit and run tactics." Chon reported pilots were taught to avoid numerically superior forces when possible, to avoid detection until prepared to engage and to utilize the environment to their advantage. Pilots learned to utilize, to their advantage, the clouds, the sun, even mountains if they were flying low enough. The successful employment of these principles, claimed Chon, led to victory in a September 1966 encounter against U.S. aircraft.

❋ ❋ ❋

In September 1966, two MIG-17 aircraft located at Noi Bai airfield near Hanoi were the intended targets of a U.S. strike force, comprised of twelve U.S. Air Force F-105s. Unknown to the Americans, the two targeted MIGs had been relocated to another airbase, Ha Bac, to the southeast, prior to the launch of the U.S. strike force. As the American planes approached Noi Bai, the force split into three groups of four aircraft each.

Two mountains were located north of the airfield: to the northwest lay Tan Vien, an 893-meter high mountain; to the northeast was Tam Dao, at 1020 meters. The two mountains were about 20 kilometers apart.

One U.S. strike group approached Noi Bai airfield from the southwest at an altitude of 1500 meters. Another, using Tan Vien to avoid detection, made its approach to the northeast of the mountain at an altitude of 600 meters. The third strike group, similarly using Tam Dao to its advantage, approached the mountain from the northwest at an altitude of 500 meters.

With the U.S. strike force so focused on Noi Bai airfield, the two MIGs launched from Ha Bac to conduct a surprise attack against the third group of F-105s. They approached this group from the southeast of Tam Dao Mountain.

Pilots scrambling to their MIG-17s

The MIGs were detected coming up from behind the group. The F-105s ejected their external gas tanks to engage the MIGs. But, Chon reported, the first MIG was on top of the third strike group before the F-105s could react. Its missile hit one of the American planes, forcing the pilot to eject.

Similarly, the second MIG found a second F-105 and fired. Its missile also found its mark as a second American aircraft went down. The MIGs immediately broke off contact. Both American pilots survived the attack but were captured on the ground.

(Chon identified one of the captured American pilots as Major Jim Cutler; the other was only known as "Damon.")

Chon credited his pilots' success to their ability to take the initiative away from U.S. pilots, forcing the Americans instead to engage the MIGs on their own terms.

Section 6:

The Missing-In-Action

Perhaps no one issue related to the Vietnam war elicits more emotion than the servicemen who remain Missing-In-Action (MIA). The MIA issue is one familiar to all Americans, although primarily from just the U.S. perspective. Little has been done to understand this issue from the Vietnamese side—both in terms of efforts undertaken by Hanoi to resolve the remaining U.S. MIA cases and in terms of the impact of Vietnam's own, and much more extensive, MIA problem. The stories that follow focus on this perspective.

Vietnamese veterans were very knowledgeable about America's MIAs—some even knowing the date of America's first Vietnam casualty and MIA. Accordingly, included herein is the story of what led to America's first MIA and the details of the unheeded warning he conveyed to superiors before his date with destiny.

The Fallen Eagles 155

Hope Springs Eternal 161

First to Know, First to Die 177

THE FALLEN EAGLES

As a combat journalist, Tran Cong Tan witnessed many different aspects of the war. From Hanoi in the North to Dong Hoi and Nhan Trach in the South, he chronicled his travels and observations in dozens of diaries he maintained during the war. Of particular interest are his eyewitness accounts of air attacks and pilots who were shot down. Sometimes, as his diaries reveal, the pilots survived and were captured; sometimes they did not. Picking up one of his diaries, Tan held it under his nose and wryly commented, *"It still smells of smoke"*—decades after they were written, the diaries still carry a lingering odor from that war.

❉ ❉ ❉

One diary entry related to an air attack the first week of February 1965, on Dong Hoi, a village of 50,000 people. Although military targets were hit, so were the village marketplace and several houses.

The diary entry reported that one plane, an F-105, was hit by anti-aircraft fire and the pilot forced to eject. The aircraft plunged to earth only 700 meters from the battery that had shot it down. When a parachute deployed, soldiers rushed to capture the pilot after he landed. Vietnamese records reported the pilot's rank as a Major but in fact, the pilot was Navy Lieutenant Commander, Robert H. Shumaker (pictured above) and his aircraft was actually an F-8 Crusader. This confusion by the diary writer was caused by the gold oak leaf, which is the insignia for an Air Force Major and a Navy Lieutenant Commander, as well as the diary writer's unfamiliarity with American aircraft. As Shumaker spoke some French, a conversation ensued with one of his French-speaking captors. The discussion was cut short, however, as the pilot was soon surrounded by angry villagers. Fearful they would be unable to keep the villagers at bay; his captors quickly led their prisoner away. (U.S. Department of Defense records indicate Robert H. Shumaker was released along with his fellow POWs in 1973. The photograph below, taken immediately after his capture, appears in the Vietnamese Army Museum in Hanoi.)

❉ ❉ ❉

Another young American pilot described in Tan's diary proved to be less fortunate.

After Shumaker's capture, five U.S. Navy planes, including one flown by Ltjg. Edward Andrew Dickson, attacked an airstrip near Dong Hoi. According to Tan, the aircraft passed over several junks, just off shore, enroute to their targets. After completing their strike, the planes flew back out to sea, firing at the same junks, as they passed over them.

The planes made a low-level pass, only 50 meters above the surface. At such a low altitude, they came under intensive fire by anti-aircraft batteries ashore and small arms fire from the junks. Dickson's plane was hit. It limped out over the horizon before crashing into the sea. Before the plane disappeared, a parachute deployed. A search by the junks for the pilot found nothing.

A few days later, local fishermen from the village of Nhan Trach, in Quang Binh Province, made a grisly discovery. The body of an American pilot washed ashore, his parachute still attached. As far, as could be determined, death was caused by injuries sustained during ejection. Decomposition, assisted by the hot sun, a restless ocean and sea creatures, took a toll on the pilot's remains.

Various personal items were found on him including a pistol, U.S. currency, family pictures, a watch, a small U.S. flag, a military identification card and dog tags. The U.S. flag had the same message written on the back in several different languages: "I am an American. Please assist me in finding food and lodging. Please help me to return to the U.S. My government will reward you." (This was a standard issue item for pilots to help them obtain assistance from the civilian population in the event they were shot down.)

Tan had drawn a rough sketch of the pilot in his diary. From the dead man's military ID card, he recorded the following information:

"Name: Edward A. Dickson

Number: 9520447

Rank: Lieutenant, Junior Grade, U.S.N.

Date of Birth: September 3, 1937

Blood Type: A"

A two meter-deep grave was dug near a coconut tree on the beach— fifty meters from where the body had floated ashore. Tan watched as the villagers carried the body from the beach, placed it in the grave and marked the site with a wooden headstone with Dickson's name inscribed.

A local resident, Mrs. Nay, whose husband was killed earlier fighting the Americans and South Vietnamese, lit incense on top of the wooden headstone. As she did, the diary entry indicated, she said a simple prayer over the grave of the young American warrior, laid to rest so far from home: *"May your spirit find its way back to your family in America."*

❈ ❈ ❈

An inquiry I made of the MIA office in Hanoi at the time revealed Dickson still remained on the MIA list. Asked if more detailed information about the gravesite was available, Tan said he remembered it well as it was a very distinctive location. He sketched a rough map of the beach at Nhan Trach. The location was distinctive, he said, because a rivulet intersected with the beach, creating a small peninsula. The coconut tree by which Dickson was buried was fifty meters up that point. Checking Tan's description against a military map showed him to be accurate. A rivulet, forming the small peninsula described, was clearly identifiable on a dated map at the indicated location.

As I was to drive up coastal Highway 1 to Hanoi from Saigon after Tan's interview—a drive that took me by Nhan Trach—I decided to see if the gravesite could be located. The effort was unsuccessful. Upon arrival, I was informed by the village chief, authorization had to be obtained from Hanoi before conducting such a search. The village chief reported that U.S. MIA Search Teams had already visited Nhan Trach three months earlier after hearing reports a pilot's remains were buried on the beach, but they found nothing. Time had erased all signs of the grave and its marker.

Upon my arrival in Hanoi on June 19, 1995, I contacted the U.S. MIA office to report Tan's diary entry describing the burial of Ltjg. Dickson. As the village chief reported and the MIA office confirmed, searchers did visit Nhan Trach in an unsuccessful effort to locate Dickson's grave. However, Tan's information represented the first eyewitness report of the burial. The MIA office said they would contact Tan to ascertain if he could assist them in a subsequent search of the area.

A few days later, I visited the Vietnam war military combat photography archives in Hanoi. The room was filled with thousands of volumes of combat photographs taken during the war. As it was impossible to review all the albums, I asked the custodian to select two volumes for me to examine. She did so, placing the two volumes on the table before me. As I turned the pages of the first, one photograph in particular caught my eye. In it, a group of Vietnamese villagers stood on a beach, examining the body of an American pilot lying on the sand—his parachute still attached. The caption identified the U.S. serviceman, discovered by local fishermen after washing ashore at Nhan Tranh, as Ltjg. Dickson.

While it is unknown if Tan's knowledge concerning Ltjg. Dickson's burial will lead to any further information to resolve his MIA status, it should, at a minimum, move the case a step closer to resolution. If so, that will only have been made possible through Hanoi's willingness to allow Americans free access to Vietnam's veteran population. The continuing spirit of cooperation between former enemies in the wake of normalized relations will undoubtedly increase such contacts, hopefully clearing the way to resolve other MIA cases as well.

❉ ❉ ❉

Tan's diary recounted the loss of two U.S. aircraft in one day.

On the morning of March 3, 1965, a sortie of U.S. aircraft attacked targets in the vicinity of Dong Hoi. Two planes were hit; two pilots were observed ejecting. Local villagers set out to capture them.

Shortly after the planes were shot down, an anti-air battery observed a rescue helicopter approach from the sea to rescue the downed aviators. At 10:35 A.M., an American was sighted eating berries off a bush and making his way up a hill. A military patrol was notified and gave pursuit. Villagers found a parachute, soaked in blood. (Tan's diary reported the villagers saw so much blood, they were not sure whether the pilot was severely wounded or if he had been attacked by a tiger.)

Later in the day, one of the pilots, holding a plastic map and suffering a leg wound, was captured by a three-man patrol. The map was confiscated and placed over the wound to stop the bleeding. He was disarmed and his pistol fired into the air three times to signal his capture to other searchers. Indicating he was hungry, the prisoner was fed by villagers.

The pilot gave his name and rank as 1/Lt Hayden J. Lockhard, U.S.A.F. Further questioning revealed he was from Ohio and served in the Air Force for two years before coming to Vietnam. When asked about the other pilot, Lockhard said his name was "Ronca", but that he was killed. (Inquiries made of the U.S. Department of Defense revealed Hayden James Lockhard was shot down, captured and eventually released at the same time as Shumaker. No match could be found under the name "Ronca," however.)

When Lockhard was brought to the village, he was attacked by an angry woman wielding a knife whose husband had been killed in the air attack. Tan recounted he was forced momentarily to stop taking notes to intervene and protect the pilot. Tan informed the woman when the pilot was airborne, he was an enemy of the people, but as a prisoner of war, he now was to be protected. The woman agreed then broke down and cried.

A later incident with the same woman, Tan suggested, demonstrated the capacity of the Vietnamese to forgive. Despite her personal tragedy that day, she later came to Tan with a chicken, instructing him *"to make soup for the pilot as he probably had not yet eaten Vietnamese food."*

HOPE SPRINGS ETERNAL

If we learned anything from the Vietnam conflict, perhaps it is that in war there are no victors. For the soldier in battle, for the civilian reluctantly drawn into the fray, for the family member awaiting a loved one's return, war takes its toll on all. The anguish, the pain, the suffering is consuming. For most of those involved, it was a nightmare that finally ended.

For those who lost loved ones, for those who were permanently disabled, for those whose support of the Saigon regime led to long-term sentences in re-education camps, there are no more uncertainties about the war. For them, their dues were paid—the cost of which is fully known. But for one group, the uncertainties still remain—and, as a result, their suffering continues. For them, every day the fate of a loved one remains unknown, Vietnam is a war they cannot forget.

It is difficult to fathom the pain MIA families feel. Though I eventually lost a brother to this war, there was solace for me in knowing how, when and where he died. It is the uncertainty in not knowing the fate ultimately befalling a loved one on a battlefield far away or the location of his remains that prolongs the pain and suffering for our MIA families.

As I traveled through Vietnam and spoke to hundreds of Vietnamese veterans, I sensed an eagerness to resolve, where they could, the remaining cases of unaccounted for servicemen in hopes of ending the suffering by MIA families. There is a true sincerity in their willingness to achieve this end. They, and their government, recognize nothing stands to be gained—and much more to be lost—by a lack of cooperation. A letter dated November 13, 1995, from Under Secretary of Defense Walter B. Slocombe to the late Senator Strom Thurmond, written after Slocombe reviewed all remaining MIA cases at that time, acknowledged Hanoi's cooperation: *"The comprehensive review has not revealed any evidence that...Vietnam...is deliberately withholding information about any case."*

※　※　※

A further discussion of the MIA issue requires an understanding of various terms applied to the status of individual servicemen who failed to return from the war and the legal significance attached to each.

A serviceman unaccounted for in the combat zone fell into one of three categories. If he was known to have been captured, he was listed as a prisoner-of-war (POW); if he was known to have been killed-in-action (KIA) but no body was recovered (BNR—"body not recovered"), he was listed as KIA/BNR; and, if it was unknown if he had been captured or killed, he was listed as missing-in-action (MIA). The general term "unaccounted for" was applied as a matter of convenience to refer to all three categories.

An unaccounted for serviceman's status changed to "accounted for" upon the occurrence of one of three events: (1) he returned alive; (2) his identifiable remains were returned; or (3) sufficient evidence was gathered to demonstrate that neither of the first two were achievable.

The classifications of POW, KIA/BNR and MIA had significance beyond placing unaccounted for servicemen into precise status groups. They were important from a legal standpoint as well as certain benefits continued in force or terminated, depending on the particular status of the individual. For example, pay and allowances for a POW and MIA continued in force, but not for a KIA/BNR. Also, various legal problems arose for spouses of unaccounted for servicemen. A POW or MIA spouse could not, in her own name, convey title to property jointly owned with an unaccounted for serviceman due to the presumption he was still alive, thus necessitating his signature to convey such title. However, a KIA/BNR spouse could convey such title in her own name as a presumption of death attached to her spouse.

U.S. law requires an annual review on the status of individual MIAs be conducted to ascertain if a serviceman should continue in that status or whether ample evidence existed to allow a finding of death to attach. For some spouses, such legal nightmares continued for years after the war was over.

By the war's end, one-half of all unaccounted for servicemen were, in fact, known to have died. The vast majority of these were cases in which remains were not recovered as a direct result of hostile action at the time. But some extraordinary cases involved situations in which the body of an American serviceman was under U.S. control, only to be "lost" later.

An example of the former case—i.e., where hostile action resulted in a failure to recover remains—involved the crash of an aircraft in enemy territory. The plane, operating with other U.S. aircraft, failed to pull out of a dive after attacking its target. None of the other pilots observed a parachute open before the plane hit the ground. Therefore, the pilot's status was listed as KIA/BNR.

An example of the latter case—i.e., where the U.S. government lost control over remains originally in its custody—occurred after a firefight as a medevac helicopter took hostile fire when it landed to remove dead and wounded. The body of a soldier was placed onboard the aircraft. As the helicopter hurriedly departed the landing zone and was flying over enemy territory, the body slid out of the aircraft, falling to the ground below. Due to intensive enemy fire, the body could not be recovered.

Another example of the latter situation involved a rather bizarre incident in which a soldier's remains were taken to a morgue at Ton Son Nhut Airbase in Saigon. As the morgue was filled to capacity, the body was temporarily placed in the base post office. When morgue personnel later returned to the post office to retrieve the body, it was missing. To this day, the serviceman remains unaccounted for.

Except for a small handful of cases, all remaining servicemen unaccounted for at the end of the war were given MIA status. Only three dozen cases were considered at that time not to qualify as KIA/BNR or MIA and were therefore given POW status.

❊ ❊ ❊

A former U.S. Army officer responsible for MIA searches shared a story of Hanoi's willingness to cooperate in resolving remaining MIA/POW cases and pursuing new leads.

In 1994, this officer related, a sighting report was received by the MIA Search Team of an American POW in a remote village. The report indicated the POW was a "dark-skinned American wrapped in chains" and escorted by armed guards.

Under the terms of the agreement between the U.S. and Vietnam concerning MIA searches, to investigate a site or a sighting, the U.S. was to give Vietnamese officials prior notice and Hanoi was to respond expeditiously to the request. The MIA Search Team gave the required notice and Hanoi granted immediate authorization to inspect the remote location where the sighting took place. In less than twenty-four hours, the U.S. MIA Search Team flew into the village by helicopter.

The quick reaction by both sides enabled the Search Team to determine the basis for the sighting. As reported, a dark-skinned man wrapped in chains was found—but he was not an American POW. He was a native Montagnard—a logger—who carried, draped over his shoulders, the logging chains typically used in his trade. The armed guards present were not there to prevent his escape; they were there to protect the loggers against bandits who were crossing over the border from Cambodia into Vietnam.

While this sighting report was a false alarm, it served to demonstrate Hanoi's resolve to act quickly to help American investigators ascertain the validity of the reports. Sighting reports such as this demonstrate how it is possible for rumors of live American POWs to circulate, in good faith. An unfortunate consequence of such reports is that families of servicemen still unaccounted for continue to foster hope a loved one may still be alive—only to see those hopes dashed.

❊   ❊   ❊

For two decades, the inability to resolve more than two thousand cases of unaccounted for American servicemen remained an obstacle in normalizing relations between Washington and Hanoi. But Vietnam's increased cooperation in their resolution resulted in President Clinton's decision in July 1995, to re-establish full diplomatic relations. (Prior to this act of diplomatic recognition, President Clinton had, as a first step, lifted economic sanctions against Vietnam. He consulted with my father, as a senior wartime commander in Vietnam, to see if he would support such an action. My father did and persuaded General William Westmoreland to join with him in a message supporting the lifting of sanctions. While my father later supported Clinton's decision to restore diplomatic relations, Westmoreland declined to do so.) It was the collective opinion of the majority of Americans directly involved in resolving the remaining unaccounted for cases that, ever since 1988, Hanoi clearly demonstrated a more cooperative attitude, justifying President Clinton's decision to normalize relations.

In the weeks prior to this decision by President Clinton, I spoke to several U.S. MIA Search Team investigators who, while requesting anonymity, shared their personal observations about Vietnam's cooperative efforts.

"When Hanoi was not cooperating early on in the process," said one investigator, *"we had a responsibility to report such conduct to the American people—which we did. Now that Hanoi is fully cooperating, we have a similar responsibility to report that fact to the American people as well. We did a good job on reporting the former; unfortunately, we have not done as good a job on reporting the latter."*

Another investigator suggested opposition to Clinton's decision based on non-cooperation by Hanoi had no basis in fact. *"Decision-makers determining whether or not the required level of cooperation has been met by Hanoi,"* he reported, *"have not been given all the necessary technical information to make the right judgment."*

Investigators believed the American press was not particularly helpful at times, as it proved eager to portray the Vietnamese in a negative light. One example involved a story reporting Hanoi denied access to a particular area to conduct a search.

"In all fairness to the Vietnamese," continued the investigator, *"we were never denied access—except in isolated cases where the demand for such access was clearly unreasonable on our part under the circumstances."* Almost all such cases in which access to a site was not given involved two common factors: (1) the site identified was near a military base, and (2) the coordinates were an American analyst's "best guess" of the site's location based on the last known position of the lost aircraft or missing individual—the accuracy of which guesstimate was disputed (many times justifiably) by Vietnamese officials.

"Often we do not know exactly where a particular aircraft crashed," conceded the American investigator. *"So the only thing to do is to go by the information in the case file as to the last reported location. For example, it might be the last point at which we had radar contact when an aircraft flew out of range, or it might be the actual target where an aircraft was conducting its last attack at the time it was lost. In any case, it represents our best estimate."*

Determining a lost aircraft's crash site, in many instances, is far from an exact science. *"A good example of how far off we can sometimes be in our estimates was evidenced by the loss of a C-47 which went down in December 1964, in Laos,"* shared the investigator. *"It was on a night mission when it disappeared. Our analysts, using the last position report by the pilot, came up with a set of coordinates as to where it may have crashed. But we could never find the crash site. Later, after Clinton lifted the embargo against Vietnam, a Vietnamese veteran contacted his government to let them know he visited some crash sites in Laos during the war. One of these was the site of the C-47 for which we were searching. The veteran kept a diary during the war in which he recorded the coordinates of the site. After determining at that time that all personnel onboard were dead, he recorded the condition of the remains as well as the names and serial numbers of the crash victims taken from their military ID cards. As it turned out, the C-47 actually crashed near Xepone, Laos, on Route 9, west of Khe Sanh—more than 140 kilometers away from the coordinates estimated by our analysts."*

To put the issue of access by search teams into perspective, the investigators related several cases which, only for bureaucratic reasons, still remain on the unaccounted for list. As such, they are charged against the total number of cases requiring resolution by Hanoi. Maintaining such cases in a state of "bureaucratic limbo," in which no new evidence is clearly obtainable but the individual's status remains unaccounted for, has proven frustrating for both sides. For example, procedures require, before a case can be closed out, the search team conduct a physical inspection of the individual's or crash site's last known location. This procedure was adopted primarily to assure families of missing pilots that, while the actual crash site was unknown, the last known position given by the pilot or tracked by ground radar was physically inspected. Thus, the team was required to go back and check flight records to ascertain a pilot's last reported position when he went down. Armed with the coordinates and equipped with GPS (Geographic Positioning System), a satellite link-up system that allows one to locate specific coordinates on the ground, the search team goes to the last known coordinates on the ground. There, a circular patterned search is conducted, spiraling out from the coordinates for a reasonable distance, to locate any evidence of the aircraft's crash site.

These searches obviously ended either in a positive finding of remains or, most often, a negative finding as nothing was found. While a positive finding closed a case out, a negative one could result in a case being closed out as irresolvable, if supported by other factors. But, if such an on-site circular search of the last known location was not undertaken for any reason, a case remained open.

The requirement to conduct a physical search of the last known location, while logical, in some cases, can be taken to illogical extremes. In such cases, it is unfair to hold the Vietnamese government to an unobtainable standard of proof.

One such case involves the loss of a U.S. serviceman at Cam Ranh Bay, a naval base occupied by U.S. forces during the war. Life at Cam Ranh Bay was more leisurely than it was in the jungles. Servicemen often took advantage of off duty hours to go swimming. One such serviceman, who went for a swim, disappeared under a wave and was never seen again. Despite a search, his body was never recovered. The cause of death was listed as drowning. However, since a body was not recovered, this serviceman remained on the unaccounted for list, even after the war. In order to close this case out years later, investigators were required to physically inspect the swimmer's last known location. The U.S. Search Team had to return to the beach at Cam Ranh Bay where the drowned serviceman was last seen.

Common sense suggests such a search of the last known location under these circumstances is futile as there can logically be no expectancy the body of a drowning victim lost decades earlier would be found. Additionally, today Cam Ranh Bay is a Vietnamese naval base and, therefore, is off limits to foreigners. Thus, U.S. Search Teams have been denied access by the Vietnamese government. This is understandable— for the facts of this case establish the serviceman achieved his unaccounted for status while Cam Ranh Bay was still under U.S. control, that the U.S. conducted a timely search for the serviceman's body when he disappeared and that no body was found.

It is unreasonable to demand access by search teams more than a quarter of a century after the loss to an area having military sensitivity to the Vietnamese, simply to be able to fulfill the last known location physical inspection requirement. Insistence on following procedures such as this in all cases creates frustrations for MIA representatives of both governments.

(Unable to resolve this case and four others, it was decided one representative from both sides would work out a solution. Reason ultimately prevailed. In the above case, it was agreed search teams would interview locals near Cam Ranh Bay to determine if interviewees had any recollections about the incident or reports about the body of an American serviceman washing ashore. After some interviews were conducted, the Vietnamese became comfortable the search team was not on a spy mission and allowed the team onboard the base to visit the last known coordinates. As for the other four cases, all of which involved Vietnamese documentation disputing the last known positions given by U.S. analysts, it was agreed Vietnamese positions would be given first priority and, if no crash site was found, discussions would be held about search teams accessing other restricted areas.)

⁎ ⁎ ⁎

One of the most frustrating cases for the Vietnamese was that involving an unaccounted for American by the name of Joseph Grainger.

Grainger, a Foreign Service Officer, worked for the U.S. Department of State in Vietnam. On August 8, 1964, while traveling outside of Saigon, his vehicle was stopped by Viet Cong forces. He and his Filipino driver were captured. The driver was eventually released; Grainger was held. Five months later, while attempting to escape, he was shot and killed. The Viet Cong buried his body in a small village in South Vietnam.

As required by the 1973 Paris Peace Accord ending U.S. involvement in the war, Hanoi agreed to provide Washington with a list of all U.S. POWs who died in captivity in South Vietnam (known officially as the

"Died in Captivity List"). Among the names appearing on the list was Grainger's, reporting his date of death as March 17, 1965, seven months after his capture.

For a fifteen-year period following the American withdrawal from Vietnam, little progress was made in resolving any cases of unaccounted for Americans. In 1987, President Ronald Reagan appointed former Chairman of the Joint Chiefs of Staff, General John W. Vessey, Jr., as an emissary to Vietnam to negotiate procedures for resolving the remaining unaccounted for cases. Agreement was reached that these were to be investigated jointly. By the following year, new information emerged on many cases—including Grainger's.

Hanoi's own investigation into the Grainger matter indicated the following: Local villagers questioned reported his body had been buried near the POW camp where he had been held. But, these villagers added, in 1967 ARVN troops flew in by helicopter, dug the body up, and departed with it. It was Hanoi's position that Grainger's case was closed as the body was returned to U.S. government control. But, as often happens when trust is lacking between governments, Washington rejected Hanoi's accounting in the Grainger case, particularly since a review of mortuary records maintained by the American military during the war failed to turn up evidence supporting Hanoi's claim.

It was the U.S. government's position in 1988 that Grainger remained unaccounted for. Hanoi was informed further investigation was required.

By June 1992, the status of Grainger's case remained unchanged. A joint American and Vietnamese team launched a new investigation. Interviews were conducted with the same witnesses. While their stories were the same, the villagers provided a few additional details. It was reported that the ARVN troops who removed Grainger's body were led to the gravesite by a Chieu Hoi (a Viet Cong defector to Saigon). The Chieu Hoi, assigned to the POW camp at the time of Grainger's death and a participant in his burial, confirmed the body was exhumed by ARVN soldiers in April 1967.

A final resolution to the Grainger case seemed impossible as Hanoi repeated its claim the body had been returned—and the U.S.

government rejected the claim. Finally, in early 1994, a Special Remains Team (SRT), comprised of both U.S. and Vietnamese representatives, pressed the U.S. Department of Defense (DOD) to check with the U.S. Department of State (DOS) on the matter since, as a Foreign Service Officer, Grainger worked for DOS rather than DOD.

A DOS representative contacted Grainger's widow to explain the problem they were having in locating her husband's remains in Vietnam. Mrs. Grainger informed the caller her husband's remains were not in Vietnam but in Arlington National Cemetery in Washington, D.C.—where they had been interred in May 1966! While the Vietnamese had been incorrect about the year the remains had been returned, they had been absolutely correct about their return. (Grainger, as a former U.S. Air Force captain, qualified for burial at Arlington National Cemetery. His headstone gives his actual date of death as January 12, 1965.)

On May 23, 1994, the Assistant Secretary of Defense for Public Affairs issued public affairs guidance on the Grainger case, acknowledging the error. Twenty-one years after his name had appeared on the "Died in Captivity List," Grainger was finally accounted for.

❄ ❄ ❄

Many other cases of unaccounted for servicemen remain unresolved and, arguably from Hanoi's standpoint, improperly so.

A relatively small number of these cases have been classified for resolution by SRT. These are cases for which material evidence exists that a U.S. serviceman was last known to have been in the sole custody of the Vietnamese. Accordingly, the burden is upon the Vietnamese to explain the final disposition of the still unaccounted for servicemen. SRT cases include unaccounted for servicemen who: appeared on the "Died in Captivity List;" appeared in photographs evidencing their captivity; were listed by the U.S. Government as KIA but whose remains have not yet been repatriated; were reported by local authorities as having their remains recovered by the central government but the remains were never repatriated.

One such unresolved case, for example, falls into this category on the basis of photographs taken by a North Vietnamese news agency shortly after the crash of a U.S. aircraft in the mid-1960s. The crash occurred in a marshy area in the city of Vinh, near a train station. According to other U.S. pilots flying that day who witnessed the crash, this aircraft went into a dive from which it never pulled out. Pictures of the wreckage provided physical evidence suggesting the pilot had failed to survive. The photographs depicted the still smoldering wreckage of the plane protruding from a hole in the ground—indicating a high-speed impact crash. The most telling photograph, however, reveals a crushed pilot's helmet, attached to which are clearly visible a human ear and partial scalp. No other body parts are visible.

The logical conclusion drawn from these photographs is that high-speed impact occurred, leaving the pilot no time to eject—a conclusion supported by the U.S. pilots who actually witnessed the crash. Such a high-speed crash vaporized the pilot's body, leaving nothing for identification purposes.

However, since a body part is visible in the photographs, Hanoi is held fully accountable for the pilot's remains. The pilot is still carried as unaccounted for, in spite of the logical conclusion that no identifiable remains were left by the crash to be recovered.

(Almost thirty years later, the crash site was excavated by a joint search team. The aircraft's ejection seat was found intact, further supporting eyewitness accounts the pilot failed to eject. Enough residual jet fuel, preserved by the marsh, was still in the hole created by the jet's impact to make further recovery attempts dangerous for the searchers. Therefore, the excavation effort was abandoned with no remains found.)

❊   ❊   ❊

The Americans responsible for resolving the remaining unaccounted for cases in Vietnam are leaving no stone unturned in their quest to bring closure to MIA families. Driven by a sense of duty to these missing servicemen, they believe every lead must be fully explored. At times, this sense of duty has caused them to place tremendous demands upon their Vietnamese hosts. It is important to recognize, in meeting such demands to resolve the remaining cases, the Vietnamese have demonstrated amazing tolerance.

Perhaps the case that best reflects the extent of this tolerance is that of Frank Nelson and his co-pilot, William Charles. (Both names have been changed to protect family privacy).

Nelson and Charles were shot down in December 1965. It is believed Charles was instantly killed in the crash but Nelson survived, as evidenced by a photograph later published of him in a Vietnamese hospital. In the photograph, Nelson appears in bed, wrapped in bandages, a tracheotomy tube inserted into his throat and his eyes closed. A doctor and four nurses (one figure is partially obscured) are seen standing beside him.

Nelson failed to survive his injuries as his name later appeared on the "Died in Captivity List" provided by Hanoi in 1973. Subsequent documentation provided by the Vietnamese listing gravesites, indicated Nelson had been interred at Quang Ninh Province cemetery.

Since the photographic evidence clearly showed Nelson was last known to be alive in the custody of the Vietnamese government, the case was assigned to SRT.

The joint team initiated an investigation, reviewing all available documentation. Informal records substantiated the finding Charles was killed on impact and his body buried in a nearby hamlet. (His remains were subsequently repatriated.) Records further supported Nelson's live capture and that the severity of his injuries necessitated his being taken to the Vietnamese-Czech Friendship Hospital in Haiphong. It was at this hospital that he later died and was subsequently buried. But SRT found no one currently serving at the hospital that had knowledge of the incident.

Unable to make progress in the investigation, SRT found itself back at square one. In re-examining the photograph, it was determined the hospital to which Nelson was taken was not the Friendship Hospital but the Quang Ninh District Hospital. SRT re-directed its focus. At Quang Ninh District Hospital, investigators were able to meet with most of the medical personnel depicted in the picture with Nelson. They confirmed

Nelson was not taken to Friendship Hospital as regulations required cases with severe injuries be sent to better-equipped hospitals. Therefore, after his initial treatment at Quang Ninh District Hospital, Nelson was transferred to Quang Ninh Province Hospital. One of the nurses in the photograph personally transported Nelson there. But soon after his arrival, Nelson succumbed to his injuries.

Traveling to Quang Ninh Province Hospital, SRT soon located medical personnel who recalled an American pilot being brought in just before he died. They reported a two-man team buried him in the cemetery immediately behind the hospital.

SRT investigators next sought out the two members of the burial team. One—an ethnic Chinese—was no longer with the hospital; the other died a few years earlier. Thus, while SRT was successful in tracking Nelson's body to a specific cemetery, it could find no witnesses who could attest to the exact location of the remains. Further investigation indicated Nelson might have been interred within a particular section of the cemetery, so SRT sought—and surprisingly received—authorization to dig there.

With local residents looking on, the site was excavated. The team soon uncovered the remains of a small child in an unmarked grave. (Using their own money, SRT members bought a headstone and ceramic casket to re-inter the body.) However, Nelson's remains were never located. His status remains unaccounted for.

While SRT's search for Nelson's remains was unsuccessful, team members expressed satisfaction with Hanoi's cooperation during the investigation. They pointed out, had roles been reversed and Hanoi demanded authorization to dig up sections of an American cemetery to search for the remains of its MIAs, it is doubtful similar authorization would have been granted by the U.S. Government—and a tremendous public outcry would have been heard if it had been granted.

�֍ ✖ ✖

A great tragedy of the Vietnam war is that most remaining unaccounted for cases, in truth, will never be resolved. As one investigator said, *"It is like asking a policeman to investigate a death that occurred thirty years earlier—in most cases with few, if any, witnesses and little or no documentation available."* It is a very difficult set of circumstances under which to attempt to resolve a case; yet we do not hesitate to impose a demand upon the Vietnamese to do so.

❖ ❖ ❖

There is a common ground Americans and Vietnamese now share. Families of missing soldiers, regardless of which side of the battlefield they stood during the war, have hope the remains of a missing loved one soon will be returned home.

As of this writing, 1,800 American servicemen remain unaccounted for in Vietnam. That total pales in comparison to the Vietnamese who, as first reported to my late father and me during a meeting with General Giap in Hanoi in September 1994, have 300,000 servicemen still missing. To understand the relative impact the MIA issue has had on both populations, one need only compare ratios. Based on the 1975 populations of North Vietnam and the U.S.—26 million and 210 million respectively—those ratios are staggering: while roughly one in every 116,700 U.S. citizens suffered the loss of a missing serviceman, one in every 87 Vietnamese was similarly affected!

For the impact to be equal, America would have had to suffer the loss of more than 2.4 million MIAs!

The recovery of a loved one's remains is important to Americans and Vietnamese alike. A visit to Vietnam's countryside reveals the cultural import attached to returning a loved one's remains to the land of his birth. Among the rice paddies, deceased family members are entombed above the very ground their surviving family continues to cultivate. Such means of burial has special meaning to the Vietnamese in the continuation of the life cycle. Burial on family land ensures the deceased's spirit passes from the earth to the crops nurtured by the soil and cultivated by the family; and, as surviving family members consume those crops, the spirit, in turn, nurtures their bodies, thus keeping the departed family member's spirit alive.

❖ ❖ ❖

Nguyen Ngoc Hung is one of those still awaiting news of a loved one's fate. Hung and his younger brother joined the army at the same time. While Hung survived some very heavy fighting, his brother did not.

Not until 1973, after encountering soldiers who served with his younger brother, did Hung learn of his death six years earlier. To this day, Hung's inability to recover his brother's remains brings tears to his eyes. Despite his personal suffering, Hung, like many Vietnamese families still searching for missing loved ones, bears no animosity towards his former enemy.

"We Vietnamese have small bodies," he explained. *"If we fill them with anger, there is no room for love."* Hung suggested it is not part of the Vietnamese makeup to allow bitterness and hatred to overshadow the hopes of the future.

Drawing on his country's past, Hung explained its future attitude towards America: *"In our history, when we were victorious against the Chinese, an emissary was sent to the Chinese emperor to apologize for the victory we achieved over his forces and to beg for his forgiveness."* To the Vietnamese, humility by the victor is an important element in building a future relationship with the vanquished.

❊ ❊ ❊

"Cuu Chien Binh" ("Veterans") is a monthly magazine in Vietnam for the retired military. Decades after the war ended, the magazine remained inundated with inquiries from mothers still searching for missing sons, wives for missing husbands, children for missing fathers or siblings. Each inquiry provided information about the missing serviceman, such as the last known location or the unit with which he served at the time of his disappearance.

These were published each month in a section of the magazine dedicated to locating missing servicemen from the war. There is never sufficient space to include all inquiries, so most are carried over to the following month, at which time the same space limitation problem again arises. Despite a backlog of many thousand inquiries, submissions continue to come in to the magazine.

The May 1995 issue of Veteran's Magazine included the following introduction for its missing persons section: *"Our country currently has 300,000 missing whose bodies were never recovered. Recently, both local people and our veterans found several remains that were moved to our national war cemetery in the city—but the number of remains located is small compared to the number still missing. The Veteran's Magazine created this section for inquiries by families with lost loved ones and veterans wishing to learn about comrades who sacrificed their lives in this war. It has been ordered by the Central Committee that during the next few years the search for soldier's remains be completed. Knowing the love and friendships the soldiers and families have for these missing heroes, the editors of this magazine are determined to fulfill the Central Committee decree by establishing this section 'Searching for Comrades' for the purpose of locating missing soldiers' remains."*

In Vietnam, as in America, for parents, wives and children of those servicemen who failed to return, hope still springs eternal the future will reveal the fate of a missing loved one.

FIRST TO KNOW, FIRST TO DIE

Some of the Vietnamese veterans I interviewed were aware of a milestone in U.S.-Vietnam relations of which most Americans are unaware: the date of America's first casualty and MIA. Each year, lost in the anniversary celebrations marking the end of World War II is the anniversary of America's first casualty in Vietnam. (In 1996, Congress officially established the starting date of the Vietnam war as February 28, 1961—the date it was believed America suffered her first official casualty—as no official declaration of war was ever made. However, the circumstances surrounding the death of a young Army Lieutenant Colonel strongly suggest he should have received this dubious recognition.)

The death of any soldier in the service of his country is a personal tragedy, but the loss of America's first casualty in Vietnam was, in many ways, also a national one. It was a national tragedy for what it signaled: "the beginning of the beginning" of America's march into the Southeast Asian quagmire. It was a tragedy for what was not heard: the warning that a dutiful soldier attempted to sound before his life was taken. It was a tragedy for the opportunity lost: i.e., the failure in the days following this soldier's death to build upon an alliance that had existed between the U.S. and Vietnam only two months earlier.

❖ ❖ ❖

A quarter of a century after invading Vietnam in 1858, France imposed colonial rule. Almost half a century later, a charismatic leader by the name of Ho Chi Minh (pictured at right) was born—a man who eventually would prove successful in rekindling his country's nationalist spirit.

By the time World War II erupted in Europe, a number of small uprisings by the Vietnamese against their colonial masters were already taking place. When Paris fell to the Germans in 1940, French control of Vietnam was tenuous at best.

The Japanese wasted no time in taking advantage of waning French control in Vietnam. They occupied northern Indochina, ostensibly with French "approval" but, in reality, did so because the French were powerless to stop them. (On July 29, 1941, France and Japan signed the "Protocole concernant la Defense en commun de l'Indochine Francaise" which allowed Japanese troops to use most of the major air and seaports in Vietnam. This document effectively recognized Japan's military presence in all of Indochina.) By August 1944, however, the liberation of Paris by the Allies was imminent. Realizing its days of occupation with French "approval" were numbered, Tokyo again acted. In March 1945, the Japanese dissolved the French government in Indochina, declaring Vietnam "independent."

The Vietnamese did not take this declaration seriously. They realized they were merely pawns in a game the Japanese were playing to legalize their own occupation of Vietnam. They also knew, with the defeat of Japan imminent, the French would soon be reasserting their control over Vietnam. From Hanoi's perspective, Japan's declaration simply meant it now had to deal with two foreign occupiers instead of just one.

On May 7, 1945, Germany surrendered to the Allies. With the war in Europe over, the Allies turned their attention to delivering the final decisive blow against Japan to knock her out of the war. The Office of Strategic Services (OSS), predecessor of the U.S. Central Intelligence Agency, planned operations in support of this effort.

In July 1945, the OSS initiated an operation to assist the under-equipped and somewhat depleted Vietminh forces of General Vo Nguyen Giap, who had been fighting the Japanese. An OSS unit, code-named "Deer Team", parachuted into Giap's jungle camp in the mountains of northern Vietnam to assist the General and Ho Chi Minh in their efforts against the Japanese. (Ironically, Ho Chi Minh's life may well have been saved by the Deer Team medic who, finding him close to death from repeated bouts of dysentery, malaria and other diseases, nursed him back to health.)

Soon after meeting with Giap and discussing what assistance could be provided to the Vietnamese, Deer Team arranged to have ammunition and weapons air dropped into the jungle camp. They also began conducting tactics and weapons training for Giap's army. Soon, Vietminh and American soldiers were fighting side-by-side, as a series of attacks against Japanese outposts were jointly undertaken.

On July 24, 1945, President Truman and other Allied leaders attended the Potsdam Conference to discuss, among other things, Vietnam's fate after Japan's defeat. They decided Vietnam should be divided along the sixteenth parallel, with Chinese forces to occupy the North and British forces the South. Less than a month later, on August 14, 1945, Japan capitulated, formally surrendering on September 2. As agreed at Potsdam, Chinese and British troops entered Hanoi and Saigon respectively.

As British forces under Major General Douglas D. Gracey marched into Saigon, another OSS team, commanded by U.S. Army Lieutenant Colonel A. Peter Dewey, 28, was dispatched to assist them. Arriving on September 4, the team's mission was to liberate Allied POWs and search for U.S. MIAs. Dewey was the right man for the job. Among his many qualifications, he spoke fluent French, a result of his having served in France behind German lines. Ironically, his mastery of the French language would ultimately play a role in his death three weeks later.

While Dewey was a good selection to represent the U.S. in Vietnam, Gracey was not a good selection to represent Britain. Having dealt with colonized peoples for most his military career, Gracey had little compassion for them. He was under orders to remain politically neutral on the issue of Vietnam's independence versus French control. But Gracey sympathized with the French, effectively helping them re-establish control over much of southern Vietnam contrary to his orders to maintain neutrality.

Gracey also served under a mandate to disarm the Japanese and maintain order in Saigon. But he soon undertook a number of actions demonstrating a severe lack of sensitivity to the plight of the Vietnamese people. First, when Ho Chi Minh sent delegates from Hanoi to meet with Gracey, the British general unceremoniously threw them out of his office. Second, he imposed martial law upon the Vietnamese, choosing to enforce it with French soldiers and Japanese prisoners, released to perform this role.

Dewey was concerned over the course Gracey was taking and his insensitivities towards the Vietnamese. He felt Gracey was headed for disaster, further fanning the flames of Vietnamese animosity against the West. Dewey and Gracey clearly looked at Vietnam from two very different perspectives; it was obvious they were headed on a collision course. Dewey would send dispatches to Washington more and more critical of the British commander's performance. Tiring of Dewey's continuing criticism and exercising his authority as commander of the occupation force, Gracey ordered Dewey to leave the country.

Dewey had only been in Vietnam three weeks—but it was sufficient time for him to form a strong belief about the country. He believed any nation seeking to control Vietnam or otherwise maintain an unwanted presence there was courting disaster. It was a belief Dewey made clear in the last report he filed with Washington prior to his departure. In it, he made a hauntingly ominous observation:

"Cochinchina (South Vietnam) is burning; the French and British are finished here, and we ought to clear out of Southeast Asia."

Dewey's departure, and ultimate ride into history, is chronicled by Stanley Karnow in his book, **VIETNAM: A HISTORY**, published by Penguin (USA) Inc.:

"Early on September 26, 1945, Dewey prepared to clear out...He went to the Saigon airport with a colleague, (French) Captain Herbert J. Bluechel, only to find that his airplane had been delayed. They came back later in the morning to check on the aircraft, with Dewey behind the wheel of the jeep—which Gracey had forbidden him to identify with a U.S. flag on the grounds that only he (Gracey), as area commander, was entitled to fly a pennant on his vehicle. Another OSS officer (in a similar unfledged vehicle) had just been wounded by the Vietminh, and Dewey was upset. He took a shortcut past the Saigon golf course. Suddenly a barrier of logs and brush blocked his path. Braking to swerve around it, he noticed three Vietnamese in a roadside ditch. He shouted angrily at them in French. Presumably mistaking him for a

French officer, they replied with a machine-gun burst that blew off the back of his head. Bluechel, unharmed, fled the scene, a bullet knocking off his cap as he ran."

The French blamed Dewey's death on the Vietminh; the Vietminh blamed it on the French and British. Ho Chi Minh, recognizing a terrible mistake had been made, wrote to President Truman, offering his condolences. That letter, in part, said, *"The incident may have been provoked by the British or the French, or it may be due to some confusion owing to darkness...We are deeply moved by such...news and promise that nothing will be omitted on our part to find out the culprits and severely punish them."*

Ironically, the first person to foresee America's involvement in Vietnam as spelling disaster also became America's first casualty of its policy to get so involved. Dewey's death claimed another distinction: as his body was never recovered, he became America's first post-World War II MIA in Vietnam.

The death of Lieutenant Colonel Dewey may have been an unfortunate mistake, but set the tone from that point on for U.S. involvement in Southeast Asia. As Washington continued to march into a quagmire, additional mistakes in policy-making followed, drawing America further in. The failure to recall U.S. troops once the futility of winning the war had become evident eventually would cost the lives of thousands more soldiers on both sides of the battlefield.

Dewey was a man of great foresight. He recognized—twenty years before the first U.S. Marines landed at Danang—that America should avoid military involvement in Vietnam. Similarly, he would have known, once defeat extricated America from its morass, when to accept the hand of friendship from our former enemies. Were he alive in 1995 when President Clinton made the decision to normalize relations between the two countries, Dewey undoubtedly would have recognized the importance of forging a new relationship with Vietnam in light of the terrible war that had turned a one-time ally into a bitter enemy.

On August 6, 1995, the U.S. liaison office in Hanoi was upgraded to a full-fledged U.S. embassy for the first time in forty years, establishing a new highpoint in U.S.-Vietnam relations. One would like to believe, among the observers there that day, not in body but in spirit, was Lieutenant Colonel A. Peter Dewey. If so, he most likely was nodding his head in quiet approval.

Section 7:

That's Entertainment

Just as U.S. troops were able to enjoy USO shows during the war, periodically so too did Vietnamese soldiers enjoy performances by traveling troupes of entertainers. While the message conveyed by these Vietnamese troupes to their audiences was usually quite different from that conveyed by the USO shows to theirs, for soldiers fighting in the war both groups of performers provided a temporary but welcome relief from the rigors of combat. The following account is taken from interviews with several Vietnamese artists and performers who dedicated the best years of their lives to performing along the Ho Chi Minh Trail and on the battlefields of the south.

The Show Must Go On 184

THE SHOW MUST GO ON

Le Thu Luong discovered early in her life the realities of growing up in a country subjected to generations of war. An only child, she never really knew her parents. Born in December 1947, in the dawn of Vietnam's war against French colonialism, she was orphaned by the age of two. Her father, a Vietminh soldier, had escaped death at the hands of the French, only to die in the jungles. Unable to obtain medication, he eventually succumbed to the malaria that ravaged his body. Less than a year later, Le's mother died—the unfortunate victim of a bombing attack by the French. The death of her parents would not be the last time the tragedy of war would take its toll on Le.

If there is a purpose in heartbreak, perhaps the loss of her parents at a tender age provided her with a direction in life. Raised by a maternal grandmother who often sang to her, Le grew up with an appreciation for the traditional folk songs of her region. Raised a poor child in her village in the Vinh Linh area, Le—by the age of twelve—had clearly developed a special talent as a folk singer.

That talent did not go unnoticed by regional authorities. Le was soon recruited for propaganda and broadcasting. Her magnificent voice, coupled with her angelic looks, made Le a natural for the communist cause—to enchant audiences with songs of passion, inspiring them on to ultimate victory, and reunification of their Motherland.

Initially performing in local villages, Le later went to Hanoi as part of a 45-member troupe to entertain soldiers there. Volunteering to join the army as an entertainer, she was sent south in March 1967. Departing Hanoi with her troupe, which included a full range of talents from singers and dancers to actors and comedians, she soon found herself making the rigorous transit down the Ho Chi Minh Trail by foot.

The departure of the entertainment troupe from Hanoi would mark the beginning of what would prove for Le and her companions to be a very demanding eight-year tour of duty—their lives filled with continuous physical hardship and emotional challenges.

The troupe made its way south along the Trail, stopping at each binh tram. As entertainers, they, unlike regular soldiers, spent several days at each of these stations to perform. For soldiers with little else to distract them from the rigors of war, visits by such troupes provided a tremendous morale boost.

Normally, these performances were held outdoors. While most soldiers sat around a makeshift stage, others found nearby trees to climb up in order to get an unobstructed view. Stages were strategically placed to take advantage of the jungle's natural vegetation to conceal performances, and the massing of troops in the audience, from aerial observation. No one had to be reminded about the consequences of failing to do so. A large group, caught in the open in daylight, spelled certain death from enemy aircraft. Performances were occasionally held underground in bunkers for the benefit of patients too incapacitated to be brought up.

Regardless of where a performance was held, it was always well received. For male soldiers who had not seen a woman for many years, the troupe's arrival was a welcome sight. Whether their attendance was motivated by an appreciation for the cultural experience or by a longing to regale themselves with the magnificent beauty of Le and the other female performers will, perhaps, remain one of the unknown mysteries of the Trail.

The troupe's trek south ended on the Trail between Quang Tri and Thua

Thien, which became its operational base. Known as the "Tri-Thien" troupe, Le and her fellow performers continuously traversed the area, moving up and down the Trail, to perform for troops within their operational area.

While her primary talent was as a vocalist, Le proved talented in other areas as well.

"I sang all different kinds of songs but also performed comedy and acting," she explained. Regardless of the form of entertainment, it all seemed to have a fairly common theme—that of individual sacrifice for the common good. For only through self-sacrifice could the ultimate victory of reunification be achieved.

"One comedy play in which I was involved," shared Le, *"dealt with the capture of prisoners by an old lady. The story emphasized that the war being waged was a people's war. A small village was the setting for the play. Many enemy soldiers entered the village, taking the old woman's goats and chickens. They were soon run off by NVA soldiers, but not before the old woman was able to capture several enemy soldiers."*

Le also performed dramatic roles. One play, entitled *"Flag,"* she felt was particularly moving. In this play, an old blind woman, despite the occupation of her village by enemy troops, held on to a communist flag that she had kept hidden in her home. Her loyalty to the north transcended her fear the enemy might discover the flag and her true allegiance to Hanoi. In the final act, as the war ends, the woman removes the flag from its hiding place and proudly flies it from the roof of her house.

* * *

An understanding of the significance of the arts is necessary to appreciate the fact that, during the war, entertainers played just as important a role in Hanoi's war effort as the front line combat soldier.

"For a soldier in the field of the arts, the lyrics of a song or lines of a play became a weapon of the war," explained Nguyen The Linh, who commanded an entertainment group from 1964-1975 that performed along the Trail. *"We did not have experience in fighting but we took*

care of the fighting soldier's spirit. While our unit was small, it was effective and its contribution was very important. All music, all poems, all plays were to motivate the soldier. Each helped to explain why we had to fight the war—and, more importantly, why we had to win."

The use of the arts as part of the North Vietnamese war effort is, perhaps, difficult to grasp fully. As American soldiers listened to songs about home, loved ones left behind, and the tragedy of war (such as "Where Have All The Flowers Gone"), North Vietnamese soldiers listened to songs about patriotism, victory for the Motherland, and the glory of fighting—and dying—for the country. The songs heard by the North Vietnamese soldier rarely, if ever, dwelled on personal heartache or loss—for that only served to distract the soldier from his ultimate mission to achieve complete victory.

Whether the message was for the soldier on the battlefield or the family back home, the theme was always the same. It gave the soldier's "raison d'etre"—he was there to make the ultimate sacrifice for country. And, despite the common roots shared by the two Vietnams, the themes of South Vietnamese songs were uniquely different from those of the North. While the Saigon soldier's thoughts were on romance, his North Vietnamese counterpart focused on what was expected of him on the battlefield.

Just as the arts provided political motivation for the North Vietnamese soldier, they also provided an important outlet for him as well. *"Art is a very important part of our culture,"* explained Linh.

"Our people's army always concentrated on fighting so we needed art to relax us. We cannot ignore this very important ingredient in our lives. In warfare, modern equipment and weapons are important—but the human factor is also very important."

Linh credits America's defeat in the war to its failure to understand the Vietnamese people and their leadership. *"It was this human factor that Americans did not understand before they became involved in the war,"* he shared. *"It was a lack of understanding that carried over into the arts as well. The arts motivated our troops and provided them with the spirit to overcome immense hardship and difficulty. The most difficult time in the war was during the food shortages. We would go for days with only a small amount of food. Things were so bad we wanted to send the women back but the women were inspired by the music to stay on. That is why we were able to fight for eleven years. It was very difficult. But we were able to overcome these hardships, in part, due to the inspiration of our music, our songs and our poems. Lyrics are an invisible yet very powerful force. Their importance and the importance of the entertainer who delivered them were recognized by the combat soldier who, even during times when food was scarce, would voluntarily surrender his own food to ensure the health of the performers."*

The Commander-in-Chief of the Ho Chi Minh Trail, General Dong Si Nguyen, recognized the importance of the arts as a motivational tool. After a particularly bloody engagement in which a regiment under his command was almost entirely destroyed, he summoned his full time poet, Pham Tien Dzuat, who served on his headquarters staff. It was near midnight as the poet stood before his commander. Informing Dzuat of the devastation suffered, General Nguyen instructed his poet to write a poem about the regiment's sacrifice. The purpose of such a request Dzuat understood—for his commander sought to give the survivors of the battle a renewed spirit and to re-motivate his command by the regiment's sacrifice. *"General Dong Si Nguyen clearly understood the main effect of literature,"* observed Dzuat.

❊   ❊   ❊

As an entertainer, Le found it was important to be adaptable. There were many times flexibility was required as word of an impending enemy attack would result in the temporary suspension of a performance.

"Several times there were bombings from the air and sea interrupting our performances. But," she added, *"we immediately continued once it stopped."* While the first air attacks were a scare for her, Le quickly learned to adjust to the situation. *"During the first attack I was very jittery. But after awhile I realized if anything happened to me, there*

were all these nice young men to care for me—so I started making the best of things and tried to enjoy the bombings."

One of these men, Le observed, had taken an immediate liking to her—as she had to him. His name was Trung Chi Thanh—political officer for the 6th Regiment. He had attended a number of her performances. They met in October 1967, after Trung finally took the initiative to talk to her.

Trung was more than twice her age, but Le immediately fell in love with him. *"He was tall and muscular,"* she said. *"Much bigger than normal—and very handsome, with a crew cut. His unit was awarded one of the highest medals for their actions during the war."*

Carrying on a courtship in the jungles among thousands of troops was not easy. It became even more difficult when Trung's unit had to relocate several kilometers away. The distance was such that it required a day and night's travel to reach Le at the binh tram. Distance, however, proved no barrier to their love—only an inconvenience with which they had to cope.

"We fell very much in love," Le explained. *"He wrote me romantic letters. Every night, a courier arrived at my camp with another letter from him."* Misfortune found Le again. In December 1967, she and Trung shared their last embrace. *"I was sick with malaria and had a very high temperature at the time. He came to visit me and brought some food and sugar. We shared our dreams. He talked about buying a car after the war so he could take me around the country to perform. It was a very emotional departure."*

The love letters, delivered by courier, continued to arrive until Trung's unit departed the area. His last letter was accompanied by a package. It included a jar of melon jam—made by his soldiers, a handkerchief and a pair of socks. His letter was apologetic, explained Le. It said, *"During this time of fighting, I have nothing to offer you except these small gifts. These I send to my entertainer so I at least can give you something during this Tet holiday."*

Trung's unit departed to join other units assembling to launch the Tet offensive of January 31, 1968. On that day, numerous attacks were launched against U.S./ARVN forces in and around Saigon. It was in the course of Trung's withdrawal from one of these attacks that disaster struck. He and his men were moving along a riverbank, unaware that their withdrawal had been detected. Within minutes, their position was radioed in to an enemy artillery unit several kilometers away. By the time Trung heard the incoming artillery rounds, it was too late. He and several of his men fell mortally wounded. Ten days after Le received Trung's last letter, he was dead.

Although the members of Le's troupe learned of Trung's death soon after it happened, they tried to withhold the news from her. When she kept asking about him, headquarters personnel told her Trung was transferred further south. One day several months later, in the course of a conversation with a co-performer, the truth slipped out. Le was devastated. In a cruel twist of fate, a war that had brought Le the greatest love of her life, also took it away from her. A beautiful love story had come to a tragic end.

Eight years later, after the war had ended, Le married the courier who had brought her Trung's last letter and gift.

❖ ❖ ❖

As a female, life in the jungle was not easy. *"Although life was tough on the men, it was even tougher on the women,"* shared Le. *"We had to deal with female problems without any basic comforts...If life was hard for the men; it was five times more difficult for the women."*

The Spartan lifestyle the women endured took a severe toll on them physically and mentally. For those used to living in the city, the impact was even more severe. No longer able to enjoy the relative luxuries of city life, their bodies became calloused by work demands and continuous exposure to the elements. For some, the hardship lasted as long as nine years. Those who arrived in the jungle at a tender age found their bodies, by the war's end, drained of their youth.

Many women who served on the Trail had a high moral code. A pre-marital sexual relationship was strictly forbidden. Many women who adhered to this code found themselves doomed to live life alone upon their return home. Physically changed by the demands of jungle life, they were less desirable to the men returning home from war who sought younger, softer brides. The story is told of one group of 40 female Trail veterans who remained chaste during their service and, twenty years after Saigon's fall, were still single, unwanted by the male counterparts alongside whom they had so loyally served.

❄ ❄ ❄

Female entertainers were a different breed, however. Perhaps because their duties put them in regular contact with male soldiers, a large percentage of the female performers met and married their spouses while serving on the Trail. One such encounter and betrothal is recounted by Pham Thi Thu Hong. A singer who entertained troops along the Trail in the vicinity of Hue City, Pham was sent south in 1963, at the age of twenty-two. She served there until 1972 when continued bouts with malaria forced her return to Hanoi.

"I met my future husband on the southern battlefield in 1963. I was an entertainer and he was a cameraman filming a documentary. His name was Nguyen Hong Sau. Although Sau attended a number of my performances, he never spoke to me. Then, one afternoon about two years after he had first seen me, he went out looking for vegetables in the jungle. He had only a bayonet with him and while searching for food was bitten on the neck by a poisonous snake. He came rushing into our camp. Another performer and I both treated his wound. We gave him a pill to offset the effect of the venom. We broke another pill in half and used it to make a salve. The salve was then placed on the wound to prevent the poison from spreading. As we treated him, I learned we were both from the same village. When we finished with him, he asked me if I could come to his camp later that day."

Pham did pay a visit on her recuperating patient that evening. He then confided to her that he had been in love with her for a long time. He had never known how to tell Pham this before but the incident involving the snakebite had provided an excellent opportunity for him to do so.

For Pham, however, love did not come so quickly. While they became good friends, it was not until three years later that Pham was finally smitten with love for her former patient. They were married after she was permanently sent back to Hanoi in 1972 for health reasons.

✤ ✤ ✤

Female entertainers lived in camps by themselves, segregated from their male counterparts. Sometimes, either for security or simply to assist the women with the hardship of camp life, a few males stayed with them. There was never a problem when the two sexes stayed together. The men respected the women's privacy and vice versa.

Sometimes the women invited the men to their camp for a meal. Le recalled an incident arising out of one such invitation. Having finished washing their underwear and hanging them up to dry, the women prepared a sweet soup—a desert made with beans. Later that evening, the men arrived. As they, all sat around an open fire, the large cooking pot containing the sweet soup came to a boil and was poured into  individual bowls. As the last scoop was served, the ladle caught a rather lumpy substance at the bottom of the pot. Examined more closely, the cooks immediately recognized it as a pair of women's underwear. Apparently, while the pot had been left unattended, someone's underwear had fallen off the clothesline near the fire—directly into the pot of soup! Discovering the soup's secret ingredient, the men proceeded to eat the underwear.

✤ ✤ ✤

Anyone traversing the Trail had a story to tell of food shortages. While such tales were less frequent for entertainers as they spent much time at binh trams where food was more plentiful, even they experienced occasional shortages. Le recalled one such shortage: *"One time we were short on food and went out into the jungle to look for something to eat. We found some mushrooms. We cooked and ate them, not realizing they were dangerous to eat. Everyone in our group got very sick and had to be treated at the hospital...Food was particularly in short supply after the 1968 Tet offensive. We often were very hungry. We had no salt, no medication, and no food. We constantly were going into the jungle to find something to eat. We hunted animals, occasionally killing elephants. While elephant meat was filling, it was not tasty."*

⁂ ⁂ ⁂

Pham Thi Thu Hong recalled a dilemma she and her comrades faced one day from the gnawing hunger brought on by a very limited food supply:

"Each of us carried an emergency ration in our pack. This ration consisted of a hard biscuit only to be eaten upon the order of our commander. To ensure we did not violate this regulation, our commander periodically inspected our packs to ensure the ration was still there.

"Our group was traveling south along the Trail. We had eaten little for several days and were very hungry. When our commander could not hear us talk, we debated whether we should eat our biscuits. We stopped to rest. I decided the four of us should share a single biscuit from one of our packs and if caught, I would accept responsibility for our action. A biscuit was removed from one pack. Fearing our commander might hear the sound of the biscuit being snapped apart into four pieces, we began making noise to hide the sound. We quickly ate our portions and, to disguise the biscuit's removal, placed dry leaves in the pouch which originally contained it."

The action went undiscovered for several days. But then their commander conducted an inspection. The four co-conspirators looked at each other in horror as the first pack was opened. When their commander began inspecting the second, the four women attempted to swap the first pack for the pack missing a biscuit. Their commander observed the switch as it was being made. Demanding to know who had eaten their emergency ration without proper authority, Pham stood up to take the blame. As she tried to explain how hungry they were, her commander reprimanded her. Normally not one to challenge authority, Pham reacted totally out of character. Taking a big gamble, she challenged her commander to reveal the contents of her own pack to everyone before continuing her reprimand of Pham. As her commander stood in silence, Pham approached her and opened up her pack. Her bluff had worked—her commander's biscuit was missing. Recognizing that Pham and the others were guilty only of splitting a single biscuit among the four of them while she had a biscuit entirely to herself, the commander quickly dropped the matter.

❖ ❖ ❖

The life of an entertainer on the Trail was not simply one of waiting for the next performance to take place. Often they assisted with daily tasks. At times, their services were required to move supplies between locations. One day, Le was involved in transporting weapons from a mountain base to a binh tram. Moving down a mountain with cargoes strapped to their backs, her group encountered another on its way up to the same mountain base. The other group had a few American POWs with them who were being transported to Hanoi. Le and her co-performers entertained the northbound group, including their prisoners. These were the first Americans she had ever seen. She recalled feeling emotionless watching them—feeling neither hatred nor empathy for their situation.

While most of Le's transits of the Trail as a porter were uneventful, some troupe members fell victim to the Trail's dangers. While transporting food supplies, two performers came under air attack and were killed.

❖ ❖ ❖

For millions of soldiers making the difficult transit of the Ho Chi Minh Trail, they knew, somewhere along the way, inspiration—in the form of their entertainers—awaited them. They knew entertainers such as Le Thu Luong, or Pham Thi Thu Hong, or Nguyen The Linh continuously travelled the Trail, waiting to perform a cultural benediction that would inspire them on to victory. To the survivors of the war, the important role these entertainers played in the overall struggle will never be forgotten.

Section Eight:

The Unexpected

In researching BARE FEET, IRON WILL, some interviews were notable for a surprise element. Of the four accounts that follow, The Assassin proved to be the most compelling to me for personal reasons that become apparent as that story unfolds.

The Assassin 196

The Capture That Was, Wasn't 204

A Novel Approach to War 210

The Shifting Sands of Cua Viet 215

THE ASSASSIN

Sometimes fate takes us down a path we might not otherwise choose to follow—as it did with my decision to return to Vietnam, changing my attitude towards my former enemies. It led me as well to my meeting

with Major General Tran Hai Phung (pictured at left). During the course of my interview with this man I was to learn, to my astonishment, how close he had come a quarter century earlier to inflicting personal tragedy upon me.

In my desire to learn more about the Cu Chi tunnels—the massive underground complex just northwest of Saigon occupied by the Vietnamese for the duration of the war—I scheduled an interview with the man who played a major role in its operation. He was the commander of the Cu Chi tunnel fighters, Major General Phung.

Having first fought in the tunnels against the French in the late 1940s, Phung was intimately familiar with the system. He provided great detail about the tunnel's history, its design, its construction, its transition from a defensive to offensive mode, etc.—all of which is covered elsewhere in this book.

Phung explained to me that his responsibilities during the war included organizing and conducting attacks against various targets in and around

Saigon—attacks initiated only after careful planning and coordination had been undertaken. I listened intently as he identified various targets he had attacked: "...the Presidential Palace (pictured at left), the broadcast house, the U.S. Embassy, the naval headquarters..."

It was the last target he listed that caused me to interrupt Phung with a series of questions for clarification that resulted in the following exchange:

"Was that the U.S. Naval Headquarters," I queried.

"Yes," he replied. As he smiled at me, I sensed he knew where I was going with my questions.

"The U.S. Naval Headquarters in Saigon," I continued.

"Yes," came his response.

"Would that have been in 1969," I asked.

"Yes," he replied, again smiling. (I felt like a panelist on the popular television game show of 1950s/1960s fame, "What's My Line," where one was allowed to continue with a line of questioning of a guest as long as the questioner continued to receive an affirmative response.)

"What was the purpose of your attack," I queried. As I waited for the response, I held my breath.

"To kill the admiral in command of the U.S. Navy in Vietnam," he replied.

I needed but one final answer to play out the irony of the moment for me. I was not quite sure I really wanted to know the answer at this point.

"Do you know who he was," I asked.

"Yes, your father."

I was in disbelief. I remembered first hearing of the attack in the spring of 1969. The attack took place on May 11, 1969. I heard about it as I was listening to the radio and the day's report on the war's activities came in. Although many years have passed since, I vividly recall the newscaster's statement: *"The Military Advisory Command Vietnam reported an attempt was made today to assassinate the commander of U.S. naval forces at his headquarters in Saigon. No casualties were reported."*

I never heard the last part of the announcer's report—remaining in shock after having heard the first part. It would take several hours before I was finally able to get through to my father's headquarters by telephone to learn he was, in fact, safe.

Little did I know then, years later I would piece together the final details of the attack that took place that day by talking directly to the man actually responsible for the attempt on my father's life.

The attack had been planned for weeks by Phung after his men had monitored activities at my father's headquarters. COMNAVFORV Headquarters, in central Saigon, was encircled by a seven-foot high, very thick, masonry wall. Each wall abutted a busy Saigon street. The walls provided some level of security for the compound, serving not only to hinder penetration by the Viet Cong from the outside but also to shield the movements of those on the inside. Unknown to the Americans within, their activities were being observed by Phung's men from other vantage points, both inside and out the compound—observers outside the compound being assisted by a spy within. Through many pairs of vigilant eyes, Phung discerned, over time, a distinctive pattern in the activities of those within the compound.

As Commander, U.S. Naval Forces Vietnam, my father's schedule was routine. For him, the day started with an early morning jog inside the compound's walls, followed by a staff briefing. A report on the previous night's combat activities then determined whether my father remained at the compound or flew out by helicopter immediately after the briefing to meet with the men involved in the fighting.

Photo# USN 1148801 Admiral Zumwalt
& RADM Salzer, 1971

Photo# NH 97203 Admiral Zumwalt at Rach Soi Naval Base, 1971

As discussed in the Prologue, a new strategy for fighting the war in the waterways of Vietnam had been implemented by my father soon after his arrival. This strategy greatly increased the Navy's effectiveness in cutting off the flow of Viet Cong supplies into the South. With supply lines cut, Viet Cong activity in the Delta region decreased, as did U.S. Army casualties. My father's success did not go unnoticed by Phung.

The trips by my father to meet with boat crews involved in the previous night's combat action at their jungle bases were normally concluded by late morning. Afterward, my father usually returned to his compound, holding additional briefings to discuss lessons learned. Following this set of briefings, usually completed by noon, the staff would break for lunch. Several staff members, including my father, would then exercise during this time, rather than eat lunch. A volleyball court had been erected within the compound, just inside a wall adjacent to one of the busy streets. Participation in these daily games allowed staff members a chance to escape, momentarily at least, from the war going on all around them.

Unfortunately, a pattern of complacency developed within the compound. In times of war, that can spell disaster. My father frequently challenged his men not to allow such routine to slip in—encouraging them randomly to change tactics and schedules to avoid falling into a pattern of predictable behavior of which the enemy might take advantage. It was one of the few times my father failed to practice what he preached.

As Phung received intelligence about my father's activities, he began developing a plan of attack. To be successful, he knew it had to incorporate certain vital elements.

Foremost was the element of surprise. An approach to the target was needed to allow the attack force to close with its target before initiating an assault. This, Phung realized, required the use of a small force.

Next, Phung knew a direct assault against the compound by such a small force would be suicidal. While he sensed perimeter security was lax, a direct assault would require a larger force, negating the element of surprise.

Lastly, the plan had to include a means of escape for the assault force. It had to be simple, providing the attackers with easy access for a quick withdrawal.

Phung's final plan contained all three elements. Selecting a two-man hit team, he ordered it implemented.

Dressing inconspicuously, the two member hit team commandeered a motorcycle. As one man drove, the other rode on the back, carrying a small package on his lap. Shortly after noon on a very warm day in May, the motorcycle turned onto the busy Saigon Street paralleling the COMNAVFORV compound wall nearest the volleyball court.

The two men knew exactly how far down the street they needed to go in order to be directly abreast of the court. Their conspirator inside the compound was a cook who had left a mark on the outside wall the day before, identifying the point inside where the volleyball court could be found. Reaching that point, only the seven-foot high masonry wall separated the attackers from their target.

The motorbike passenger quickly glanced at the security guards. One standing at the next street corner had been distracted. The driver of the motorcycle reduced his speed. As he did so, his passenger immediately threw the package he was holding—a satchel charge—over the wall, directly onto the volleyball court inside the compound.

The hit team's positioning for the attack and the toss of the satchel charge were very precise the explosive falling close to center court. The driver immediately accelerated, speeding past the slower moving traffic in order to escape the beehive of enemy activity he knew would soon follow.

Seconds later, an explosion rocked the compound. The satchel charge sent commuters running for cover as earth and debris thrown into the air settled onto the adjacent street.

Above: Vice Admiral Zumwalt's living quarters in the COMNAVFORV compound. To the left behind the trees, is the headquarters building, to the right following the driveway, is the volleyball court and 7-foot high masonry wall. The satchel charge exploded approximately 40 feet from the quarters' entrance.

Above: Vice Admiral Zumwalt with his nephew, Ltjg. Richard Crowe, outside USN headquarters, Saigon, Vietnam, 1969.

Phung's attack involved months of intelligence gathering as well as careful planning. It was well executed—yet it failed. Just as my father allowed his activities to fall into a routine, Phung fell out of one. The general had made one simple, yet critical, error—he had failed to verify target location before initiating his attack.

Moments before the staff were to play volleyball, my father was called away to a meeting at Military Advisory Command Vietnam (MACV)  Headquarters (pictured at left). Thus, the scheduled volleyball game was cancelled at the last minute. Fortunately for my father, but unfortunately for Phung, the satchel charge exploded on an empty court.

As my interview with General Phung concluded, we stood and shook hands. *"The next time you see your father, please give him my apologies,"* the general said. *"But tell him I was only doing my job as a soldier."* As a military man, I understood what Phung was saying. I thanked him for his apology, and added, *"The fortunate thing, General, is that you missed!"*

I reflected on the irony and emotions of the moment. Here I stood face-to-face with a man who twenty-seven years earlier had tried to kill my father. Yet, I now stood shaking his hand in friendship. As General Phung departed, I was overcome by one last emotion. It was one of compassion and forgiveness for a former enemy whom, I knew all too well, was really, only doing his job as a soldier.

As my interview with General Phung occurred before my father's death, I called him from Saigon that evening to share what happened. I ended by saying, *"By the way, Dad, I gave him your new address!"* I heard a hearty laugh on the other end of the line.

THE CAPTURE THAT WAS, WASN'T

Many years after the war, Sergeant Nguyen Ngoc Huan read an article in the Vietnamese newspaper about a former American POW. It mentioned a U.S. Navy pilot by the name of John S. McCain of Arizona who had recently been elected to the U.S. Senate. McCain, the article reported, was shot down over Hanoi on October 26, 1967. It was a date Huan remembered well: for fate had brought Huan to Hanoi earlier that month, allowing him to play a role in capturing an American pilot shot down that day.

As Huan read the newspaper article, he reflected back on the events of October 26, 1967 and how, for a brief moment, he believed, he had held within his hands the fate of a man who would go on to become a highly respected U.S. Senator. On that day, as the pilot whose aircraft was hit only moments earlier descended to earth in a parachute in the skies over Hanoi, an angry Huan was preparing to kill the American before he landed.

Huan recalled seeing flames erupt from the aircraft, the pilot ejecting over a small lake in the center of Hanoi. Racing towards the lake with the pilot still several hundred meters overhead, Huan stopped at the shoreline and raised his rifle. Aiming at the helpless pilot, he slowly squeezed the trigger.

"Had I actually pulled the trigger," Huan thought to himself as he read about McCain's election, *"I would have ended the American's political career before it even started."* It is a thought Huan has reflected upon many times in the years since McCain's election to the Senate, as the name of one of Vietnam's most famous ex-POWs occasionally appeared in the Vietnamese press.

What follows is Huan's account of how he found himself in Hanoi at that particular time and his actions leading to the capture of a young, injured American pilot who dropped in on him that October day.

Those familiar with the details of John McCain's capture will quickly recognize that Huan's account differs significantly from what is known about it. Yet, in a somewhat startling revelation, it was discovered that both accounts—with one major exception—are true!

❊ *❊* *❊*

Huan's army career began in April 1963, with his enlistment into one of the NVA's most famous divisions—the 308th. (The French had surrendered to the 308th division at Dien Bien Phu in 1954.) In May 1964, he was assigned to the 959 Corps, operating from a base in Som Nua, Laos. This unit had two primary responsibilities: to provide guides for motorized convoys passing through the area and to provide security for visiting high-ranking officers. Huan performed his responsibilities well, never losing a convoy or senior officer in his charge.

Personal security for visiting senior officers fell to three man teams formed specifically for this mission. Team size was limited to three men as anything larger might draw attention to their movement. Each team member was trained extensively in the use of various small arms.

Armed with the latest intelligence about enemy units operating in the area and familiar with the local terrain, Huan safely guided his charges to their battlefield destinations. While successful in avoiding contact with enemy ground forces, Huan was less fortunate in avoiding air attacks.

"We were bombed many, many times in Laos," Huan recalled. *"Day and night, the bombs kept coming. We could not even sleep."*

Although Huan was lucky to survive such air attacks, many of his comrades were not. The memory of these bombings and of the friends lost was something he would never forget. These memories weighed heavy on his mind that October day in 1967, as he stood poised with his rifle, ready to take the life of the helpless pilot descending down to earth in his parachute.

In early October 1967, Huan's security team was escorting a general officer, along with his secretary, cook and personal doctor, from Laos to Hanoi for meetings the general was to attend. Departing the first week of October, they traveled both by foot and vehicle up the Ho Chi Minh Trail.

Escorting a general, Huan discovered, had certain advantages, including priority access to vehicles and portions of the Trail. Such access enabled the group to complete its trip in just one week. Once in Hanoi, Huan was able to relax in the relative comfort of a military barracks while the general attended his meetings.

On the morning of October 26, Huan remembered Hanoi was fairly deserted. Reports had circulated that U.S. warplanes might attack that week; so many residents were playing it safe and had left the city. Despite these reports, Huan was not worried—for he had already survived numerous bombings in the jungles. Besides, his attention was on enjoying a luxury he had been denied for a long time in the jungle— a hot shower.

"We were very young and eager to fight at that time," admitted Huan. *"As such, we sometimes took chances we should not have, becoming calloused towards danger."*

It was 10:00 A.M. as Huan headed for the shower, ignoring the sirens warning of an imminent attack. The sirens were soon followed by the sound of anti-aircraft batteries opening up on the approaching aircraft. Irritated that his hot shower was being interrupted, Huan went outside to observe the activities. Glancing skyward, he saw an aircraft take a hit.

"Looking to the east, I saw a plane in flames and a parachute open up over Truc Bach Lake," Huan recalled. He rushed back to the barracks to retrieve his fully loaded AK-47. With weapon in hand, he ran towards the descending parachute.

"Like a tightly wound spring that had now been released, I...took a short cut and ran as fast as I could to Quan Thanh Temple (pictured at left) *on Youth Road. As I arrived by the lake, the parachute was a hundred meters above the water. I saw from the pilot's face he was in great pain."*

As the pilot made his descent, Huan raised his rifle.

"My thought at that moment was only about the deaths of my comrades in the jungles of Laos caused by American pilots such as this one. We suffered greatly at their hands. The anger inside me grew."

With surprising candor, Huan said, *"I had every intention of killing the pilot. I even thought about doing it in a way to ensure he suffered as much as possible before dying. I had my finger on the trigger and moved closer to get a better position from which to shoot. My only thought was to kill him...all I had to do was pull the trigger and he would die."*

However, as the pilot came closer, something held Huan back from completing his role of executioner—he found himself unable to take the American's life. With his rifle trained on the pilot, he held his fire and watched as the pilot landed.

"As I took those last few steps to position myself before firing, I remembered the orders of my commanding officer—that all POWs were to be treated humanely," Huan reported. *"That momentary hesitancy probably saved the pilot's life."*

"There were few trees on the shore but the pilot's parachute made a rustling noise as it brushed against some branches," Huan explained. *"He just missed landing in the lake, ending up on his back with one leg flat and the other with his knee up in the air...I looked directly into his eyes. He was in a daze. I think for a second he thought I was going to shoot him but I saw no concern in his expression that I might do so. I still had my rifle pointed at him, as I was concerned he might be armed. When I saw his dazed look, I realized he was injured."* As Huan's anger subsided, it quickly turned to compassion.

What motivated him, at the last minute, not to shoot? Huan feels two factors came into play over which he had no control—his professionalism as a soldier and his understanding of the pilot's situation. *"I was just doing my job as a professional soldier,"* he explained, *"which included having empathy for a fellow human being."*

Realizing his prisoner was unable to offer resistance; Huan unzipped the pilot's flight suit and pulled it off. In doing so, he saw the pilot had suffered a severe leg injury.

"I saw a hole in his calf. It was so large I could see a vein. When I took the suit off him, all he had on was his underwear. I yelled to a young girl who was coming towards us to bring bandages. She returned with

bandages and another girl who wrapped his wound. Meanwhile, I searched through his personal belongings and confiscated a small gun containing a chambered round. I also found keys, pictures, a small knife, some U.S. currency ($21.00) and dog tags. A few minutes later, a vehicle drove up and, after placing the pilot inside on a stretcher, drove away."

That was the last time Huan saw the pilot. Not until reading in the newspapers many years later about the election to the U.S. Senate of a former American POW who had been shot down over Hanoi on October 26, 1967, did Huan tell friends it was John McCain he had captured that day. As he continued to relate his story about McCain's capture, it was picked up by the Vietnamese press as well.

"For the first time I realized I not only captured, but came close to killing, a future U.S. Senator," Huan exclaimed. Since his election to the Senate, McCain has become "the" one pilot every North Vietnamese soldier in Hanoi seems to lay claim to have captured during the war.

While Huan appeared to be truthful in relating his account, it was clear his story was at odds in many respects from what is known about McCain's capture. McCain did sustain severe injuries that day—a broken right knee and two broken arms—not a calf injury. He ejected

over a lake in Hanoi, landing in the water, not on the shoreline. He was captured by a group of soldiers who swam out into the lake (his capture pictured at left), not by a sole captor; and, after his capture, he was greeted by an angry crowd which bayoneted him and smashed his shoulder, not by a young woman who cared for his wounds.

Confronted with the numerous discrepancies in the two accounts, Huan insisted his facts were correct—the capture taking place exactly as he described.

If true, there is only one explanation that supports Huan's claim.

On the morning of October 26, 1967, twenty U.S. warplanes set out to attack various targets in and around Hanoi. McCain's A-4E Skyhawk was not the only aircraft lost that day—two others, an F-8 "Crusader" and a second A-4E Skyhawk, were also shot down. The pilots of both these other planes ejected and were captured as well. While one of the other two pilots was contacted and confirmed he was not Huan's captive, the other was reluctant to talk. Therefore, it could not be confirmed whether he was the pilot captured by Huan that day.

Huan never knew that three American pilots had been shot down and captured on October 26, 1967. He always assumed there was only one pilot shot down and captured that day. Since subsequent newspaper reports about Senator McCain always reported that date was when the future Senator was shot down, Huan always assumed McCain had been "his" prisoner.

Today, Huan realizes the capture he thought was of McCain, was not. While Huan no longer lays claim to capturing McCain, he does take comfort in knowing an American pilot lives today because Huan decided to exercise restraint and not pull his trigger that fateful day.

A NOVEL APPROACH TO WAR

THE SORROW OF WAR, a novel by former NVA soldier Bao Ninh, was the first literary work written about the Vietnam conflict from the enemy's perspective. The novel's protagonist, Kien, returns home from the war, attempting "to come to grips with the savageries he has witnessed, to make some sense of death, love and loss—and of his own survival."

Soon after the novel appeared in the U.S., a book critic commented: *"The violent upheavals of war have given painful birth to many great novels. The greatest novel about the experience of WWI—some would say of any war—was* **ALL QUIET ON THE WESTERN FRONT***, written by a German. It spoke not only to the author's countrymen but also to all who fought. Bao Ninh's* **THE SORROW OF WAR** *may not be the greatest novel of the Vietnam War, but the powerful tale of lives destroyed by war has gathered tremendous international acclaim and seems destined to speak as compellingly to Americans as to Ninh's countrymen."*

This book critic had never met Bao Ninh. Therefore, he had no idea how chillingly accurate his observation was.

Having read **THE SORROW OF WAR**, I met with Bao Ninh to discuss, among other topics, his motivation for writing the book. In interviewing him, I quickly came to realize from where Ninh had drawn his main character—for Kien seemed to have much in common with his creator.

"We were both from Hanoi and we both fought in the Central Highlands. But," he modestly added, *"Unlike me, Kien was brave."* Ninh was humble, for having volunteered for military service, before he was old enough to serve, he—like the fictitious Kien—had demonstrated his courage.

Born and raised in Hanoi, Ninh witnessed his first air raid as a young teenager. That experience instilled in him a desire to serve his country. So, in 1969, at age 17, he volunteered for the army. Under age, he needed parental permission. While his father consented, his mother did not. He joined anyway.

He compared himself to the young American Vietnam war veteran, Ron Kovic, depicted in the movie "Born on the 4th of July."

"Although very young, I was eager to fight," he recalled. *"And, as a man at seventeen, I had a duty to fight. Our country was divided in two—a festering wound to our nationalistic spirit. We were motivated to fight for unification—our young people rallying under the flag of nationalism."*

Ninh recognized America's youth also had their own motivations for fighting, motivations that were entirely different and, in the end, he felt, entirely wrong. *"Americans were motivated to fight communism...but we were not communists,"* said Ninh. *"I did not feel I was a communist. Americans were fighting nationalists in Vietnam—not communists. But soldiers are the same from country to country,"* he concluded. *"While they have their individual rallying cries, in the end, when we face death, we are really all the same."* (Ninh's statement is supported by one World War II era U.S. Department of State representative, Abbot Low Moffat, who headed its Southeast Asia Division. He observed of Vietnam's leader, *"I have never met an American, be he military, O.S.S., diplomat, or journalist, who did not reach the same belief: that Ho Chi Minh was first and foremost a Vietnamese nationalist."*)

Reflecting on his training, Ninh observed, *"As in any army, new recruits had to be trained. Forced to forget family and life at home, they were taught how to use a rifle, how to obey orders, how to bear hardship...we knew roughly how to shoot."*

His training completed after only three months, Bao Ninh was sent south. But he and other recruits received their first "baptism by fire" long before reaching their destination. *"Along the Ho Chi Minh Trail,"* he explained, *"we constantly faced aerial bombardments."*

Upon his arrival in the Central Highlands, Bao Ninh was assigned to a three man guerrilla cell—part of a twelve man squad. While his unit occasionally operated as a company size unit, squad size operations were the norm.

Bao Ninh had mixed feelings about the fighting capabilities of U.S. forces he engaged. For example, he respected some Army units, such as the 1st Air Calvary with which *"we tried to avoid contact"*; other units were far less capable or their actions were oftentimes predictable. In reference to the latter, Ninh noted, *"Even as new recruits, we quickly came to see some Americans were very predictable in their operations."* He gave as an example the way the Army established its artillery positions on the battlefield: *"U.S. soldiers were not flexible. They arrived by helicopter, landed on a hill, cleared it, set up their artillery battery and then fired indiscriminately."*

Ninh described his first ground combat experience as *"a small battle in which I discovered combat is not at all like it is in the movies—we just shot at each other and ran."*

Ninh's squad was divided into four three-man cells with each having responsibility for certain targets. As a young recruit, he was assigned to the same cell as his squad leader. Soon after joining the army, his squad was operating around Plei Me where 200 U.S. troops were dug into positions on high ground. The Americans' defensive perimeter was marked by a number of foxholes. During daylight hours, his squad identified the exact position of each foxhole. When darkness fell, the four cells took up their positions. The squad leader, armed with a captured M-79 grenade launcher, was to signal the attack.

As the men gained their night vision, they attempted to locate their respective targets. Ninh's first battlefield lesson was, *"U.S. troops quickly lose their vigilance."* A careless American soldier enabled the squad quickly to get a bearing on their targets. Partially hidden in his foxhole, he unwittingly gave away his position as he nonchalantly lit a cigarette. Ninh learned his second battlefield lesson: *"in combat, he who chooses to smoke at night chooses to die."*

The squad leader aimed his M-79 at the burning embers of the unwary soldier's cigarette—and fired. As the round exploded on target, the other squad members opened up on their targets. Although he was unable to see at what he was shooting, Ninh joined in the fireworks. As they received return fire, the squad immediately withdrew. Darkness temporarily gave way to daylight as the Americans fired flares into the air. The flares revealed the squad's now abandoned positions, occupied only moments earlier, as the unit safely withdrew deep into the jungle.

The next morning the four cells rendezvoused at a pre-scheduled location. They had suffered no casualties.

This was not the only time Ninh's squad took advantage of a lack of vigilance by U.S. troops. Early one morning his squad was astonished to find a group of Americans gathered together in a clearing, kneeling in front of an officer who was talking to them. Not often did Ninh's squad find such a "group" target of opportunity. They immediately took the Americans under fire. Only later did he learn the soldiers were assembling for Sunday worship services. He thought it a bitter irony that a man's life could be taken at the very moment he prayed to God for his safekeeping. While the incident initially bothered him, in time, he came to accept it—for that was all he could do. *"War is brutal and illogical,"* he rationalized.

An avid reader, Ninh was asked what books influenced his own writing. He reported one book in particular had affected him deeply. He read the book during the war, having acquired it under rather bizarre circumstances. In 1973, his unit engaged in a firefight against ARVN troops. When the fight was over, Ninh and his comrades searched the battlefield for anything of value. Coming across the body of one ARVN soldier, Ninh rummaged through his rucksack for food. Among the items he removed was a book. He put the book in his own rucksack, but did not get a chance to read it until much later. When he finally did, he felt it ironic the book that came into his possession as the result of a bloody battle conveyed a powerful anti-war message. He was deeply affected by the book, which later motivated him to write **THE SORROW OF WAR**.

When asked for the name of the book he read, Ninh reported it was **ALL QUIET ON THE WESTERN FRONT**—the very same work to which an American book critic had equated Ninh's novel, **THE SORROW OF WAR!**

In the years since the war, Ninh saw many depictions, in film and literature, of the Vietnam war and the men on both sides who fought it. He felt the American movie "Platoon" was good but unfairly cast all North Vietnamese soldiers as brutal. Ninh observed that while brutal individuals fought on both sides of the battlefield during the war, brutal armies did not. Like courage, he added, brutality is an individual trait.

The jacket of **THE SORROW OF WAR** says of Bao Ninh: *"During the Vietnam War he served with the Glorious 27th Youth Brigade. Of the five hundred who went to war with the brigade in 1969, he is one of ten who survived."*

Bao Ninh attributed this representation to an overzealous publisher's creative mind. While three to four hundred young people from his region joined the army together, Ninh indicates he does not know how many actually survived the war.

In both Kien and Bao Ninh, one discovers war had a significant impact upon them. Robbed of their youthful innocence, they returned home to pick up the broken pieces of their lives. It is a story not too unlike that of many American veterans of the same war. In putting their lives back in order after returning home, veterans on both sides shared the same concerns and desires—to provide for themselves and their families, to enjoy peace and prosperity, to be happy. *"While war is brutal and illogical,"* concluded Bao Ninh, *"perhaps the ultimate 'sorrow of war' is we learn, only after the shooting stops, how much we share in common with our enemies."*

THE SHIFTING SANDS OF CUA VIET

Tong Huy Tinh joined the army in 1971 at the age of eighteen. A member of the civil forces before his enlistment, he required little additional training before being sent down the Ho Chi Minh Trail to join his comrades in the south.

Tinh was more fortunate than many—for his transit took less than a month. Departing Hanoi by train, he arrived in Vinh, from where he and other new recruits boarded trucks carrying them to the Giang River. There they waited until nightfall to cross the river on the Long Dai ferry.

On the other side of the river, Tinh's unit, the 320 Division, began its final move south by foot. Following standard procedures—designed to limit their exposure to air attack along the Trail—the division broke up into smaller, company-size units.

"The most vivid recollection for me," said Tinh *"was when we split up into smaller units for the final part of the trip. We said good-bye, not knowing if we ever would see each other again. Saying good-bye was harder than transiting the Trail."*

Carrying 50-kilogram packs, the physical challenge began. *"Before long,"* shared Tinh, *"we were climbing slopes so steep we had to use rope."* After a grueling journey, they arrived in Laos.

Due to his previous experience with the civil forces, young Tinh was appointed squad leader. As his division immediately engaged in heavy fighting, the young squad leader quickly became an experienced combat veteran. But the most difficult aspect of Tinh's responsibilities involved welcoming new recruits. For he well knew they were, in many cases, replacing the dead or severely wounded, whom he had welcomed only days earlier.

During the next two years, Tinh's division moved often—from Laos to Quang Binh, to Vinh Linh and, finally, to Quang Tri. In January 1973, they arrived at Cua Viet. It was here the division took on a most extraordinary assignment—attacking ships of the U.S. Navy's 7th Fleet.

Cua Viet is situated on the coastline (map below). South Vietnamese forces were dug in along the beach, supported by U.S. Navy ships sailing just off the coast within full view of Tinh's division. The division was told to take these ships under fire.

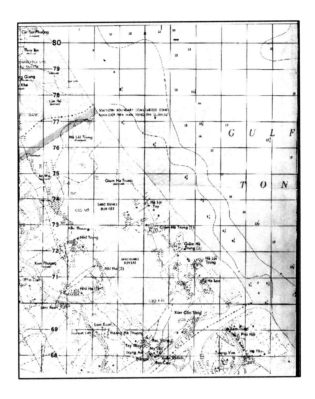

This was a tall order. Tinh recalled the ships brazenly sailed back and forth, paralleling the shoreline, sometimes in columns of two. There was concern the ships might be used by South Vietnamese forces to support a subsequent amphibious landing, so harassment fires of the vessels were periodically conducted. Tinh's mission was to let the U.S. Navy know heavy resistance awaited any amphibious landing force.

Responsibility for conducting the harassment fires was given to Tinh's regiment, which broke down into platoon size units. Under cover of darkness, the units moved to within one kilometer of the shoreline. The night was spent digging in along the beach. To defend against a possible assault from the sea, six tanks were assigned to Tinh's unit. The tanks were buried in the sand up to turret level, with vegetation used to camouflage the turret.

To its surprise, at sunrise the next morning, Tinh's unit discovered their defensive position was only one kilometer away from an ARVN position. Normally, such a discovery would have immediately resulted in an attack being launched against the South Vietnamese. But Tinh's unit was under orders not to reveal their strength levels. If any action was to occur, it was up to the ARVNs to initiate it.

The South Vietnamese—who discovered the presence of Tinh's unit at the same time that morning—did not initiate an attack either. Tinh never understood why. He thought that perhaps the South Vietnamese were under similar orders not to reveal strength levels by engaging the enemy.

"It was a strange situation," Tinh recounted. *"It was as if a silent truce had been signed. We would occasionally fight at night, but by 3:00 A.M. each morning, all fighting came to a halt."*

To harass U.S. Navy ships, the only weapon capable of doing so was the DKZ 82 (pictured at right), a long-range mortar normally used against tanks. Each squad in Tinh's regiment was armed with such a  weapon. One night, the squads took up positions along the beach from where they could attack the ships. They waited for a target to sail into range.

As their eyes adjusted to the night vision, squad members scanned the horizon for the passing silhouette of a U.S. Navy ship. Blackout conditions were observed on the ships, making them all but indiscernible shadows. Attempting to hit an enemy tank with a DKZ 82 was difficult enough but, as Tinh quickly learned, trying to hit a barely visible ship at sea was yet a greater challenge.

Each squad was authorized to fire at will. Tinh's squad soon acquired a target. Before engaging it, however, his squad heard blasts from other DKZ 82s launchers along the beachhead. Tinh knew time was now a factor. They had to fire their launcher and quickly relocate to another position—for the prey would soon become the predator, as the targeted ship would respond to the attack. Firing their DKZ 82, his squad immediately moved to its alternate position.

The anticipated return fire never came. Tinh realized his unit's close proximity to the ARVN position on the beach perhaps afforded them some unintended protection. Concerned about hitting nearby ARVN troops by mistake, the ship had opted not to return fire.

During the course of the next two weeks, his unit continued to operate in this manner, only varying the time of their night attacks. Each squad fired up to twenty rounds a night. It was a strange battlefield scenario, thought Tinh: *"At night, we fought U.S. Navy ships which failed to fire back at us; during the day, we rested in full view of South Vietnamese forces that refused to attack us."*

Of the six tanks assigned to Tinh's unit, five were eventually destroyed by the ARVNs in the limited nighttime engagements that occurred. Later, the fighting grew more intense. Now with two years of combat experience, Tinh had become a seasoned veteran, prepared—or so he thought—to cope with any adversity. But he soon discovered one aspect of fighting on the beaches of Cua Viet for which he was totally unprepared.

When a lull in the fighting occurred, both sides used the time to undertake the unpleasant, but necessary, task of burying the dead. A location on the beach was selected by Tinh's division as a cemetery site. Burial parties were routinely dispatched to perform the task of burying the dead. On occasion, Tinh accompanied the burial party. While burying fallen comrades was nothing new to him, he discovered a somewhat gruesome aspect attached to doing so at Cua Viet.

Often, a few days after such burials, remains were found still exposed in their graves. With further body decomposition having occurred in the interim, it was a ghastly sight to behold. The exposing of these remains proved not to be an act of man but, rather, one of nature. Regularly shifting coastal winds at Cua Viet wreaked havoc on the beach, moving mounds of sand around and uncovering graves in short order. In so doing, nature uncovered in Cua Viet a horror of war man sought to hide.

As winds would expose the remains, burial parties would return to rebury their dead.

"I undertook this responsibility on many occasions," related Tinh. *"Sometimes it seemed not to matter how deep we buried a body. Having to do this a third or fourth time, however, witnessing further decomposition of a friend's remains each time was a very unpleasant experience."*

Years after the war, images of a friend's decomposing body, reappearing from a sandy grave, remain firmly etched upon Tinh's mind.

"There are times," he said, *"when I still see their faces."*

Section 9:

"Iron Will" Personified- The Ho Chi Minh Trail and Cu Chi Tunnels

Some American critics argue, had the Vietnam war been fought properly, without political constraints, it could have been won by the U.S. Prior to my first trip back to Vietnam in 1994, I believed that to be the case. Today, I do not. My conversion took place only after I came to understand the unwavering commitment by the Vietnamese to fight that war for as long as it took to achieve reunification.

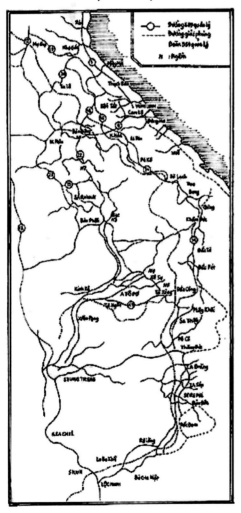

Nowhere was that determination more evident than in the attitudes of the men and women who lived and fought on the Ho Chi Minh Trail and in the Cu Chi tunnels. To understand their resolve to maintain the Trail and to occupy the Cu Chi tunnels is to truly understand their "iron will."

What follows is an historical account of the evolution of both the Trail and Cu Chi tunnels, primarily through the personal experiences of the soldiers who lived and fought there—experiences that tell a story of commitment, of patience, of ingenuity, of courage, of hardship, of suffering and of personal sacrifice. It was this phenomenal and uniquely Vietnamese iron will that propelled them to victory in their war against the U.S.—one not winnable by an America lacking a corresponding dedication.

As the final chapter in this section relates, Hanoi—recognizing it alone possessed the will to stay the course to victory—declined offers of combat forces from its allies to assist in the effort (with one brief exception), opting instead, unlike its South Vietnamese counterpart, to fight its own fight.

The Always Invincible (sometimes invisible) Ho Chi Minh Trail 222

The War Down Under 295

Going It Alone 317

THE ALWAYS INVINCIBLE (SOMETIMES INVISIBLE) HO CHI MINH TRAIL

Introduction

It is indisputable that the key to Hanoi's success in the war against America was the Ho Chi Minh Trail. In fact, asked after the war what the U.S. might have done to affect a different outcome, General Vo Nguyen Giap responded greater success would have been achieved by cutting off the Trail.

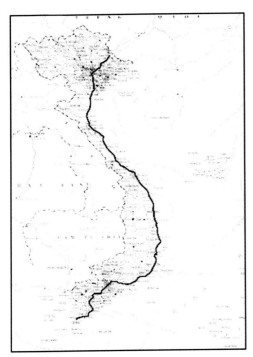

The Ho Chi Minh Trail was the rather remarkable network of roads, communication lines and fuel pipelines, stretching thousands of kilometers, over mountains and through jungles, at points crossing the Vietnam border into Laos and Cambodia before re-entering Vietnam, by which Hanoi fed its war effort in the south through a constant flow of men, supplies and equipment.

In the early years of the conflict with South Vietnam, before U.S. involvement, the existence of the Trail was a well-kept secret.

But over time, as men and materiel from the North continued to flood the South—without having transited the easily accessible north/south route (Highway No. 1, pictured above) along Vietnam's coastline to get there—Saigon began to realize that Hanoi was obviously using another route. Identifying the Trail's exact routing was a very difficult game of "hide and seek," not only for South Vietnam but also for the U.S. after its entry into the conflict. Hanoi proved immensely successful in keeping details about the Trail secret during the war, both by employing innovative deception techniques (some effectively making parts of the

Trail "invisible") and severely limiting dissemination of information to its own forces.

With the fall of Saigon in April 1975, the extent of Hanoi's success in maintaining secrecy concerning the Trail's exact location became clear. The Ho Chi Minh Trail's commander, General Dong Si Nguyen, when shown a map taken from Saigon's military headquarters indicating its routing, smiled with satisfaction. Although the US and South Vietnamese governments knew of the Trail's existence for more than a decade by the time Saigon fell, the map revealed to General Nguyen there were major segments of the road network that had never been discovered by the enemy.

When the Americans did discover portions of the Ho Chi Minh Trail, they found themselves locked in a contest of wills with Hanoi. This contest pitted Hanoi's determination to keep the Trail open against Washington's to either close it or significantly reduce traffic flow. To achieve this goal, the U.S. embarked upon the most massive bombing campaign in history—one designed to destroy the Trail, disrupt traffic flow and break morale. But, despite the number of bombs dropped, significant portions of the road always remained intact—along with Hanoi's willpower to continue the fight.

The idea of building the Ho Chi Minh Trail was not a new one. Almost two centuries earlier, Emperor Hue conceived of such a concept while fighting the Chinese. It proved to be an effective means of circumventing superior enemy forces occupying more accessible areas of Vietnam, such as along its coastline. Some four hundred years earlier, the Vietnamese leader, Nguyen Thai, had observed, *"For the weak to fight and win over the strong, for the few to fight and win over the many, we must force the enemy to fight our way."*

This observation was never lost on those leaders, like Emperor Hue (photo of statue at right), who followed Nguyen Thai. As students of history, they saw—through the effective operation of the Trail— an opportunity to force the enemy to fight the way the Vietnamese wanted them to fight. Americans, unfortunately, failed to extract this lesson from

Vietnam's history.

A study of Vietnamese history should have forewarned American leadership in the 1960s as to the consequences of committing U.S. ground forces to a war there. If nothing else, it would have prepared Americans for what lay ahead, providing a better understanding of Vietnam's national character and psyche.

Nowhere was this spirit more evident than among the men and women who served on the Ho Chi Minh Trail. Overcoming the hardship of life in the jungle, of separations from family that—for some—lasted the entire war's duration, and of devastating bombing attacks, these soldiers kept Hanoi's lifeline to the war effort open during the entire conflict.

The Trail's evolution is a remarkable one. It is one characterized by accounts of individual sacrifice for the common good and provides enormous insights into the Vietnamese national psyche or "iron will." It underscores America's ability to disrupt, but inability to prevent, Hanoi's ultimate march to victory.

※ ※ ※

For centuries, armies invading Vietnam have learned a costly lesson—while the country's topography appears to advantage the invader, in reality it benefits the defender. A quick look at the map explains why. Vietnam is a country 1609 kilometers long. Its width, at its narrowest point, is 50-70 kilometers, and, at its widest, 200 kilometers. The country's narrow, flat terrain, extending along most of the eastern coast, has provided an ideal route by which invaders from the north could access areas in the south.

More often than not in Vietnam's history, these invaders were the Chinese, whose armies drastically outnumbered those of the Vietnamese defender. With such limited resources, Vietnam developed a defensive strategy, allowing it to fight the invader on its terms. This involved using the jungles and mountainous areas in the western part of the country to the defender's advantage. Such a strategy, by which the Vietnamese concealed their military movements, enabled them to choose when and where to strike the enemy. It was inevitable, therefore, that the concept of a secret road network for shipping men, supplies and equipment from the north of Vietnam to the south eventually evolved.

Known to the North Vietnamese as the Truong Son Road—the name taken from a mountain range through which it passed—this road network came to be known to Americans as the Ho Chi Minh Trail. (The use of the word "road" or "trail" is somewhat of a misnomer as its existence as a mere trail was very short-lived, quickly expanding into a very extensive road system.)

It is clear the outcome of the Vietnam war was determined not by what took place on the battlefields in the south or by the bombings of Hanoi in the north—but by what took place along the Ho Chi Minh Trail. Its existence was a testimonial to the ingenuity, extraordinary fighting spirit and unrelenting determination of a people willing to endure untold sacrifice in pursuit of ultimate victory.

Early in my research for this book, I received my first insight—as well as a somewhat puzzling clue—to the ingenuity of the Trail architects. I met an elderly Chinese Vietnamese gentleman in Ho Chi Minh City (formerly Saigon) who had lived in Vietnam for most his life. Our meeting led to a discussion about my interest in writing about the war from the Vietnamese perspective. Upon learning this, his eyes lit up. He suggested as I meet with Vietnamese war veterans, that I inquire about the "invisible" roads and bridges of the Ho Chi Minh Trail. Reluctant to provide me with further details, he—needless to say—had piqued my interest.

I would later learn there were few Vietnamese veterans who possessed detailed knowledge about the "invisible" bridges and fewer more about the invisible roads. I would have to conduct dozens of interviews before I would be able to understand to what it was the Chinese Vietnamese gentleman alluded. The details concerning the Trail's invisibility are shared later in this chapter. They are a fascinating revelation of the sheer brilliance, yet utter simplicity of design, employed on the Trail. I learned too that such brilliance was the rule rather than the exception for those responsible for keeping the Ho Chi Minh Trail operational.

A full understanding of the magnitude of work required to keep the Trail functioning, creates a healthy respect for those tasked with doing

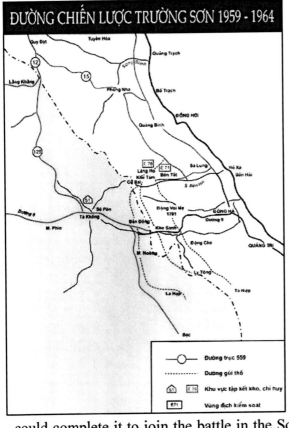

ĐƯỜNG CHIẾN LƯỢC TRƯỜNG SƠN 1959 - 1964

it. Their ability to perform this mission continuously throughout the war under the conditions they faced, overcoming extraordinary hardships imposed by both man and nature, was a true testimonial to their strength of character.

This iron will was exhibited by soldiers who traversed the Trail (a portion depicted at left)—in the early days—by foot, carrying their own supplies, navigating thousands of kilometers over every type of terrain imaginable, concerned not with how difficult their journey was but rather with how quickly they could complete it to join the battle in the South. Silently, methodically, they trod the Trail. Every step was filled with danger from enemy air attacks, disease, wild animals and food shortages. For many, it was a one-way trip.

Creation of a Secret Land Route to the South

The July 21, 1954 Geneva Accords marked the end of the war against the French after their defeat at Dien Bien Phu. Vietnam was partitioned and immediately afterwards, Hanoi attempted, through negotiation, to reunify North and South. As violence by governments in both the North and South caused the Saigon government to launch a bloody purge against pro-North sympathizers, Hanoi realized armed conflict would ultimately be necessary to accomplish what negotiations were failing to achieve.

In March of 1959, the Secretary General of the Communist Party of Vietnam held a meeting to discuss the reunification issue. This meeting led to the decision that a secret route needed to be established for transporting men, weapons, ammunition, food, etc. from North into South Vietnam.

With the issuance of Decree No. 15 of the Central Communist Party, the Ho Chi Minh Trail became a reality. Tran Cong Tan, a writer, historian and frequent wartime traveler of the Trail, reports the decision was made that *"Hanoi would send reinforcements to help its comrades in the South"* since the Saigon government's purge was receiving U.S. support. (Washington had started training the South Vietnamese army in 1955.) The decree effectively provided a charter to create a secret passage, stretching from the north of Vietnam (just south of Hanoi) to the south, over which assistance could be sent to win liberation for the South.

To map out the Trail's initial course, Hanoi selected a soldier who had distinguished himself in fighting the French, Colonel Vo Bam (pictured at right). Bam was a natural choice for the assignment as he was intimately familiar with the region, having traversed it numerous times while operating with the Vietminh forces there.

Colonel Bam organized the 559 Corps—a unit taking its numerical designation from the month and year of its establishment, May 1959. The 559 Corps became the command structure for the Trail, charged with responsibility for planning, creating and organizing a passageway.

The first operational battalion established within the 559 Corps structure was the 301st. This battalion was formed by a group of 500 volunteers. Not only were they familiar with the area through which the Trail was to be cut but also with the local villagers and cadres of resistance fighters in the region. Before the war against America was over, the ranks of the 559 Corps would swell to more than 100,000.

Bam's initial cut of the Trail incorporated a series of intermittent footpaths and trails that had been beaten down through the region over the centuries by animals, local natives, traders and smugglers (see picture below). In effect these trails were a series of "dots and dashes"  on a map which Bam now connected together. He attempted to do so in a way that used the surrounding terrain to maximize secrecy yet minimize travel time. Where both could not be achieved, the former took priority over the latter.

The construction of the first Trail is documented in a compilation of diaries and memoirs by some participants in the effort. It provides a good picture of just how desolate the region was.

(Hanoi's sense of urgency in opening the Trail was evidenced by the secondary mission given this initial group of trailblazers. Not only were they to carve out the first trail, they also were to transport the first supplies and arms south at the same time. It was clear no time was to be wasted in opening up the flow of the supply pipeline.)

※   ※   ※

"That spring (1959), a group of scouts comprising two officers and three men set out from Khe Ho forest at the foot of the Truong Son Range, north of the 17th parallel. Their guide was a man of the Van Kieu national minority, who carried a machete and a crossbow with bamboo arrows steeped in poison capable of killing big game.

"The six men split in two smaller groups, and worked their way southwards through the brush. At sunset, they halted by a field of maize. An old Van Kieu man emerged from the maize gestured them to follow him up to his tiny hut.

"The following day, at dawn the guide from the northern bank of the Ben Hai River (the river which was the line of demarcation separating North and South Vietnam at the 17th parallel) set off for home and the old guardian of the field of maize led the outfit farther south.

"*Day after day, they carried on their trip, piloted by Van Kieu guides of different ages, now a taciturn middle-aged man, now a jovial lad wearing a loin cloth of coarse material, now an old man smoking a pipe, a crossbow slung over his shoulder and arrows stuck in the chignon behind his neck. Sometimes, it was a girl in*  brightly coloured clothes...Those Van Kieu people* (some of whom are pictured above), *long since settled in the Truong Son area, always found a way to communicate between villages a day's march apart on either bank of the Ben Hai River, in spite of all the obstacles set up by the Saigon administration. From 1954 to 1958, they had served as messengers, passing on news of the struggle of the South Vietnamese people to the North and bringing, in return, the heartfelt encouragements of their Northern countrymen and women.*

"*The scouts set up a secret base in the West of Thua Thien. After a night's rest, they hurried back, this time without any guide, finding their way with the aid of compass, staff maps, blazes and their own memory.*

"*Upon their return to Khe Ho forest, a column of porters was already there, ready for departure.*

"*The column set out on a morning of May 1959.*

"*The men carefully picked their way along the flank of the Eastern Truong Son, pushing farther and farther south. At each stage, a small detachment parted from the main body and settled in a remote position. This established a sequence of relays, each a day's march away from the other. Hidden amidst the high trees, the relay posts consisted of never more than three huts on stilts, built like lookout posts for looking after the crops. At night, in each high-perched hut, five men slept on the floor, a few others lay dangling above in their hammocks while the rest hung theirs in an intricate tangle below the floor.*

"*Day after day, on different portions of the route, men plodded on, indefatigable, carrying on their backs boxes of ammunition, bundles of rifles and other goods wrapped in waterproof sheeting...On average, each of them carried 50 kilograms. Some transported 80 kilograms up and down the hills over long distances.*

"For secrecy's sake, they had to take endless precautions so as not to leave the slightest sign of their passage...Every time they caught glimpse of some woodcutter, they made a detour to avoid him...

"This trail had what was later called a 'neuralgic point [sic].' That was the place where it crossed the Highway 9 defence [sic] line running from Khe Sanh to Lower Laos. This strategic highway bristled with enemy positions and was controlled day and night by armoured patrols. The transport columns used to cross Highway 9 at dusk or between midnight and daybreak, guided by scouts who knew it well and would signal the opportune moment through a secret telephone line. The crossing point lay between two enemy posts, so near them that the laughter and curses of the soldiers there could easily be heard.

"In order not to leave traces on the asphalted road, the transport men chose to use a wide culvert under the highway, which came out near the source of the Thach Han River. There a sampan would be waiting, hidden somewhere, ready to transfer the goods to the southern bank for the men of the next relay post to carry them farther south towards the front.

"August 1959. In a thick forest on the Truong Son Range West of Thua Thien, representatives of the South Vietnamese revolutionary movement received the first load of arms coming from the North. The volume was not considerable, only 280 kilograms, but the Southern combatants were deeply moved to hold in their hands these weapons which had been conveyed at such a risk and in such adverse conditions."

❊   ❊   ❊

It was fitting that the first leg of the Trail completed linked points in the north of Vietnam with Quang Ngai Province in the south—for this was Colonel Bam's home province. Later, the 301st Battalion physically cut the Trail through to Quang Ngai, further establishing the series of relay posts along the way, expanding what were initially footpaths into roads capable of accommodating vehicular traffic. Completed in 1964, this road expansion greatly increased the flow of supplies south as the first vehicles began to use the Trail.

Within a three-month period during the latter half of 1959, the battalion demonstrated the Trail's strategic value by moving more than 21,000 small arms from Hanoi to Quang Ngai.

In 1959, the flow of men and supplies south along the Trail had commenced. It would continue, virtually unabated, for sixteen years, until Vietnam was reunified.

The Secret Discovered—The Bombings Begin

Despite the thousands of personnel who traveled the Ho Chi Minh Trail in its early days, its existence remained secret for several years. Saigon suspected a secret route existed, as two things were obvious: (1) the guerrillas in the south were well armed and supplied and (2) those arms and supplies were not being shipped on the country's primary north-south route along the coastal highway. Search operations by the South Vietnamese to locate the Trail were mounted into the dense jungles and mountain areas. Forewarned of this effort (such advance notice of operations by the South Vietnamese, and later the Americans, was common during the war), Hanoi temporarily halted its supply columns as it sought a new, more desolate route further west. Ironically, Saigon—by forcing the Trail's movement west—enabled Hanoi to take greater advantage of the terrain and concealment to establish a more durable and permanent one, ultimately allowing a much greater volume and faster flow of supplies south.

Even after the existence of a Trail became known, much about its actual operations remained cloaked in mystery. How was it organized? How were convoy transits conducted? Where did the convoys enter/exit the Trail? How much traffic could it sustain, etc.? Not even sophisticated U.S. aerial photo equipment could provide answers.

By 1965, the Vietnamese were aware the Americans knew of the Trail's existence as they felt the sting of U.S. air power along some of its routes. One of those on the receiving end of these U.S. air attacks was Colonel Ho Minh Tri, 473 Division commander, who was responsible for maintaining one of the lengthiest segments of the Trail.

"In 1965," Tri explained, *"the Trail was heavily damaged by U.S. air forces. We were visited regularly by U.S. bombers...There was a period of time we took very heavy casualties."*

As the traffic increased, so did America's bombing activity.

"Although the U.S. used every kind of bomb available, we believed the Trail would exist no matter what," Colonel Tri said with pride. However, he acknowledged, running convoys on the Trail came at high cost.

"In 1965-1966," he estimated, *"only forty percent of the traffic sent made it through."* By 1967, only twenty percent survived. By studying U.S. tactics and taking other measures such as bolstering air defense capabilities, Tri reported the situation dramatically shifted after 1968 as survivability improved to eighty percent.

As Tri reported, the bombings did not deaden Vietnamese resolve. The Trail grew in leaps and bounds—if one section of the road closed due to bomb damage, an alternate route appeared almost overnight.

Listening to Tri, one envisions the evolution of the Trail in the wake of U.S. bombings as not dissimilar to the flow of water heading downhill: coming to an obstacle in its path, it is only briefly interrupted—never really stopped—as it eventually bypasses any obstacle that lies in its way.

The Early Days—Transit to the Front by Foot

Phan Luong Truc was a pioneer of the Trail. In 1964, it took Truc, then a Lieutenant Colonel, five months to complete the demanding trip by foot. Years later, as a Major General, he described that journey as *"one of the most difficult times in my life."*

In addition to the obvious physical challenges, were the mental ones. Air attacks quickly tested a man's metal—as well as his mental state. At times, bombardments took a soldier to the brink. Another traveler by the name of Tu Son, who first transited the Trail in 1964, maintained a diary about his experiences there. In the diary, he shared an exchange he had with a straggler he encountered from another unit following an air attack. *"'Good luck,' I said to him.*

"'I'll need it,' he replied candidly. 'Experience has taught me that a man may go through twenty-four different states of mind in the twenty-four hours of the day. Just the other day we came under a B-52 bombing. The sight of my friend lying dead by my side scared me, and I was strongly tempted to desert. A few hours later, however, I decided to continue searching for my unit. So I am not sure what I'll be thinking a few hours from now. Just now I know I must carry on looking for it.'"

Major General Truc reported another challenge. *"When I traveled the Trail, I carried my own food as there was always a problem with food shortages,"* he said. Although binh trams provided food on occasion, re-supply was very limited. So, for the most part, travelers were left to forage for themselves. Each soldier was advised to maintain at least ten kilos of rice. If, upon arrival at a binh tram, he possessed less than that, he was topped off—but only if sufficient food supplies were available. Travelers could never count on being re-supplied.

"We carried dried fish sauce powder which was in a special container, to be added to our rice and mixed with water," continued Truc. *"We ate wild vegetables we found and occasionally wild animals we encountered...including elephants, deer, pythons, fox and tigers, although the tiger meat did not taste very good. Sometimes we conserved rice for a particularly long transit. But we relied on tribal villages we encountered for some food such as corn and tapioca."*

It was not unusual to stop and barter for food at tribal villages. Truc shared the details of a negotiating session he conducted with two impressionable young children from a local tribe.

"Before my trip, I was given vitamin pills in a bottle. But if we put the bottle in our pack, it made it heavier. So we used a rubber condom to carry the pills in our packs.

"One day I arrived at a tribal village to look for fruits to barter for our clothing, cigarettes, or anything else. My close friend and I could find nothing. We left the village and stopped to rest under the shade of a big tree. I pulled out the condom containing our last two vitamins, which my friend and I then ate. At that time, two children from the village who had been collecting fruit in the jungle came walking towards us, carrying two bunches of bananas with them.

"I offered them a shirt for the bananas but they said no. I then took out a pair of shorts from my pack and offered that too, but again they shook their heads. As I had a real craving for the bananas, I thought it might be funny to blow up the condom like a balloon and offer that to them. They quickly accepted my barter. We made the exchange; and while we ate bananas, the children, standing a few meters away, repeatedly inflated and deflated their new toy.

"After finishing our bananas, I felt guilty we had cheated them on the exchange. So we called them over to us. The children thought we were beckoning them because we wanted the 'balloon' back, so they ran off. We followed them back to the village, located their hut and gave their parents the clothing we initially offered to the children. The parents were very grateful for our effort. As we left, the children were still playing with their new toy."

At one point on the trip, Truc arrived at a creek. Standing at the water's edge, he saw evidence of an earlier traveler who had apparently stopped to wash his rice before cooking it. They had carelessly left a few grains on the creek's bank. Food was in such short supply at that time that he carefully picked up the abandoned grains of rice, adding his newly discovered treasure to his own supplies.

"We learned to value every grain of rice," he commented.

In the early days of the war, larger groups of soldiers transited the Trail together. There were about three hundred men in Truc's group in 1964. This large group broke down into three separate 100-man subgroups. The subgroups maintained a distance of a few kilometers between each other as they traveled.

But as bombings along the Trail increased in intensity and took their toll, the size of the subgroups was decreased—sometimes as small as only three men each. The expression of "safety in numbers" had no relevance along the Trail—for large numbers invited air attacks—and certain death.

✳ ✳ ✳

Neither gender nor age was a barrier precluding one's passage on the Trail. Women traveled alongside their male counterparts. Children occasionally did so as well, most notably when parents in the South sought to send their children North to continue studies in a safer environment—away from active fighting. Duong Thi Xuan Quy (pictured at right), a female journalist who departed Hanoi for the south in 1968, maintained a diary in which she noted an encounter with some young travelers:

"*May 29 (1968).*

"Met a group of thirteen children coming from Gia Lai. They have traveled for a month and a half. The sight of them with their tiny packsacks fills me with emotion. The youngest is a boy of eleven· with course hair and skinny limbs. The oldest is only fourteen. They are going to the north to study. They carry their own supplies of rice that they cook themselves. Fortunately· their hammocks are light because they are made of nylon. The children· however· are first.rate walkers. They could outdistance us easily. And they remind me of my Ly (Quy's 17-month-old daughter she had left at home). *Oh my child· one day I'll tell you about the children I met today.*

"All sorts of people travel down the Truong Son (Ho Chi Minh Trail)· *soldiers· civilians· men and women. But never before had I met children here."*

Quy's written promise one day to share with her daughter her encounter with these children that morning in May 1968 was never fulfilled. The following year, Quy was killed in Quang Nam province when her unit was attacked by South Korean troops.

⁂ ⁂ ⁂

The enemy was not the only danger or discomfort Trail travelers faced. They also confronted "all creatures big and small"—ants, leeches, deadly snakes, wild animals, etc. One maintained constant vigilance so as not to unwarily step where one best not. Most travelers, unlike their South Vietnamese and U.S. counterparts who were issued boots, wore sandals, affording no real protection against these dangers.

Major General Truc explained a traveler became so focused on covering as much distance as possible each day that it often tended to block out the pain and discomfort associated with the pace. So preoccupied was Truc with his journey, he failed to realize at one point he was carrying a small predator with him—one which continued to grow in size until he finally had to notice it.

Taking a rest following a rather difficult day, Truc pulled out a handkerchief to blow his nose. A large amount of blood was disgorged. As he attempted to locate the source of the bleeding, he discovered something attached to the inside of his nose. A tick had made its way into his nasal cavity, embedding itself there. The pressure he had applied while blowing his nose had ripped the tiny predator's body open, leaving the head buried. It would be several days later before the head could be removed. Thereafter, Truc made it a point to examine himself daily for such unwelcome hitchhikers.

※　※　※

When not combating the enemy or the creatures of the jungle, Trail travelers were challenged by other forms of discomfort.

Quy, the female journalist, noted some of these in her diary:

"May 13. Post 14"

"The boils on my back hurt me the whole of last night. Could neither sleep nor think clearly. Impossible to lie on my back and it was torture to lie on my side. Had to rock the hammock frequently to ease the pain. Felt hot all over. Haven't had a bath since Post 1. Will stay here until tomorrow morning and will cross the river at four."

Later that same day, she made another entry:

"Have lost my appetite for several days now. Left my portion unfinished this morning. Never thought it could take so much effort to eat.

"'You cannot go without food-' people keep insisting. And they tell me to take prophylactics regularly. 'You cannot afford to be ill now.'

"Ill- oh my! What a dreadful thing to fall ill now! The more I think of it- the more I'm worried. I must not break down- not even with colic. I'd be left behind. Yesterday I craved for a fresh drink- but the fear of colic prevented me from gulping down the can of unboiled water I was holding. Must take great care of my health now."

Three days later, Quy provided an update on her festering boils:

"May 16.

"...The two boils on my back have erupted- one all by itself- the other assisted by Huong (a friend). Have had them covered with sulfamide powder and a bandage- but still they hurt like mad each time my pack touches them."

As if the boils and insects alone were not enough, the weather often added to the misery. As Quy related elsewhere in her entry:

"May 18.

"It's a scorcher and there are no trees along the road. My skin is peeling and I'm tired out. My knees and ankles give me great pains. It began with the left knee as I was going from Post 15 to Post 16- but I had to hurry up to catch up with the rest of the group. Set off at noon on May 16 and arrived at Post 16 at eight in the evening. I limped along and it was six when I crossed Highway 9."

No matter how bad things got for a traveler, someone always seemed to have it worse. Quy's diary entry of May 16 tells of one who failed to complete the journey:

"Then there was that lonely grave I saw on my way to the potato patch- behind a bush at the foot of the hill. The low mound of

brown earth was adorned with a small oval wreath. The frame of the wreath was made of a single strand of bamboo and strengthened by two sticks laid in a cross. There were two flowers skillfully cut from paper. Guess they were made by a girl. Who made these flowers for you· unknown soldier? There was no tombstone to show your name and dates. Only these paper flowers. You who planted that potato plot· and you who made these paper flowers· do you mind if I write about you?"

During the final year of her young life, Quy's hardships seemed to be eased by fond recollections of her daughter:

"May 9.

"Ly· my child. You are seventeen months old today· a day so dear to me. Is the sun shining at Me (Quy's home village) too· my child? Are you still there· or have you moved to Hanoi? Here I'm in a jungle· which is glowing sunshine as if it· too· were celebrating your seventeenth month. As soon as I woke up· I thought of you. My child is seventeen months old now· I told myself. So you've grown a month older without my being there. How were you in the past month· dear? Were you well?...I suppose you've forgotten me· I hope you have so that you don't miss me. Myself· I think of you all the time and I miss you so much I think I cannot bear it any longer. Just this morning I cried out· 'My child's seventeen months old today!' And what a day! I haven't seen the like of it for a long time. It's bright and dry. Do you have this kind of sea,blue sky over there· dear? Such a fine day! Summer has come to stay. How will you live this summer? Last year I used to tuck you in at seven in the evening and would fan you for hours to keep you cool. I wonder if Granny does this for you now. Do you still have a warm bath every day? Oh· there's no end to my worry about you. This morning I got up at five and prepared to go at six. But at five past six· the head of the post said departure was postponed til tomorrow. I was overjoyed. A free day and today of all days· to celebrate your seventeenth month!"

A May 18 entry by Quy:

"...Under the bridge I could distinctly hear water gurgling. Then I recalled to mind the bus station at Kim Lien the day I brought Ly back to Hanoi from the countryside. It was odd; whenever I felt tired- I began thinking of my child.

"My little girl- you know- she's only seventeen months old- but she can use the tip of her tongue to push out the ill-flavored filling inside a polyvitamin tablet."

❄ ❄ ❄

Parts of the Trail seemed insurmountable. One diary entry cited the *"impenetrable forests...the steep peaks...the diseases"* challenging all travelers. It is estimated disease claimed ten percent of the Trail's early foot transporters who carried on their backs tons of critical weapons, ammunition and supplies. Many, committed to completing the transit quickly, walked until they dropped from sheer exhaustion. Over time, survivors learned to pace themselves.

During the first years of the war against the Americans, even after the Trail was enlarged to accommodate vehicles, soldiers were rarely transported by truck. The number of trucks was limited so use was reserved for the primary mission of transporting badly needed supplies and equipment to the southern battlefields. Soldiers were left to walk. Trucks were invaluable in maintaining the massive flow of supplies through the pipeline; the soldier, while also a necessary element in the war effort, took second billing.

❄ ❄ ❄

Tran Cong Tan was a frequent Trail traveler. By the war's end, he traversed its full length a total of fourteen times—six during the French war (when it was just a series of intermittent foot trails) and eight times during the American war. *"During the revolution against the French, I made the trip on foot and by elephant; during the war against the Americans, I sometimes traveled on foot, sometimes by car and sometimes by convoy,"*

said Tan.

He described the Trail's routing at that time as *"starting at Than Hoa; extending around Truong Son Mountain into Laos and Cambodia and ending in South Vietnam at Loc Ninh. The primary route initially was several thousand kilometers long; however there were many branches off the main one so that the road system covered a total distance* (in the later years) *of around 18,000 kilometers."*

For those who made the journey by foot, Tan said, *"there was singing once the trip was completed."* One could well understand why.

A Trail Traveled by Knowns and Lesser Knowns

The Ho Chi Minh Trail was a road well traveled. The vast majority

who used it were common people—the soldier performing his daily duties, making his way south; but there were some well-known people as well. Among the Trail's list of "Who's Who" was Fidel Castro (pictured at left and below). His transit occurred in 1973—after the Paris Peace Accords were implemented—so air attacks no longer posed a serious problem. Upon visiting

Hanoi, Castro insisted on transiting a portion of the Trail in tribute to his Vietnamese comrades-in-arm. In honor of this, the first part of the Ho Chi Minh Trail to be paved was named after the Cuban dictator. (To this day, many Vietnamese veterans still maintain an affinity for Castro and the support he demonstrated for their cause.)

Royalty traveled the Trail as well. After visiting China in 1972, Prince Norodom Sihanouk and his Queen (pictured at the top of the following page) returned to Cambodia via the Trail. They flew from Hanoi to Dong Hoi in Quang Binh, where their trek began. It took several weeks to complete as they passed through Laos before reaching Cambodia.

Visits by VIPs were dissuaded. General Dong Si Nguyen, Commander-in-Chief of the Trail, shared a story about an unnamed Chinese dignitary at the vice minister level who contacted his staff concerning a visit.

"No one on my staff dared to advise him how dangerous such a trip was," said Nguyen. *"They phoned me for advice and I instructed them to arrange the visit for him—but only on condition he call on me first before he traveled the road. He did so and I proceeded to advise him that, should a bomb be dropped behind you, you must not stop your vehicle. Should a bomb be dropped in front of you, you must stop and go to a nearby shelter. Should the pilot's intention clearly be to attack your vehicle, you must increase your speed and run for your life. I told the Chinese VIP if he accepted this advice, he could continue with his visit. To his credit, he was undaunted and proceeded with his transit. I understand he was bombed from behind during the trip."*

The "Binh Trams"

The Ho Chi Minh Trail was organized into sectors of responsibility, known as "binh trams" or military stations (one is pictured at right). Each contained a military post, commanded by a major or lieutenant colonel, falling under the command of 559 Corps. The binh tram commanders had total responsibility for their sector. This included repairing it, clearing it of mines and unexploded bomb ordnance, defending it against attack from the air or ground, transporting material and equipment over it, etc.

The actual size or ground distance of a binh tram was determined by the surrounding terrain. Generally, they were no more than 200 kilometers in length. Each was self-sufficient, complete with its own food warehousing, ammunition storage facilities, transport repair, engineering corps, air defense unit, field combat hospital (pictured at left), etc.

The Safe Areas

Once the Ho Chi Minh Trail was first expanded so as to be able to accommodate vehicles, the shipment of supplies along the Trail was organized in such a manner that these supplies were ferried through each binh tram on convoy vehicles belonging exclusively to that binh tram. This made the transport very time consuming. For a binh tram commander would begin by picking up a shipment of supplies at a safe area located at the extreme northern end of his sector of responsibility. From there, his convoy would start heading south to another safe area at the extreme southern end of his binh tram. Upon reaching this point, the convoy off-loaded its cargo and picked up a new one—usually consisting of wounded soldiers, prisoners or other personnel on their way to Hanoi—before heading north again, back to the northern safe area. Meanwhile, the off-loaded southbound supplies were picked up by vehicles belonging to the adjoining binh tram. This process was repeated, relaying cargo from binh tram to binh tram, until the passage of a shipment of supplies down the Trail was eventually completed.

The Trail was dotted with numerous safe areas that had been built to provide convoys and their cargoes with temporary refuge. The manner in which these safe areas were constructed clearly reflected an appreciation by the Vietnamese that the war was going to be a long one. Where the Trail meandered through mountainous terrain, safe areas were dug into the sides of mountains (pictured at right). These effectively were underground garages. While some were capable of accommodating an entire convoy of 50-100 vehicles, policy was always to spread the risk of loss. Thus, a safe area was broken down into a number of individual sites situated over several hundred meters. Each of these individual sites rarely sheltered more  than a few vehicles at a time. Each vehicle was separated by bulwarks constructed of timber frames and sand bags. These served to protect each individual vehicle from the shrapnel of an exploding bomb or from another burning truck.

Where possible, natural caves were used. Sometimes they housed trucks and cargoes or, if not easily accessible from the road, they accommodated personnel.

※   ※   ※

One very large cave near the Trail used to shelter personnel was the Cha Lo cave. It was located on the Vietnamese side of the Mu Zia Pass, near the Lao border, in Quang Binh Province, off of Road 12. (Road 12 was part of the Ho Chi Minh Trail network, stretching south from Ha Tinh, situated north of Quang Binh Province to Ba Na Phau in Laos.) It housed a headquarters unit and, due to its massive size, became a troop entertainment center.

Nguyen Sinh, a journalist who once spent a month at Cha Lo, described it as follows:

"The cave was located at the (Mu Zia) pass. Nearby were the remnants of an old cable car system built by the Germans after World War I in compensation to the French but which fell into disuse after World War II. One could still see the poles used to hold the cable in place. The road (Road 12) was repaired in 1953 but was not regularly used until 1965, when it became a branch of the Trail. The cave itself was so high up the mountain from the road I had to climb for nearly two hours, carrying supplies, to reach it. It was of enormous size, capable of holding a

thousand troops. The cave extended several hundred meters back into the mountain. It was so large we called it the 'opera house.' It was a very safe place as its depth under the mountain made it impenetrable by the bombs dropped from American planes. Some renovations were required inside the cave, which were made by our army engineers using dynamite to further expand capacity. Kerosene lamps provided lighting. Although we also had generators, they were only used for special occasions such as performances."

Some soldiers, permanently stationed at Cha Lo, rarely saw the world outside during their lengthy tours. Perhaps even worse for them was the lack of female companionship.

"Many went two to three years without ever seeing a woman, even when plays were performed," reported Sinh. *"Whenever performances involved female roles, smaller soldiers with nice complexions performed them. One night it was learned a unit of female soldiers was moving through the pass along Road 12. The men were eager just to catch a glimpse of these women as they walked by, even though it meant taking a long, two-hour climb down the mountain. After making the climb that evening, they were met by a thick fog that obstructed their view of the road. They were denied the chance to see these women, even for just a brief moment. They had to content themselves with listening to their voices before making the long climb back up the mountain."*

Early occupants of the cave had to find a water source. While it eventually was located, it proved unlucky for one resident.

"Initially, there was no water available in the cave," explained Sinh. *"But later, we discovered an underground stream towards the back, in a deep hole. To access the water at the bottom, we carved out 40 steps, much like a ladder. In March 1966, the first B-52 attacks were mounted against the Mu Zia Pass. Outside the cave, a dog was wounded during one such attack, losing its tail. After bandaging the dog, a soldier carried it up the mountain to our cave to show it to us. We thought how fortunate the dog was to have survived. A few days later, however, the animal was found dead, floating in the water in the back of the cave. Trying to get water, it fell in and was unable to get out. Such were the fortunes of war."*

Sinh could not remember the dog's name, but said it definitely was not "Lucky."

* * *

Where the Trail was level, safe areas had to be dug underground. Large bunkers were constructed, again designed to accommodate only a few vehicles at a time. Dug to a depth of four meters, they were fortified with overhead protection two meters thick while providing quick and easy access. Although capable of shielding vehicles from exploding shrapnel, the bunkers were incapable of withstanding direct hits.

Most safe areas, however, were not so extensively constructed; instead, they merely provided concealment for the discharge or pickup of cargoes and virtually no protective shelter. They used the surrounding vegetation as a natural form of camouflage.

In some instances, trees and other foliage were cut down as camouflage to conceal an area underneath, as the existing vegetation did not entirely cover it. While a useful technique, it was eventually abandoned after several convoys were destroyed—and the Vietnamese had learned why. After such foliage had been cut down, it would immediately begin to decay. U.S. reconnaissance aircraft—using special infrared equipment—were then able to detect from the air the heat generated by the decaying foliage. When that heat signature created a discernible pattern (such as lineal, suggesting an effort to conceal a road, or spatial, suggesting a safe area), suspicions were aroused that the cause of the decay was man-made rather than natural. The result was that the suspected area was then placed on a B-52 target list. Instead of cutting trees, the Vietnamese learned to dig trees up and transplant them to conceal their safe areas in order to avoid the detection problem.

Transport by Man, Beast and Machine

Some rather unique means of transport evolved during the Trail's sixteen-year history: from human "pack mule" in the early days, to elephants, to specially configured bicycles capable of transporting several hundred kilos of supplies, to large Soviet and Chinese transport trucks. Initially, the Soviet trucks were the old GAZs used at Dien Bien Phu; but these were later replaced by more modern vehicles—most notably the five to six ton capacity Russian ZIL, providing greater cross-country efficiency and fording capabilities. The transport system over the Trail truly became an evolutionary process—for as each transit was made, new ways were constantly sought out by which larger cargoes could be moved more expeditiously.

Before the Trail accommodated motorized traffic, foot was the main mode of transport. Awards were given to soldiers who carried the heaviest loads. The commitment of these foot transporters was, perhaps, best exemplified by Nguyen Viet Sinh, whose cargo load averaged 45-50 kilograms each trip. Over a four year period that encompassed 1,089 work days, it was estimated he had carried over 55 tons of supplies on his back for a distance of 41,025 kilometers—the equivalent of walking once around the equator with a cargo load equal to his own weight. For his efforts, Sinh was awarded the title of "Hero of the People's Armed Forces."

Despite the dedication of men such as Sinh (pictured at left), there was general recognition that the supply flow had to be increased. Elephants were used to a limited extent; but while they succeeded in increasing volume, they failed to increase speed. Therefore, bicycles, specially modified for use on the Trail, were designed. The bicycle transporters, like the foot transporters before them, constantly sought to break their own load records. One bicycle transporter, Nguyen Dieu, averaged 100-150 kilograms per load, setting a record in 1964 of 420 kilograms. As one historical diary entry noted, *In the hands of the transport men, ordinary bicycles worked wonders."*

These bicycles were designed so that no cargo space was wasted. Loads were distributed across the handlebars, seat and back. Control was maintained via two wooden sticks strategically attached. One served as a handlebar extension,  necessary as the regular handlebars disappeared from view under their massive loads, and was positioned on the same side on which the transporter stood. This provided them with a means of guiding the bicycle.

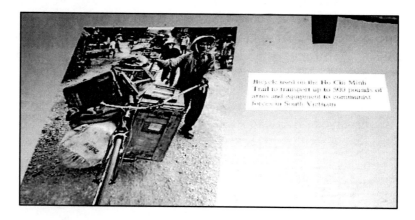

The second stick was attached on the same side of the bicycle as the first, but at the rear, behind the seat. This allowed the load to be guided and easily pulled.

Understandably, tires rarely lasted long under such weight, distances and terrain. When they failed, they were simply replaced by cloth rags tied around the tire rims.

The Exit Ramps

While Colonel Ho Minh Tri, the former binh tram commander, made a full circuit of the Ho Chi Minh Trail on only one occasion, he made thousands of trips within his own binh tram.

"There were," Tri reported, *"six major exit points off the Trail."* Tri's binh tram, one of the largest, encompassed three of the exits—Quang Nam, Danang and Khe Sanh.

The Khe Sanh branch opened as U.S. Marines set up a base in an area bearing the same name. *"Before then,"* he reported, *"use of the Trail was limited to the west; but after Khe Sanh we opened a branch to the east."* It became Tri's responsibility to keep this branch open as well.

The Heart of the Binh Tram

When first assigned command of his binh tram, Tri was ordered to organize a new division—the 473rd. It had but one mission—to keep his binh tram operational and everything on it moving. Division 473 pulled together, under one command, units performing this mission independently elsewhere along the road. Once the division had been established, Tri found himself in charge of one of the largest binh trams on the Trail.

Division 473 consisted of eight regiments, totaling 15,000 soldiers, all of whom played an integral role in keeping the supply pipeline open. Included were four regiments of engineers to repair, clear and otherwise keep the binh tram fully operational; one regiment of antiaircraft personnel to defend against air attack; two transport regiments to ferry people, material and equipment along the Trail; and one infantry regiment to provide security for the division.

Activity along the Trail broke down into two distinct activities—the movement of the convoys and the maintenance/de-mining/construction operations of the engineers. A delay by the latter completely shut down the former. The engineers served as the heart of the binh tram's operations.

When a portion of the road was destroyed, Tri's engineers sprang into action. Lacking heavy equipment such as bulldozers, they often had to work by hand, filling in bomb craters, clearing fallen trees, removing unexploded ordnance, etc. If a road suffered extensive damage, making repairs too time consuming, engineers focused on building a pre-planned, alternate route to by-pass the damaged section. All available assets were committed to complete the repair/clearing operations to reopen the road in time for the next convoy. Such maintenance work rarely took longer than a day to so complete. Colonel Tri's engineers felt it their duty to meet such a demanding schedule—for they knew their comrades' lifeline in the south depended upon getting convoys rolling again by nightfall.

The Nighttime Bombings

As I learned from an historical diary, nightfall offered little respite to those on the Trail. *"Night did not stop the fighting. Trucks ran with small lamps screwed onto the chassis; young people, a lantern in their hands, guided the vehicles through the maze of bomb craters, time (delayed) bombs, blocks of stone, or through the fords. The enemy came to drop flares and the landscape lighted up, every detail of the terrain becoming visible as in broad daylight. Crossroads, fords and bends were particularly aimed at by enemy planes.*

"The only solution in the face of this deluge of rockets and bombs: to pass. Trucks no longer had their windshields—and their frames were riddled with bullets. They ran, covering 10, 20 at most 30 kilometers a day. If a truck broke down and blocked the way, they unloaded and had it rolled into the ravine alongside the road in order to let those who followed pass..."

A well-known North Vietnamese poet, Pham Tien Dzuat, spent several years on the Trail, primarily at the headquarters of the Trail's commander. In 1969, he wrote a poem in tribute to those men and women who bravely endured the night bombing attacks:

"The Moon In Circles of Flame
Delayed action bombs rip up the hilltop. The sky is molten in red circles
of flame.
Through the explosions, I watch
The moon rise straight up from the crest of the hill.
Trees sway under the lightning's flash.
By the guard station engineers sit and rest.
A young soldier sings.
He knows a young woman is listening in a nearby trench.
Shadowed in canvas, trucks tumble down through the lightning. Over
the hill a moon burns red in circling flames.
Friends, the engineers are deep and quiet men.

The smell of cordite hangs in the chords of their song.
The hail of the marble bombs will taper, the rain
of shrapnel on our helmets will grow weak.
Along the road all night, I hear the whisper, whisper,
the soil's veins merging, my country's two halves joining.
I see the halo of the moon, my country
rising higher and higher through the circling fire."

The Changing Trail

From the American perspective, the Ho Chi Minh Trail grew like a cancer. If an aerial bombardment successfully blocked North Vietnam's supply flow in one direction, it simply grew in a new direction. As another historical diary entry records: *"In order to pass, one road was not enough. There had to be many roads lengthwise, roads running across, links; as soon as a portion was bombed, one had to take immediately another in order to escape from enemy planes. (To go) a distance of one thousand kilometers they had to build a network of 16,000 kilometers."* Detour signs, with arrows providing new direction, were always in ready supply.

"If one branch was closed down," explained journalist Tran Cong Tan, *"the engineer corps immediately opened up an alternate route mapped out ahead of time. They were determined to keep the roads open."*

With the Trail constantly being redirected, those who traversed it earlier rarely saw the same Trail later. A diary entry by traveler Tu Son described his transit north seven years after his trip south:

"We did not walk the same path that we took to the front seven years before (1964). We left the headquarters...on the morning of November 14, 1971, and arrived at the meeting-point in the evening...Great changes had occurred since our outward trip. Most of the time we took jungle trails which, of course, were now broad enough to walk two,

sometimes four, abreast. From time to time, we used carriageable roads for a change, which were much easier to walk on.

"As far as the going was concerned, things had improved enormously. But security was much more of a problem. There was no end to air and artillery attacks, and the most terrible were the showers of pellet bombs..."

Mine Clearing Operations

With the varied arsenal of U.S. ordnance showered upon the Vietnamese during the war, there was rarely a dull moment for the engineers.

"Initially," binh tram commander Colonel Ho Minh Tri reported, *"we took major casualties trying to remove* (air dropped antitank and anti-personnel) *mines with our shovels."* Unwary engineers did not realize their metal shovels were triggering the magnetic mines. As they began to appreciate exactly what they were up against, engineers stripped naked before attempting to defuse them. Tri pointed out survival motivated his people to quickly learn new techniques with which to counter the mines.

One of the first techniques used was to hook a battery up and detonate it in place. But this often damaged the road, delaying convoys as repairs became necessary. Familiarizing themselves with the design of the mines, engineers then began to learn how to disarm them. After being dropped from an aircraft, a mine's exact location would be marked with a flag. Explosive ordnance disposal (EOD) units assigned to each binh tram would then be dispatched to disarm it.

Tri explained as the level of Vietnamese sophistication in disarming mines increased, so did U.S. countermeasures. His men always were on the alert for changes.

Vietnamese ingenuity constantly aimed at turning a negative into a positive. That was why, Tri said, *"We preferred to disarm rather than detonate these mines so that we could use the parts—such as the circuitry—for other purposes."*

Different binh trams used different approaches to clear mines. While Tri's engineers focused on disassembly, engineers on other binh trams preferred to blow them in place.

Lieutenant Luong Cong Dinh was assigned to the Trail in January 1968. He remained there until the fall of Saigon in 1975. As an engineer who guided convoys safely through his binh tram, Dinh also was responsible for clearing ordnance. *"I was based at Savannakhet in Laos,"* explained Dinh. *"Whenever a part of the road was bombed, one of our squads went out to repair it...They would either blow ordnance in place or defuse it. Different kinds of bombs and mines were used. The U.S. dropped...magnetic mines and regular bombs...But our task was mainly to destroy these as we rarely got involved in disassembly."*

Regardless of which procedure was used, the first step was locating the mine. There were times when this proved to be more of a challenge than at others. As Dinh explained, *"The most difficult time to clear ordnance was after it rained. We did not know how many or what kinds of ordnance were dropped on the Trail.* (Mud covered up the ordnance making it impossible to determine visually if mines were dropped on the roads.) *Together with my comrades, I was responsible for clearing five to six kilometers of the Ba Nha Pass in October 1969...To clear the road; it was decided to use a 'test' vehicle first to traverse the road to determine if any magnetic mines were present. I volunteered to accompany the driver of this truck...* (who) *was a volunteer as well. When we entered the truck, we had no doubt we would die that day— and we were prepared to make the sacrifice...The driver drove very slowly...for about 150 meters. Suddenly, there was a very loud explosion. The truck had hit a mine. Although the vehicle was shaken, it did not overturn...Everyone watching thought we were killed as part of the truck was destroyed. But, fortunately for us, the mine was quite deep under the mud so the explosion was cushioned. We determined the mine was buried so deep for several reasons. First, as it fell to the ground, its stabilizing fins failed to deploy, causing it to be imbedded into the ground upon impact. Second, the mud created by the rains buried the mine. And, third, other ordnance which exploded nearby further covered this mine with soil."*

Miraculously, the only injury Dinh experienced was a perforation of his left eardrum.

"Later we used a group of six engineers—three on the left and three on the right—to search for mines," he continued. *"They cleared them by hand...In some cases; they just decided to open another route."*

Dinh and his fellow engineers lacked high-tech equipment with which to locate mines. They depended solely on their instincts, their courage, their ingenuity—and their luck.

Another mine-clearing procedure used, Dinh explained, was to *"take empty oil drums and roll them down hill to detonate the magnetic mines."*

Variations in techniques were employed as related by frequent Trail traveler and journalist Tran Cong Tan:

"Once the mine was located, a specially protected truck was used to detonate it. Heavy wood was attached to the vehicle's sides, undercarriage and around the engine. A driver and assistant driver entered the truck, both wearing Russian-made flak jackets and helmets. Tied behind the vehicle was a very long line—about 500 meters in length—that the truck pulled behind it. The line could be adjusted when clearing parts of the road that were not very straight. The purpose of the line was to provide a safety factor for the truck as a weighted oil drum was attached to the line in order to detonate the mines. The drum had to be of sufficient weight to cause mine detonation. Our engineers studied these mines and knew exactly how much weight was required to do this. The drum was then filled with the appropriate weight, usually scrap metal—wheel rims, engine parts, etc.—some of which came from other vehicles destroyed earlier along the road. The drum was pulled over the mine, causing it to explode. If the driver used a shorter line to navigate a short stretch of straight roadway, he normally accelerated to increase the distance between the truck and the eventual blast that followed. The driver needed to allow for a 50-meter blast danger area. Sometimes he failed to outrun the explosion—but this technique was effective nine out of ten times."

Another variation of technique involved using personnel in place of trucks. Four or five young volunteers would dig a foxhole just outside the blast danger area. The weighted drum would then be situated on the other side of the mine. A line attached to the drum was fed back to the foxhole. The volunteers would climb inside and pull on the line, exploding the mine as the drum rolled over it.

Yet another technique developed by the Trail engineers employed the use of a specially designed armored car, developed by a man named Vu Dinh Cu. Approximately thirty of these vehicles were built.

"These cars were old armored army vehicles," explained the Commander-in-Chief of the Ho Chi Minh Trail, General Dong Si Nguyen, *"which we used to lead a convoy. They were designed to trigger a magnetic mine from a distance of about ten meters. After each bombing, our engineering corps examined the terrain to mark locations of mines or unexploded ordnance. These magnetic cars were then used to trigger them. They worked very well and were seldom destroyed, unless they were directly over a mine when it exploded. We always held one or two of these vehicles in reserve, especially at the hot points. Thus, there was a constant battle between the enemy's ingenuity in designing mines and our ingenuity in countering them."*

❊ ❊ ❊

But minesweeping operations along the Trail were not always completed satisfactorily. That is something to which Brigadier General Nguyen Don Tu can personally attest. After NVA forces took the provincial capital of Quang Tri on May 1, 1972, Tu—then a Lieutenant Colonel—was immediately put to work as part of the planning staff to coordinate the attack on Hue City. The NVA Commander, General Vo Nguyen Giap, had already approved the operation.

"General Giap only planned such an attack if he felt the logistical support was there to mount it successfully," explained Tu.

Evidently, Giap felt good about the logistical situation. For on May 7, Tu was ordered to make the trip down the Ho Chi Minh Trail from Quang Tri to the west of Hue City. He accompanied General Nguyen Khoa Diem (pictured at left), Commanding General of the Special Forces—the sapper units with a well-established reputation as fearsome fighters. Four battalions of Special Forces were massing to the west of Hue City in preparation for the planned attack. Along with General Diem was the 5th Military Zone Commander, General Tran Van Quang.

"We were in a four-vehicle convoy," said Tu. *"A truck loaded with engineers led the way to clear obstacles. My jeep* (in which General Diem rode) *was next, followed by a second jeep and a truck carrying our luggage and supplies. It was night. There was a distance of one hundred meters between the engineer truck and my jeep. It was our second or third day into the trip and we were no more than twenty kilometers south of the 17th Parallel. Suddenly, following a loud explosion, the vehicle in front of us erupted into flames. The truck of engineers hit a magnetic mine."*

Tu reported all ten engineers and the driver were instantly killed. To avoid a similar fate, the group *"decided to abandon our jeeps and make the rest of the trip on foot."*

The trip by foot took them three weeks to complete. Moving now in daytime as well as night (their mobile transport limited them to nighttime movement), for concealment they sought out what little vegetation had been left on this part of the Trail by the defoliants. *"This sometimes required that we climb down some steep hills to seek the concealment of trees and high grass by the rivers,"* said Tu. It made the group's forward advance a difficult and relatively slow one. But the memory of the devastating destruction of the truck a few days earlier always provided Tu and the others with ample motivation to err on the side of caution rather than speed. (Unbeknownst to the Americans, a man who would eventually play a key role in North Vietnam's final drive south to Saigon—General Diem—had come very close to being denied that role. Spared the unfortunate fate of his ten engineers, General Diem survived to participate in Hanoi's final victory. But he did not totally escape unscathed, however. For a few years later, Diem died of cancer believed to have been caused by his exposure to chemical defoliants. In fact, two of the five members of a small group operating together with Diem during much of the war later died of cancers linked to this exposure.)

✳ ✳ ✳

The dangers along the Trail from mines came in many different forms.

Magnetic mines posed a serious danger to convoys, but not necessarily to foot soldiers as detonation normally was activated by metal contact and vehicle weight. But foot soldiers were not neglected as an abundant supply of anti-personnel ordnance was dropped along the Trail too, making life miserable for all travelers.

One anti-personnel mine which instilled great fear among the Vietnamese was known as a "tentacle mine." Dropped from the air, upon impact and as if exercising a mind of its own, the mine threw out several snare lines, each about eight meters long, in various directions. The snare lines, in effect, became booby traps—trip wires which triggered the detonation if the wires were tripped, spraying the area with hundreds of small pellets. An inexperienced soldier, unfamiliar with this mine type, upon observing a trip wire, unwittingly tended to move away from it and directly into the path of another wire, thus triggering the device.

Another anti-personnel mine encountered by the Vietnamese was the "leaf mine," so named by its appearance.

General Dong Si Nguyen said the effectiveness of such mines along the Trail was short-lived. *"By the time they were dropped, we had caterpillars plowing the areas where they fell. The engineering corps again was involved—and they had fun. They crackled like firecrackers when set off by the heavy equipment. We preferred handling leaf mines this way as opposed to defusing them, which was a much slower process and more dangerous. And on the Trail, every minute counted."*

The Bombings Continue

A traveler who successfully transited the Trail had no guarantee he would survive a later passage. Each demanded caution as danger came in many different forms.

Tu survived a near death experience from an undetected mine during his transit to Hue. But his return trip underscored the need to maintain constant vigilance.

After arriving at their destination, Tu and the others learned General Giap had called off the attack on Hue. Intelligence was received the U.S. was preparing to launch heavy B-52 strikes. While such strikes had multiple targets, Giap knew with certainty what some of the targets would be—among them parts of the Ho Chi Minh Trail and the forces defending Quang Tri. (This was the start of what was a five-month bombing campaign by the U.S. Air Force, known as Operation Linebacker I. It was designed to provide tactical air support to ARVN forces to reverse gains made in the recent NVA offensive.)

Now eager to return to their troops in Quang Tri, Tu and his fellow travelers returned up the Trail by vehicle. Traveling at night, they knew to expect B-52 strikes at any time. Based on this expectation, whenever the terrain allowed, Tu instructed his driver to move off the Trail. Paralleling the road at a distance of about one kilometer, the vehicle maneuvered through some lightly forested areas. Driving in this manner that particular night probably saved the lives of Tu and his fellow passengers. For no sooner had the vehicle moved off the road to make one of these parallel jaunts, when a B-52 payload fell on the Trail. (Flying at very high altitudes and at night, B-52s, unlike tactical bombers, could not be heard or seen by those on the ground as the planes approached their targets; usually the first sign of such an attack was the whistle of the bomb seconds before it fell to earth or the explosion that followed.) One of the bombs from a B-52 fell only 500 meters away from Tu's vehicle.

"It was like an earthquake suddenly struck," recounted Tu. *"Our jeep shook violently from the concussion of the bomb."* Confident the attack was over, Tu's convoy returned to the road, continuing the ten-day transit back to Quang Tri.

"At another point in our trip," Tu related, *"we were taken under fire by tactical aircraft. We abandoned our vehicles. One man dove under the truck carrying supplies and baggage. The truck was hit several times but the bullets were stopped by the baggage and he emerged uninjured."*

(The group returned to their units at Quang Tri to wait out the bombings. It was a long wait as the North Vietnamese proved unwilling to give up the provincial capital for which they had fought so hard. Tu estimated of the four NVA divisions there—one of which was held in reserve—the casualty rate was an astounding 50%. But, he added, new recruits quickly came in to replace them on a one-for-one basis.)

As to what a bombing on the Trail was like, Tu Son's diary entry shares the following:

"We suffered one such attack at Post 54-A at nine on the evening of January 4, 1972. I was lying in a hammock beside Thai Ha, a painter, when I heard what seemed to be an approaching storm. This was followed by many sharp explosions as if thousands of grenades were raining on us. We only had time to fling ourselves upon the ground, and there we lay still at the mercy of the bombs, which kept up their concert for a full forty minutes. Bombs were dropping everywhere, with steel pellets humming murderously through the air. One man completely lost his head (figuratively). *Throughout the bombing, he* (Thai Ha) *cursed aloud, blaming the people at the post for the absence of shelters. When the raid was over, he was shown an individual shelter that he had failed to see in his fright. It was just beside his hammock."*

You Never Know Who Is Listening

Not everything dropped on the Trail by the Americans was an explosive. On occasion, the payload had a different mission. Such was the case with listening devices. These served as human ears, effectively listening for all activity along the Trail. This included vehicles or troop movements, both of which were discernible within the device's limited range. Binh tram commanders established special teams to ferret out these devices. The teams became skilled at locating and, when deemed appropriate, removing them.

"Sometimes the devices were dropped into an area that was really not important to us so we deliberately triggered them," Tri said with a smile. *"They were difficult to detect, something which could only be done visually."*

Troops were trained to watch for the devices being dropped and special observation posts were established on high ground to keep vigil for the aircraft carrying them. These were some of the same devices used in the electronic fence established along the 17th parallel—the brainchild of Secretary of Defense Robert McNamara. Known as the McNamara Wall, the purpose of this fence was to monitor activity along the border with North Vietnam to determine where exactly troops and supplies were crossing over into South Vietnam.

General Dong Si Nguyen discussed the Wall's effectiveness: *"As to the McNamara Wall, the devices dropped looked like real jungle plants. They were dropped over an area as large as 100 kilometers covering our transportation network. We spent seven days trying to arrive at a solution. We brought vehicles to the area and ran them back and forth throughout the day (to make listeners believe the area was active). The Americans dropped these devices for a few months more before finally stopping. The exercise cost us a number of vehicles as American warplanes attacked the areas where we were running our trucks back and forth to fool them. While we distracted the Americans in this manner, the actual convoys were then able to safely move by means of a different route."*

The Life and Death Link

Besides the military station situated in each binh tram, there were a number of listening or observation posts. The distance between these posts varied depending on the topography of the particular section of the Trail involved. At some points, they were only 15-20 kilometers apart.

Survival on the Trail depended extensively on quick communication free of disruption or monitoring by the enemy. This normally was done by way of battery-operated radios or landline (wire) phones. The latter were primarily used to prevent the U.S. from picking up transmissions. (Use of any other radios was strictly limited to emergency or high priority communications.) From time to time, bombings severed the landlines so personnel were immediately dispatched from the binh trams to locate and repair the breaks. This system proved very effective in linking posts together while limiting U.S. intelligence-gathering capabilities.

※ ※ ※

Sergeant Tran Van Thuc was intimately familiar with the Trail's communication system. In 1972, he was assigned to a binh tram near Khe Sanh. He provided insights as to what life was like for those responsible for maintaining these lines:

"Prior to 1972, it was very difficult to move from the north to south due to control by (South Vietnam) *President Thieu's forces,"* he explained.

"But after 1972, the NVA took control and things improved. The station to which I was assigned was the largest troop receiving station on the Trail. It was established as a temporary stop for troops moving back and forth between Vietnam and Laos. It served solely as a service stop for units to pick up needed supplies before continuing on. (Binh trams, on the other hand, provided many more services to its transient visitors who could remain for longer periods than visitors at the receiving stations could. Due to the nature of the receiving station, they were fewer in number than binh trams.) *Because we had so many storage areas and facilities for these supplies, a station occupied a very large area—about five to seven hectares. These facilities were widely scattered as a defense against air attacks."*

While good communications up and down the entire Trail was imperative, there was a special need at Thuc's station due to its significance as the largest receiving station on the Trail. Their success hinged directly on the ability of higher headquarters to reach the station to let them know when and what units to receive. It was also important to ensure the station's timely receipt of shipments of food, ammunition, weapons, etc., to support these units.

"I served in communications as part of a team responsible for checking and maintaining all the lines from my station to all connecting stations," said Thuc. *"These wire lines ran all the way north along the Trail from the southern battlefields to Hanoi, through stations like ours. A break anywhere disrupted those communications, so we were constantly sent out to check the lines."*

Due to the major role played by Thuc and his fellow linesmen in maintaining an effective communication system, they enjoyed special status. All other individuals or units moving into a receiving station or binh tram, even when permanently assigned to it, were required to carry a letter with them authorizing their movement. Thuc was not required to do so. The job of maintenance required that linesmen be able to move quickly, accessing many different stations to check out possible breaks and they were allowed to move about freely.

"My area of responsibility primarily covered an area with a fourteen-kilometer radius from my receiving station," explained Thuc. *"Sometimes, when there were no breaks, we went out and back in one*

day; other times it took much longer. There were basically two lines we tested—ground lines and elevated lines. The latter, elevated by using poles cut from trees or bamboo, were our fixed lines. The ground lines were just for temporary communication so they could be rolled back up for reuse. We only used an elevated line in an area considered extremely safe as otherwise the enemy might find it and follow the line to our post."

Where lines crossed rivers, they were fed through lengths of pipe fitted together and weighted down with rocks.

As for tools, linesmen had basic necessities, such as testing equipment and wire cutters. Sometimes a special jolt was needed to teach them how to use their equipment properly.

"We had testing equipment which let us know if a line was working or not," said Thuc. *"If it was not, it let us know which end of the line was lighter, indicating a break, and we followed the line on that side until we located the break. To test a line, I cut through the insulation and attached testing equipment to the wire. The easiest way for me to do this was to use my teeth. I did that until one day I was biting through the insulation just as someone was using the line. I received a jolt that knocked me to the ground."*

Following that shocking experience, Thuc learned it was much less painful to use the cutters with which he had been provided.

Linesmen such as Thuc operated as a three-man team. Although team members occasionally changed, a very close relationship developed among them, even when a member was a "rookie."

In September/October of 1972, Thuc's team was out checking lines. The team's newest member, Cuong, was a young man, just recently married, whose wife was pregnant with their first child. The "rookie" was full of energy and anxious for his first mission. Returning to their station from the La La River in Quang Tri, they reached Luong Kim hamlet, situated in the lowlands, when they suddenly came under air attack. As bombs fell, the team sought cover. A bomb exploded near the team. All three men were hit. Cuong collapsed, mortally wounded. Thuc, fifteen meters away from him, doubled over in pain as a piece of shrapnel sliced through his stomach. The third team member received a head wound. Despite his own injury, Thuc rendered what assistance he could to Cuong. As the young man lay dying, he made a request of Thuc. He told Thuc to seek out his wife after the war to tell her she must remarry. This must be done, he said, so his child will have a father.

"After liberation, I located Cuong's wife," reported Thuc. *"I went to her house and explained I was with her husband when he died. I conveyed to her his dying wish. It was difficult for her to accept. For while she recognized the need to remarry in order for her child to have a father, she was torn by her faithfulness to Cuong not to do so. It was a dilemma many young widows faced after the war."*

Although working the communication lines was a team effort, there were times it was also a very lonely assignment. In late 1972, Thuc's team was out longer than anticipated. Thuc stayed behind near a river while his two comrades returned to their station to pick up additional supplies. However, heavy rains fell after their departure, flooding the area and preventing them from rejoining Thuc. He had to spend a month in the wild by himself, working on the lines while living off the land.

"It was a lonely existence," related Thuc. *"I was in the jungle by myself. I got very hungry. I went fishing with my rifle, shooting the fish. It was cold. I had only one uniform and had to wear it all the time when it was wet."*

The nights were the worst for Thuc. As a fire could reveal his position to the enemy, he could not even enjoy the heat of such a fire at night. He was overjoyed once the rains stopped and he was able to reunite with his comrades.

The linemen were proficient land navigators. Initially, they depended on maps and compasses to navigate the terrain; but after becoming very experienced, they were able to find their way through the jungles without using them. Looking for a bent tree here, or an unusual rock there, they learned to cross long expanses without having to use maps. They became so familiar with the surrounding area that many were used as *giao liens* to escort groups along the Trail into the receiving station or another binh tram.

Thuc's job did have its lighter moments. *"I was working on a line I was tied into,"* shared Thuc. *"After making my connection, a call came across the line. I asked who it was. A voice on the other end said 'tao day,'* (Vietnamese for 'It is me'). *Not knowing who 'me' was, I asked again, who was on the line. Again, I received the same response, 'tao day.' As long as he persisted in giving the same answer without revealing his identity, I persisted in asking who was calling. After the third time, however, the voice on the other end got very angry. When he shouted 'tao day' again, it finally dawned on me who it was. In a momentary lapse, because the words had a double meaning as both a phrase and a person's name, I recalled 'Tao Day' was also my boss' name! I immediately pretended to develop a technical problem and disconnected to allow time for my boss' anger to subside."*

❋   ❋   ❋

Binh tram commander Colonel Ho Minh Tri believes the communications system in place on the Trail saved his life on a night he was out in his sector. He was in a four-truck convoy running under cover of darkness. A security guard stationed at an interim listening post waved them to a halt. They were informed another listening post reported an inbound aircraft flying north up the Trail, towards Tri's southbound convoy. Within a few minutes, the aircraft would be overhead. Tri quickly ordered the convoy to a position along the road where it was afforded concealment, as little protective cover was available. He ordered his men out of the vehicles and into nearby shelters located next to the Trail. (Personnel bunkers were dug all along the Trail, positioned at various intervals.)

Within minutes after reaching the bunkers, the men heard an AC-130 gunship fly overhead (one is pictured at right). Specially designed to conduct night attacks, the aircraft attacked the parked and recently abandoned convoy. *"The aircraft fired at my truck with devastating accuracy,"* said Tri. *"Most of our vehicles were damaged or destroyed."*

While trucks were lost, the effective early warning communications system in place along the Trail enabled Tri and his men to survive.

But there were rare times too when the Trail's communications system failed to relay advance notice of impending attacks. As Tri explained, one convoy commander was less fortunate: *"I was supposed to take a convoy down the Trail to Hue, but was unable to do it. So a good friend went instead. He and five others were attacked without warning by U.S. planes. All were killed."*

So went life—and death—on the Ho Chi Minh Trail. As fate dealt one man life, it dealt another death.

The Pipeline

North Vietnam's war effort required a constant supply of fuel. Providing that fuel for operations in the south posed a challenge—a challenge, once again, to which Hanoi arose.

Most of Hanoi's fuel requirements were met by Moscow. From the Soviet Union, fuel was sent by ship to Haiphong where an aboveground pipeline carried it to Hanoi. Beginning in 1965, this pipeline fell under constant air attack. The aboveground system, therefore, had to be changed.

A new pipeline was constructed which ran predominantly underground, from Haiphong directly to Vinh. Parts of it remained aboveground, as dictated by the terrain, to maintain adequate pressure flow. From Vinh, the line continued along Highway 15, through Quang Binh Province and Heaven's Gate, where it linked up with the Ho Chi Minh Trail at Chu Le (west of Quang Binh).

On the Trail itself, the underground pipeline started as a straight line until reaching Kham Muon Province, in Laos, where it split into two lines. Kham Muon was considered a "hot spot," an area subjected to heavy aerial attack by the enemy. The split enhanced survivability so if one line was hit, the other remained operational.

At the split in Kham Muon, one line went east to the Phong Nha Cave while the other went to Road #23 in Muong Phin (Laos). The two lines rejoined further south at Xoi and continued on to Co Village along the

Trail, passing under the Lam River. By the war's end in April 1975, it stretched all the way from Haiphong to Chon Thanh District in Song Be Province, west of Saigon. In Song Be, it split again—one line heading to Bu Gia Map in the extreme northern part of Song Be and the other southwest to Tay Ninh.

From Haiphong to Tay Ninh, the pipeline extended a distance of 2500 kilometers and included seven large storage areas.

How could the construction of such a pipeline be undertaken and not detected? While part of the line ran through jungle and mountainous areas where construction activity was easily concealed, part ran through open areas. To conceal construction in these open areas, villagers flooded their fields. Trenches were then discreetly dug and pipe laid under water without fear of detection.

The location was eventually discovered by the Americans—and attacked. But in most cases, Hanoi's early warning system enabled those responsible for maintaining the lines to take protective action. Alerted of an imminent attack, stations shut off the flow of fuel. This prevented the loss of thousands of gallons of fuel that otherwise might be lost during an attack. But stopping the fuel flow caused a problem, as there would be inadequate pressure within the line to restart the flow again after an attack. To address this, water would immediately be pumped into a pipeline whenever fuel was shut off in order to maintain constant pressure levels.

The pipeline's architect, Major General Dinh Duc Thien, conceived of this system after reading a book about a similar line constructed in the Soviet Union to transport fuel to Siberia.

To Travel by Day or to Travel by Night?

When the Ho Chi Minh Trail was widened to accommodate vehicles, convoys initially ran during daylight hours. But U.S. control of the skies increased the risk of daylight transits. Finding convoys on the Trail during daylight hours was like "shooting fish in a barrel." As losses mounted for Hanoi, change was necessary. Hanoi decided to switch from day—to nighttime—transits. The survivability ratio immediately improved.

In the early days, convoys would typically consist of between 50-70 vehicles. But policy required commanders to break them up into smaller groups. Each was assigned a departure and arrival time at checkpoints within the binh tram. To maximize cover of darkness, the groups transited between 6:00 P.M. and 6:00 A.M. At 6:00 A.M., convoy activity would come to an abrupt halt. Nighttime transits were aided by the use of special blackout lights on the vehicles. Providing very limited visibility—a few feet at best—they made detection from the air much more difficult. But, this also made the transit very slow.

Tran Cong Tan, the journalist, reported that on a good night, a convoy might cover 40-50 kilometers; on a bad night, only three to four. The latter situation occurred when extensive bomb damage delayed road repairs.

Tan reported once convoy transit was restricted to nighttime, *"there were only two times when they ran during daylight hours—in bad weather, which prevented U.S. reconnaissance aircraft from flying, or through binh trams with heavy air defenses."* (The former point was underscored by the Trail's commander, General Dong Si Nguyen, who commented, *"Whenever weather forecasts announced the coming of the northeastern wind, when clouds were low and rain drizzled, we ordered convoys to roll on by day—and at night, in the moonlight. Convoys were on the roads with thousands of vehicles."*)

Other than these two times, a daylight run by a convoy during the early war years was an act of suicide—a run through a gauntlet of death.

At the height of the war, nighttime activity on the Trail resembled a freeway at rush hour. Tan estimated convoys with as many as three hundred trucks might move through one binh tram in a single night. *"On special occasions, like Tet, when we wanted to transport supplies to the battlefield quickly,"* Tan explained, *"the level of activity increased to convoys of almost 500 to 600 vehicles or greater."* Then, at sunrise, the 6:00 a.m. curfew went into effect and all vehicular activity came to a halt, turning the Trail into an abandoned highway—except for the repair teams which sprang into action.

General Nguyen pointed out, *"Sometimes opportunities were brought to us by our adversary. The night flares, for example. There were flares every night, being dropped every other hour, for about thirty minutes over a thirty square kilometer area. Over more important points, flares were dropped every hour—also lasting thirty minutes. It was procedure for our convoys to wait until 6:00 P.M. to start moving. With flares lighting up the sky, we took off. There were times when we would be attacked and lose as many as forty trucks. But then we gave the order to switch off all lights and continue to roll. This, in addition to our own deceptive lighting practices, proved capable of confusing the enemy. The method worked very well, especially in 1972 when the intensity of the flares was increased* (so that not even convoy blackout lights were needed). *I jokingly told my men to send a thank you message to the American pilots."*

While the Trail accommodated traffic going in both directions through most binh trams, at some points the roads narrowed, limiting convoys to a single lane. In such cases, those trucks heading north, usually with wounded and prisoners, had priority over those heading south with supplies and troops. Some high-ranking officers transiting by vehicle were given priority on occasion; but even then, it could take two months to complete the journey.

The type of cargo moving down the Trail varied. Mostly consisting of small arms, food, ammunition, medical supplies and troops, larger cargoes eventually began making the transit as well. As the war progressed, tanks and heavy artillery guns were shipped, with the manner of shipment dictated by the urgency of their need on the battlefield. Initially, they were disassembled for shipment, with reassembly completed once they arrived further south. But if an immediate operation was pending, they were shipped fully assembled.

The Air Defense System

With the road repair and clearing operations completed as darkness fell, another group of soldiers sprang into action. These were the air defense personnel—the people who manned the antiaircraft guns and SA-2 (surface-to-air missile) launchers. Maintaining a constant vigil, the gunners kept their weapons trained skyward, ready to defend convoys on the Trail against any airborne intruder.

Convoys took heavy losses in the initial years of the Trail's existence due to the lack of an integrated air defense system. It was a costly lesson learned by the man who commanded the forces on the Ho Chi Minh Trail, General Dong Si Nguyen. He explained how this changed during the war: *"We had to bring into use all our knowledge of tactics, as a military art, along the Ho Chi Minh Trail. As I use the term 'military art' here, I mean offensive tactics.*

"Between 1964 and 1966, during our weak period, the roads were cut almost continuously. Our anti-aircraft fire was very weak and inefficient, road construction and repair was done at night instead of daytime and the roads were characteristically one-lane.

"Before I took command of the Trail, I realized most of what we had done was simply to resort to the tactic of 'avoidance.' It took me a few years to learn we had to do things differently. During that time, I saw people killed, trucks destroyed and supplies fail to reach their destination. Finally, after 1966, we changed our way of thinking and came to realize we could achieve our goals along the Trail by engaging the enemy with combined forces. Thus, we combined anti-aircraft guns, foot soldiers, and engineering units together—all in greater quantity. After that, we no longer avoided the enemy but sought him out in the air. Later, we not only had anti-aircraft guns, but missiles as well to protect the Trail against air attacks.

"Up to this point, everyone was fighting enemy planes any way they could. But now, they were ordered to fight as mobile units, positioned at strategic points along the roads and bridges. Units that did not follow this principle were deemed sub-performers. The result was our logistical lines were better protected.

"Before this, we were afraid of the American planes. Often our antiaircraft guns began to fire when the planes were still too far away. Also, we were taking to the road individually or in very small units, which gave us mixed results. But, with the arrival of more anti-aircraft guns, we became more confident and were able to fight as larger units and at night. Our units very quickly grew, from battalion size to regimental, reaching division size by 1972.

"As we got better and better at air defense, U.S. planes were forced to strafe from far away and to resort more heavily to bombing with far less accuracy. Generally speaking, the U.S. air force was efficient in the bombing of the Ho Chi Minh Trail—but we too became more efficient in our self-defense."

Those responsible for the air defense of the Trail soon witnessed a role reversal take place with the American pilots they fought. Observed one NVA veteran, *"We knew things had turned around when our fear subsided and the enemy's did not. On occasion, we were able to monitor radio communications in which pilots* (untruthfully) *assured their seniors their payloads were dropped on the Trail when, in reality, they were flying elsewhere to drop their bombs for fear they might be shot down."*

General Dong Si Nguyen added, *"We then relied on two anti-air support systems—one consisted of guns; the other missiles. These were augmented by a network of camouflaged roads that incorporated a large-scale deception system. But,"* he admitted, *"It must also be said that we suffered heavy losses."*

To many Vietnamese, the conflict with America was a chess match. Whenever the Americans increased the level of play by introducing new technology onto the battlefield, the Vietnamese relied on ingenuity in response. As General Nguyen put it, *"It was a war of containment and anti-containment. On one side, there were the Americans; on the other, there was us: the one side trying constantly to interrupt the supply line heading south the other desperately trying to keep it open. Both sides continually changed tactics and, of course, both paid a price."*

The chess match on the Ho Chi Minh Trail rose to a new level in the late 1960s as America introduced a new airborne weapons system. This system was so effective against nighttime convoys that even hardened drivers who had earlier overcome their fear of being bombed were revisited by that fear.

As the war progressed, the Americans realized most convoys were completing their transits of the Trail. This was due to two measures General Dong Si Nguyen implemented: a vastly improved air defense system and the use of darkness to conceal convoy activity from U.S. reconnaissance aircraft. In the chess match being played along the Trail between the two sides, the North Vietnamese had made their move, changing the complexion of the air defense war; now it was time for the Americans to make their counter move. This meant developing a means of stripping these convoys of their nighttime concealment.

❊ ❊ ❊

Late one evening in 1967, a twenty-truck convoy was overdue in reaching its checkpoint on the Trail. Hours later, checkpoint personnel heard the rumble of truck engines. As the convoy approached, it was apparent something was wrong as only two of the trucks arrived at the checkpoint—the remaining vehicles destroyed in a devastating air attack.

Upon hearing of the attack, senior Vietnamese commanders believed several aircraft were involved. They felt there was no other explanation as to how so many trucks could have been destroyed. But survivors reported a solitary plane was the culprit—an aircraft with amazing, and a never-before seen, deadly accuracy.

This was not the first report received by General Dong Si Nguyen in which a convoy was so decimated by an air attack. The pattern was always the same—vehicles were moving on the Trail at night, in full compliance with blackout procedures, when a single plane suddenly would swoop down on top of them. Immediately engulfed in a sea of devastating machine gun fire, the convoy was powerless to react. It was as if the aircraft had a capability to peel back the cover of darkness, exposing the convoy below.

As stories of this plane's effectiveness continued to instill terror among his men, General Nguyen was angered by his drivers' reaction during these attacks. As they heard the aircraft approach, they would abandon their vehicles and run for cover.

Pham Tien Dzuat, an enlisted man who served as a journalist and poet at General Nguyen's headquarters during the war, recounted his commander's reaction upon learning of his drivers' cowardice in the face of the enemy air attack.

"General Dong Si Nguyen is a brave man," Dzuat said. *"As such, he would not tolerate cowardice in others. It upset him to learn his men were leaving their posts as soon as they came under attack by this aircraft. He told them, 'We are all soldiers and if we die we have to die in the performance of our duties—we do not run away from our responsibilities.' The drivers told him the American aircraft was equipped with some kind of heat-seeking device, capable of seeing convoy vehicles at night even though their lights off were off.*

"The general was adamant no such aircraft existed with that capability. To prove his point, he announced he would accompany the convoy scheduled to go out the next night.

"The convoy that night was a particularly big one. It consisted of two battalions—more than 300 vehicles. As it was moving south down the Trail under cover of darkness, it was detected by the enemy. The attack was by the same type of aircraft which had been successfully used before. We knew it was the same because there was a very distinct sound we always heard just as the plane began to fire and just as the rounds hit their targets—it was almost like the noise of an explosion. As the aircraft's guns opened up, a tremendous wall of fire was released, reaping havoc and destruction upon the convoy. Most vehicles were destroyed. Many drivers who remained with their vehicles died that evening. Despite the barrage of fire, General Dong Si Nguyen remained with his vehicle, which was also hit many times.

"The experience was a sobering one for the general. He was not afraid to acknowledge his error when he knew he was wrong. Back at his headquarters, he did so. He said he was a poor peasant for not listening to what his soldiers had tried to tell him. He told his staff, 'the Americans can send a man into space so I should never have doubted

the possibility of their developing technology such as this. But,' he added, 'we can defeat it.' He was right and we did."

As with victory, even in defeat, lessons are there to be learned.

The aircraft responsible for decimating General Dong Si Nguyen's convoys was the U.S. Air Force AC-130A Spectre (pictured at left). It was a simple modification of a cargo aircraft, the C-130. The modification included special equipment that transformed the plane's normally passive role of cargo transport into the active role of attack aircraft. It was a night stalker, capable of locating a target in total darkness, locking in on it and destroying it with its guns. It was assisted in its attack mission by a night observation device, or Starlight Scope, an infrared sensor known as FLIR (Forward-Looking Infra-Red), a target-tracking computer and a 20-kw searchlight.

A prototype aircraft conducted the first attack against a target on the Trail on November 9, 1967. The consequences were devastating for the Vietnamese who lost every vehicle in a six-truck convoy.

Based on the prototype's success, the U.S. Air Force began a program to convert several more C-130s into AC-130As. Follow-on versions were equipped with more advanced gear, including a new fire-control computer and a moving target indicator (MTI) radar. These provided the plane with a capability to survey the ground below for a heat source anywhere along the Trail. In a truck engine, that was normally an operating spark plug, although it proved capable of detecting heat from a still hot engine after the ignition had been shut off. Once detected, the information was passed to the aircraft's onboard computers as radar tracked the convoy's progress. This equipment was inter-linked with the plane's four 20mm Gatling-type guns (later two 40 mm Bofors cannon replaced the aft 20mm guns), which then directed fire onto the target. The AC-130A and its follow-on versions effectively stripped General Nguyen's nighttime convoys of their cover of darkness, allowing the pilot to see every vehicle in the convoy on his monitor.

A description by a former AC-130A crewman of the wall of fire created by the aircraft's guns provides one with an awesome appreciation as to its effectiveness: *"If the AC-130 made a single pass over a football stadium, its guns blazing, the entire stadium grounds would be raked with fire—each 20 mm round imbedded in the field no more than two inches apart."*

No doubt, the AC-130 was an extremely effective weapons platform—so much so that General Nguyen's drivers initially lost confidence in their ability to counter it. In the ongoing chess game being played along the Trail between the two adversaries, with the introduction of the AC-130, the advantage clearly went to the Americans. General Nguyen's convoys became easy prey once again.

Following his own personal experience with the AC-130, General Nguyen wasted no time in improvising a strategy, however, to counter the enemy's new technology. Two plans were initiated—one tactical, one strategic.

The tactical plan evolved as General Nguyen and his staff were eager to know exactly how the aircraft functioned. How was it able to locate convoys in total darkness, laying down such an effective and efficient wall of fire? Unable, obviously, to examine an intact AC-130 to get answers, General Nguyen opted for the next best thing—to examine the wreckage of one.

"The AC-130 was a great achievement for the U.S.," said Dzuat. *"The order was given to shoot one down. Every unit with a machine gun was ordered to shoot at it—even our engineers. I do not understand why it was so difficult for us to do so. The plane flew low, sometimes as low as 100 to 200 meters; it was large and it was very slow. But we never were able to shoot one down with our machine guns."*

After years without success, a new plan was formulated.

The new plan called for an ambush. An infantry platoon, equipped with special weaponry, was assigned the task. In April 1972, the Vietnamese introduced the SA-7—a portable, shoulder-fired surface-to-air missile—into the war. Effective up to a maximum altitude of 1500 meters, the missile used the same basic infrared heat seeking technology as the AC-

130. This new technology, with its low altitude accuracy, made it ideal to play the role of AC-130-killer.

In June 1972, this NVA platoon, armed with the SA-7, positioned itself on high ground along the Trail near Hue. North Vietnamese intelligence determined this position put it directly under the normal approach route AC-130s took in that area to seek out their nighttime prey. From this position, the Vietnamese had a clear shot at the aircraft.

The ambush was set. A lookout was maintained every night. On the evening of June 18, the platoon's vigilance paid off. An unsuspecting AC-130A Spectre lumbered along the anticipated flight path. An account from Robert F. Dorr's book **AIR WAR SOUTH VIETNAM** provides details of the incident from the perspective of one American survivor who was onboard the aircraft:

"The gunship was flying southwest of Hue, next after Quang Tri as a likely target of the communist assault—its crew believing that it was high enough to escape harm from the missile. Sergeant William B. Patterson was the lookout for the aircraft, which had the call-sign 'Spectre II.'" Patterson lay on the aft cargo door, actually hanging out into the airstream so that he could spot the telltale flash of light when a missile was fired.

"Everything worked the way it was supposed to. Patterson gave the warning when an SA-7 was fired and came rushing up at the AC-130, its rocket motor burning with an eerie blue-white light—boring straight at the gunship rather than porpoising back and forth the way SA-7s usually did. The pilot fired a decoy flare (decoy flares are used to draw the heat seeking SA-7 missile to the flare rather than the heat of the Spectre's engines) *and began an evasive turn but the SA-7 reached 'Spectre II' anyway, colliding with the number three engine.*

"The violent, booming explosion shook the aircraft. The AC-130 bucked, threw its nose up, and settled again as the right inboard engine separated from the wing. There was a confusion of voices on the intercom as crew members reported the AC-130 heading downward and beginning to disintegrate.

"Sergeant Patterson rolled back into the aircraft, unhooked the restraining strap which kept him from falling out, and reached for his chest-pack parachute. At about that time the right wing came off and the aircraft started into a cartwheeling roll. Patterson managed to hook only one side of his parachute to his body harness, in his haste attaching it backwards, when new explosions sent him hurtling into the black void outside."

Immediately after the plane crashed, NVA soldiers rushed to the crash site. Debris was scattered over a wide area. In rummaging through it, they found what they wanted—documents detailing the inner workings of the aircraft. These were rushed to Hanoi for further study. The secret to the AC-130's success was out.

(The North Vietnamese reported, among the AC-130's crewmembers who failed to escape, the bodies of two civilian technicians were found. American MIA records indicate, however, that all casualties onboard were military personnel. This confusion may have stemmed from the absence of rank insignias and other military identification on the bodies as the two might have been involved in clandestine operations in Laos and Cambodia.)

Sergeant Patterson was fortunate. Picked up by air rescue several days after his forced ejection from the disintegrating aircraft, he was one of three men to survive the ordeal.

Simultaneously with the tactical plan to go after an AC-130, General Nguyen initiated his strategic plan to counter its effectiveness.

Perhaps adopting the golden rule, *"Do unto others as you would have them do unto you,"* the general decided to do to the Americans what the Americans had done to him—take away their nighttime efficiency. With the AC-130 so effective at night, thought Nguyen, why not deny the aircraft its nighttime operational advantage? The solution was simple—do not put convoys on the roads at night! This meant convoys returning to daytime runs. Earlier in the war, this practice proved disastrous. But there was one big difference this time when General Nguyen tried the daylight runs—they got through intact!

To counter the introduction of the AC-130, General Nguyen responded with the introduction of the "K" (the first letter of the word "kinh," meaning, "hidden") road system (discussed later in this chapter).

The Invisible Bridges

A large-scale deception plan was implemented throughout the war by the Vietnamese to deceive the Americans as to the exact location of the primary roads forming the Ho Chi Minh Trail. Such a plan evolved as a matter of survival for the convoys. Its success, perhaps, was best reflected by American uncertainty as to how many major north/south roads actually existed within the Trail's network. It was believed there were three to five such roads. But, in actuality, at its high point, the Trail incorporated seven primary north/south routes (including the K-road system). General Nguyen explained the reason for the confusion:

"From 1967 (prior to the K-road system), *there were three main routes—real ones—and at the same time three deception routes,"* he said. *"On the side of the west Truong Son in Laos and Cambodia, we had five; on the eastern Truong Son, that is the Vietnamese side, we had one. On the deception routes, we used old battered trucks as decoys and painted them to attract American planes. We would move small convoys on the decoy routes, as we would do on the real routes, soon increasing their size to company level. The concept worked well as decoy convoys were destroyed and real convoys made it through. We obviously did not mind losing the decoys. We continued these tactics for six or seven years with great efficiency. We often changed our tactics in the use of our decoys.* (This was done, as General Nguyen knew if decoy convoys were repeatedly deployed in the same manner, the Americans might become suspicious.) *For example, we changed the timing of the decoy convoys from night to day and vice versa or concentrated them in one spot one day and scattered them the next. The Americans could find no pattern to our conduct."*

The deceptions to conceal the real convoy routes from the Americans presented the Trail architects with numerous challenges. While most of the surrounding terrain could be used effectively to meet these challenges by providing natural concealment, there were points where the terrain was devoid of vegetation. In such cases, the Vietnamese relied totally upon their ingenuity. No where was that put more to the test than in creating ways of concealing river cross points for the convoys.

The Trail architects knew it was inevitable: no matter how effectively they concealed a main route, at some point the road had to emerge from the jungle to cross a river. And, *"bridges, as a rule,"* General Nguyen pointed out, *"because of their high visibility were the part of the road system most often attacked."* Architects knew they had to deceive the enemy into believing no bridge existed where one did. The challenge was how to do this—how to build a bridge, invisible to the enemy while maintaining its utility. As difficult as the challenge was, the Trail architects rose to the task.

When bridges were discovered by the Americans, it created other problems for General Nguyen as well. For not only did it result in it being attacked and destroyed, it also ran the risk of revealing where the Trail's main land routes were situated leading to the bridge. This caused major delays for the convoys as bridges had to be rebuilt or new crossing points established elsewhere along the river. It was clear to General Nguyen that a more clandestine system for crossing rivers, where possible, had to be devised.

One such type of invisible bridge design explored by the Vietnamese in mid-1965 was fairly simple. Colonel Dang Huong, Deputy Commander of the 559 Engineer Corps, described the focus of this early experimentation in an article he later wrote.

"As a measure against surprise attack or observation by reconnaissance planes," he said, *"the military authorities decided on experimenting with two-cable (suspension) bridges only."*

The design consisted of two cables, set apart the width of a vehicle, and stretched taut across the river. With the bridge's mass limited to just the two cables, it was invisible from the air.

This technique was designed to transport Chinese (CA10) trucks that, at least early in the war, were in abundant supply. This vehicle had single wheels in front and double wheels in the rear. To transport the CA10 across the cable bridge, tires were removed or deflated and pulled inward, leaving the vehicle's rims in place. Positioned with its two inside rear rims sitting directly on top of each cable (see picture below), the vehicle was then pulled across the river, using the front rims as pulleys.

The first test run failed as Colonel Dang Huong described: *"What we thought of was very simple: a system of supports on either bank to tie down two cables...and a system of strainers to regulate the arc shape and the symmetry of the cables. The basis for our early calculations relied only on the durability of the cables, for neither did we think of nor were we able to calculate the elasticity of the cables. This led to Captain Nguyen Trong Quyen's car overturning during the test run. Fortunately, although it was high tide and the car overturned in the middle of the river, Captain Quyen managed to get out safely. The vehicle turned 360 degrees but later was used again after repairs were done."*

While time was needed to transport a vehicle across, its success was measured by the fact not a single cable bridge was lost during the war. It was later abandoned, however, due to the excessive amount of time required to get vehicles across a river using the system.

One of the most ingenious designs conceived was used to cross the Ben Hai River, the waterway that separated North Vietnam from South Vietnam along the 17th parallel.

In June 1967, the Hien Luong Bridge, which crossed the Ben Hai River along Coastal Highway No. 1, was attacked by U.S. aircraft. An important link in Hanoi's road network for moving men and supplies into South Vietnam, the bridge was partially destroyed during the air attack. Trail architects went to work on a design for replacing it that would avoid a similar fate from befalling it in the future. They ingenuously developed a "peek-a-boo" crossing platform known as a "buoy" bridge.

In 1968, with Hien Luong Bridge still out of commission, a new crossing point was established where Road #43 intersected with the Ben Hai River, five to six kilometers upstream from where the bridge had been destroyed a year earlier. Road #43 was one of the Trail's main north/south routes. The Americans knew the Vietnamese convoys had to cross major rivers at some point and the Vietnamese obviously knew the Americans were aware of this. Therefore, part of the deception plan was to keep the Americans focused on false crossing points. This included building decoy bridges for the Americans to find for the specific purpose of being destroyed—for if no bridges were found they would also become suspicious. Some had limited utility but most did not—incapable of supporting much weight.

"These decoy bridges were attacked again and again," explained General Nguyen. *"The Americans then sent their reconnaissance planes in to make sure they were destroyed before being satisfied. They were immediately repaired to keep the Americans thinking we were determined to keep convoys moving across them."*

The actual convoy crossing took place several kilometers upstream from the defunct Hien Luong Bridge, at a point where the river's banks were 170 meters apart. When darkness fell, the real bridge "emerged" from the depths of the river.

Sergeant Tran Van Thuc, a lineman and Trail guide who made the crossing many times, described how it functioned. *"As darkness fell, soldiers stationed at the cross point turned on diesel-powered* (air) *pumps located on both banks. As they did so, a bridge slowly emerged from just underneath the river's surface."*

The design was ingenious: A platform was secured atop several layers of inflatable truck inner tubes. The tubes were tied together, each interconnected with a short air hose. The entire mass of inner tubes, in turn,

was connected with long hose lines to the shore pumps. Such a design allowed the bridge to be raised to the surface, secured into position and used to transport traffic at night. It had the added dimension of "invisibility"—for just before daylight, the buoy bridge was deflated, causing it to slip back under the water where it remained hidden from the enemy's view until it was needed the following night.

Taking roughly two to three hours to inflate, the bridge required significantly less time to deflate. When lowered, the tubes were only partially deflated, so the bridge did not rest fully on the river bottom, leaving the platform suspended a meter or so underwater. This reduced the inflation time required the next evening, while still allowing it to remain completely hidden from view. There was little danger the bridge would be snagged by marine traffic on the river, for the war brought much of the boat traffic to a standstill and the traffic that did run had sufficient clearance above the sunken bridge.

Routinely the buoy bridge was raised in the evening around 6:00 P.M. and lowered by 4:00 A.M. the following morning. Only the notice of possible nighttime reconnaissance activity in the area by the enemy disrupted this schedule.

Sergeant Thuc saw the bridge in operation for the first time in 1971 as he took a small group north. He knew of its existence long before then. He recalled experiencing immense pride watching it rise out of the water the first time. To him, it represented a great resourcefulness by his people in fighting a militarily superior enemy. There was another source of satisfaction for Thuc too. As a young boy, he had witnessed the destruction of Hien Luong Bridge by American planes years earlier; he was also able to bear witness its resurrection.

For the duration of the war, the Americans never knew the buoy bridge existed. Its use after the U.S. withdrawal in 1973 continued with one significant change—with American air power no longer a threat, it remained inflated, until later replaced by a more permanent structure.

⁕ ⁕ ⁕

The key to maintaining river crossing points functioning was deception. The buoy bridge was but one innovative means for accomplishing this. Others were employed too. Similar ingenuity gave birth to the "submarine" bridge (pictured below). This was a more permanent bridge platform; built just beneath the water's surface where, again, it became "invisible" from the air while maintaining its utility.

Submarine bridges were used mostly during monsoon season in low-lying areas of the road that were impossible to ford during rainy season. Constructed just under the water's surface where it was completely hidden by floodwaters, it was only observable by a person standing at the water's edge. Passage over these occurred mostly at night, making transit particularly perilous. Guides (usually volunteer members of the Youth Brigade) had to lead the convoys across. Two guides, wearing white reflective clothing, stood at either side of the bridge so drivers could gauge the bridge's location and width. The drivers then navigated their vehicles between the two human markers. When flooding stopped, the bridges were dismantled and hidden in the jungle for future use.

Other variations of the deception plan called for floating bridges. *"Sometimes, at a designated spot for crossing over,"* explained General Nguyen, *"we made four or five similar bridges, only two or three of which we really used. These were made with buoys and pontoons of*  *bamboo and were concealed by using river plants found abundantly in the area. They were floated into position when needed. From their aircraft, the Americans only saw the fake ones, which they attacked."*

A constant in the deception plan, whether for bridges or roads, was to maximize use of natural surroundings.

"We were artists drawing from the natural landscape," said General Nguyen. *"We knew the slightest miscalculation or irregularity in what we chose to use as camouflage resulted in our being discovered. The routine was repeated day in and day out, with both sides constantly observing and being ever watchful. Two wars were actually being waged—a fighting war and one of deception—both of which were waged ferociously."*

Hanoi would dispatch on occasion its own aerial observer to assess the concealment effort.

The required length for a bridge seemed to pose no significant engineering difficulties to the Vietnamese. A pontoon bridge two kilometers in length was built across the Long Dai River south of Quang Binh (pictured at the top of the following page). When the Long Bien Bridge in Hanoi was hit in 1967, a pontoon replacement (known as the Chuong Duong Bridge), stretching almost three kilometers in length, was constructed.

The Road Deceptions

The deception plan implemented by General Nguyen included the roads as well. Open expanses of the Trail, both natural as well as those chemically induced, presented new challenges to the Trail architects responsible for concealing the roads' existence.

"Where the roads were in the open, our engineering corps placed dead tree branches on them to give the appearance the road had already been bombed," shared General Nguyen. *"We even dug our own bomb craters to create this appearance too, while the real road—covered with these branches—actually went around the craters."*

The Vietnamese were constantly exploring innovative ways of further concealing convoy routes. One of the more ingenious techniques was described by Tran Cong Tan. *"You cannot openly hide a road that is visible—but if you make that road invisible, you can hide it in the open,"* said Tan with a grin. (The secret of the invisible roads, first mentioned to me by the Chinese Vietnamese gentleman mentioned at the start of my research, was finally to be revealed.)

During the war, U.S. reconnaissance aircraft monitored Trail activity. For much of that time, convoys only moved at night, with evidence of their transit—tire tracks left behind on the dirt roads—usually being visible the next morning. These tracks were often visible in aerial photographs or to the observer's naked eye. When such activity was detected, the road was bombed and the Vietnamese were left with undertaking very time-consuming repairs. They sought to implement a plan that would allow convoys to pass through areas undetected by the Americans. This would only be possible if the convoys were able to leave no tire tracks on the roads. But how was this to be accomplished?

Examining maps of the area, the Trail architects experienced another flash of brilliance. The maps revealed parts of the Trail's main north-south roads, during the dry season, were paralleled by relatively shallow rivers and streams. If incorporated into the deception plan, these waterways, as a natural part of the environment, would raise no suspicions with the Americans. Thus, the focus was on how to incorporate, to the Trail's benefit, the natural course of these waterways.

The architects saw, with a little work, the beds of these rivers and streams could be used as hidden roadways. By having their engineers'

grade the beds, convoys—under cover of darkness—could then travel down roads made "invisible" by the water flowing in the riverbeds. Thus, a convoy's tire tracks also were hidden from view. As the picture to the left shows, this was done to hide transit routes when using bicycles for transportation as well.

Nothing could have been more simple—or ingenious! Not only did Mother Nature provide the architects with ready access to a highway, at the same time, she provided a natural means by which to disguise the road's existence!

Without grading equipment, soldiers worked on clearing riverbeds of all large rocks and other obstructions during the day with their hands and a few tools. Traveling at night in these graded river roads, the convoys made excellent time as drivers did not have to worry about mines or other unexploded ordnance. The natural terrain of some of the beds was such that a convoy could go twenty kilometers without having to return to the main road. Each morning, after convoys traversed the underwater roads, binh tram soldiers performed the daily ritual of grading them.

As journalist Tan suggested, his people *"had to be very creative all the time; they had to think constantly about ways of overcoming U.S. technology—for their survival depended upon it."*

While this technique worked during dry season, it was abandoned during monsoon season as water levels and currents rose considerably. During rainy season, the convoys were forced to return to the main roads once again.

Use of these invisible roads went undetected by the Americans for the war's duration. They remained, perhaps, among the Trail's last great secrets. Trail architects took a unique approach to their job. Where others would have seen natural obstacles as barriers limiting the Trail's advance, they chose to see them as challenges to incorporate into its design. They refused to be defeated, not by man or by Nature, carefully scrutinizing each aspect of the surrounding terrain to maximize its inclusion within their grand deception scheme.

Waterborne Delivery Systems

The development of invisible roads was but one more evolution in a multifaceted effort to enhance the Trail's operation. Where a waterway might be too deep to be pressed into use as an invisible road, not all was lost. In yet another example of resourcefulness, Trail architects effectively used parallel waterways as waterborne conveyor belts. Tightly wrapped in plastic, supplies were set afloat on the waterway for recovery by troops downstream notified by landline that the supplies were coming.

⁂ ⁂ ⁂

Sampans and motorboats were also used to expedite the supply flow south where possible. While such stretches of navigable waterways were relatively short, engineers worked to maximize their use. The Sekong River, situated predominantly in Laos and spilling into the Mekong River, was expanded in this manner. What began in 1966 as a river system with only eighty kilometers of navigable waters had, by

1973, been improved into a system stretching more than two hundred kilometers.

The Xeng Phan Pass—A Test of Wills

The operative word for the Trail architects was "adaptability"—retaining flexibility so as to use natural barriers to one's advantage, to redirect the Trail where such natural barriers could not be so used, and to not allow the enemy to dictate the direction the Trail would take at any given point. But, there were points on the Trail where this was just not possible. One was the Xeng Phan Pass, south of Bhu La Pha in Laos.

In the early days of the Trail, there was no way to get around Xeng Phan Pass. From 1965 to 1966, it was the Trail's only "gauntlet." It was here the road narrowed due to an extremely steep drop on one side of a mountain pass and an equally steep rise on the other. Convoys had to traverse this narrow pass—and the Americans knew it. If any single point on the Trail represented a test of completely divergent wills, Xeng Phan Pass was it.

The pass received regular attention from U.S. bombers. Hanoi records, during one thirty-day period along a 2000 meter stretch of the pass, *"the enemy dumped 21,197 high calibre bombs, including 4,000 anti-personnel bombs. On average, it (the pass) received 707 bombs every day, or one every two minutes..."* Convoy drivers regularly ran a gauntlet of exploding shrapnel.

Hanoi's historical diary describes the passage and heroic efforts of one determined driver:

"At night, files of trucks drove through the flames, ferrying various goods: rice, cloth, medicines...even flammable materials such as gasoline, ammunition, explosives...Typical of the drivers' intrepidity was Hero Do Van Chien (pictured at left). For the 40-kilometer trip (between bases) over Xeng Phan, the set norm for drivers was one return trip per night; they had to be back at the base and hide their

vehicles before daybreak. Do Van Chien broke this norm, opening the 'More Trips For the Front' movement. On many nights, he made two return trips over Xeng Phan. Thus, between sunset and sunrise the next day, apart from loading and unloading halts, he drove over a total distance of 160 kilometers of mountain trails, and in a single night, had to pass the hot spot of Xeng Phan four times where a large-calibre bomb and scores of smaller ones were dropping every minute."

The K-Road System

When the AC-130 proved its devastating capability to attack convoys in hours of darkness, General Nguyen changed his strategy. Convoys no longer ran at night. They were ordered instead to return to daylight transits of the Trail.

Daylight convoy runs conducted in the early years of the war resulted in a very high casualty rate. General Nguyen knew to avoid a similar result now, a new road system was required—one totally hidden from view using natural concealment. This led to the concept of the "kien" (hidden) or "K-Road" system.

While other major road systems of the Trail were camouflaged in part, camouflage on the K-road was the rule—not the exception. It incorporated many of the deceptive techniques previously used, but added new ones as well.

In order not to arouse the enemy's suspicion, construction of the K-road took place slowly. It relied almost exclusively on natural vegetation— existing, replanted or grown—to conceal the road's existence. However, too much "sudden" growth viewed by an aerial observer might raise suspicions that man—not Nature—was at work. When sections of the K-road passed through areas where normal vegetation was lacking or where it existed before being destroyed by chemical defoliants, indigenous plants were relocated. A fast growing vine known as the "potato flower" was cultivated for this purpose. Transplanted and draped over sections of the new road, it immediately started to grow in place.

"This hidden road went through jungle forests," said General Nguyen, *"where we planted trees ourselves and watered them regularly once a week to keep them green. Use of the road was reserved for division size troop movements. The road ran from Quang Binh Province directly to Tay Ninh."*

Introduction of the K-road resulted in an additional benefit and significant change in operations along the Trail. Previously limited to operating within the length of a single binh tram, off loading cargoes at its southernmost point before heading back north empty, convoy trucks now transited the entire length of the Trail. There was no need for the "safe areas" built along the other main roads, as the entire K-road was a safe area. The need to transport supplies down the Trail in relays, laboriously loading/off loading cargoes, was eliminated.

Upon completion, the K-road system extended over a thousand kilometers, providing Hanoi with a seventh north/south route. Immediately upon completion, General Nguyen decided to run a large convoy of five hundred vehicles down the road to test his new strategy. The transit was completed without loss and, with no further need to off-load, in record time.

Of General Nguyen's decision to run daylight convoys once again and the overwhelming success of doing so, General Vo Nguyen Giap commented, *"Only a brave and clever man could order this kind of tactic knowing he bore all responsibility for his decision."*

"The Americans never really knew much about this K-road system," said poet/journalist Pham Tien Dzuat. *"That demonstrated our military cunning."*

Dzuat made another observation that, with the benefit of hindsight, is hard to dispute. *"I believe if one wants to prevail over his enemy,"* he said, *"one must first understand him well. I do not believe the*

Americans ever understood us or what we were capable of doing." Dzuat's observation was not a new concept. It was a principle espoused two thousand years earlier by the famous Chinese military strategist, Sun Tzu.

The Turkey Shoot

As the value to Hanoi of the Ho Chi Minh Trail increased, its mission expanded. In the allocation of assets, higher headquarters gave it top priority.

"Our job was originally to protect the road," explained General Nguyen. *"But as Trail operations expanded, we fought to get more land—so we defended by attacking. The General Headquarters considered the Ho Chi Minh Trail a high priority battlefield and we received priority treatment. There was no limit to the number of troops we could have, in ammunition, in vehicles for convoys, in directives and in assistance.*

"The Trail was a central focus for the whole territory, distributing supplies to three parts of the region: to the north, to the embattled south and to Laos and Cambodia. It was an immense area to cover, known for its ferocious battles, its climate and its rugged territory."

Whenever a threat to the Trail's survival arose, all available assets were committed to its defense. One such threat occurred in 1971, in southern Laos. Known as Operation Lam Son, it was a combined air and ground attack that sought to neutralize the Trail. A new contest of wills ensued—one for which the South Vietnamese would pay a heavy price. General Nguyen detailed what happened: *"I was responsible for the defense of the western Truong Son area. There were not only attacks from the air along the Trail, but were also battles on the ground. Two of these were on a large scale. One was in 1971, in southern Laos, where U.S. and Saigon forces engaged us in battle in an effort to stop the flow of supplies. The second was on the frontier with Cambodia. The campaign in Laos was particularly interesting because we had the unusual opportunity to fight helicopters. The U.S. had to call the campaign off after only twenty days due to severe helicopter losses.*

"Helicopters are very easy to shoot down. Knowing this, we mobilized three air defense divisions. As only twelve helicopters arrived the first day, our air defense forces were told not to fire at aircraft with anything but their rifles and machine guns. On the second, third and fourth days, the number of helicopters was about the same. Only on the fifth day did dozens of helicopters appear over an area of eight to one hundred square kilometers. We were ready for the kill, employing all our air defense weapons. Twenty helicopters were downed in one day. The battle stopped; an entire South Vietnamese division surrendered." (Again, this is an incident in which both side report numbers of helicopter losses that do not equate—for reasons delineated earlier.)

An "Unsolved Mystery"?

Some mysteries still remain about the Ho Chi Minh Trail. One that has been the object of much speculation is the death of General Nguyen Chi Thanh.

Thanh (pictured at left), born in 1914, was a teacher who became involved in the revolution against the French. Arrested by them in 1943, he served two years in prison before being released by the Japanese. A confidant of Ho Chi Minh, he was given various responsibilities after the French war including organizing the Communist Youth Union. Later he headed the General Political Directorate of the People's Army of Vietnam (PAVN) and was a member of the Party Central Military Committee. Better known as a politician than soldier, he was made a four-star general by Ho Chi Minh before taking his first troop command—commander of the North Vietnamese Army in the south.

But General Thanh died in 1967. As reported by the Vietnamese government, after taking his command and then being ordered back to Hanoi that summer for meetings, he suffered a heart attack and died. The report seemed credible as the 53-year-old general did have a history of heart problems.

But rumors have persisted Thanh did not die in Hanoi—that he really died on the Trail, the victim of a "500 pound (B-52) heart attack." The rumor was denied by the Vietnamese government.

One Vietnamese veteran claims to have firsthand information about Thanh's death. A former NVA captain serving on the Trail at the time claims he knows Thanh died on the Trail.

"I should know," he said. *"My unit dispatched a squad of men to escort the general's body to Hanoi. I understood Ho Chi Minh was very distraught over the death since he personally asked General Thanh to take the command. He did not want it to be known that such a senior level ranking officer had been killed by the Americans, as it would hurt morale. So the body was brought back to Hanoi. We later heard it had been reported by the government that he died of a heart attack while in Hanoi."*

The captain claims his men escorted a bronze casket to Hanoi. Protocol required remains of a regimental commander or higher-ranking officer be returned north so the family had a gravesite to visit. Bronze caskets were reserved exclusively for very senior officers. (Lower ranking officers and enlisted were buried where they fell in the south, with the more senior of them interred in wooden caskets if available.)

While the source of General Thanh's demise is, today, of little consequence, most Vietnamese veterans clearly believe he died in Hanoi. The truth undoubtedly will remain one of the Trail's "unsolved mysteries."

A Facelift and the Push to Saigon

In Hanoi's written history of the Trail, it appears Vietnam's leadership saw the 1973 Peace Agreement simply as a vehicle by which to get America out of the war, allowing Hanoi to press forward to victory. Immediately after the agreement was signed, changes were implemented on the Trail. Existing units were reorganized and assigned new missions. Before the 1973 agreement, the Trail's objective was to keep as many routes open as possible; after the agreement, it was to close as many as possible as US air power was no longer a threat. Only those roads offering the most direct access to the south were kept open, with a focus on improving the roads and bridges along those few routes.

This reorganization and new focus resulted in Hanoi's utilization of just two of the existing seven primary north/south road systems. One was

West Truong Son, extending into Laos and Cambodia, before reentering Vietnam; the other was East Truong Son, lying entirely within Vietnam's borders. Both were connected by a series of east/west roadways. With U.S. air power no longer a factor, paved roads and reinforced steel bridges brazenly emerged for the first time. (As reported earlier, the first paved portion of the Trail was named in honor of Fidel Castro who visited in 1973.) By 1974, the eastern route provided Hanoi with direct access to the south in less than two weeks—a vast improvement over the three to six month transits of earlier years.

As the final drive on Saigon took shape, the Trail became a beehive of activity. Convoys no longer were staggered, instead traveling bumper-to-bumper in broad daylight on unconcealed roads. Soldiers no longer walked the Trail but traveled in vehicles to expedite their arrival at the front. Tanks and heavy artillery, no longer disassembled for shipment, made the transit fully assembled, ready for immediate use upon arrival at their destination.

As Saigon fell on April 30, 1975, Hanoi's goal of reunification was finally achieved. With victory complete, Hanoi then did something neither Saigon nor Washington was able to do for the previous sixteen years—it closed the Ho Chi Minh Trail.

Conclusion

General Dong Si Nguyen stated, *"The Ho Chi Minh Trail has become part of Vietnam's history which every Vietnamese will remember forever. This is the road that led us to independence and unity."* He is deservedly proud of the accomplishments achieved by those who served.

Today, the Trail remains a testimonial to the will of a people to fight for what they believed in, no matter what the cost nor how small the chance for victory. Silence now enshrouds the Trail, belying the magnitude or significance of the activity that once took place there. The hundreds of thousands of men and women who ensured its security are gone—their task now left, perhaps, to the spirits of long departed comrades whose unrecovered remains provide a constant reminder of their ultimate sacrifice.

Life for those who maintained the Ho Chi Minh Trail was not easy. It was a unique breed of soldier who served. He was a soldier, as journalist Tran Cong Tan described, for whom survival depended on his invisibility to the enemy. He had to *"learn to walk without footprints, talk without sound and cook without smoke."*

Those who served on the Trail did so voluntarily. That service terminated, Tan added, only upon the occurrence of one of three events—*"death, near death, or victory."*

For two decades after the war, a small group of determined Vietnamese soldiers continued to travel parts of the Ho Chi Minh Trail by truck. No longer transporting instruments of war, their cargoes were the recently located remains of comrades left behind. The search for these remains was tedious, not only because little documentation existed as to where they were but also because, with the passage of time, the jungle had reclaimed much of the Trail, making recognition of earlier battlefields difficult.

There was a sense among these soldiers they were not alone as they searched for their comrades' remains. On more than one occasion, it was reported, a truck broke down for no apparent reason. As the driver worked to repair it, other soldiers set out in search of food, unexpectedly stumbling upon a burial site while doing so. Soon after the soldiers returned to the truck to report their discovery, and just as inexplicably as the vehicle's engine broke down, it started up again. As engine breakdowns would occur, soldiers thus learned always to initiate a search of the surrounding area for additional possible burial sites.

For those who traveled the Trail in search of remains for a generation after the war, the collective spirit of those who had died defending it continued to live on.

These searchers located more than 30,000 remains. They have quietly been transferred to a cemetery in Quang Tri Province. It is the country's largest national cemetery and provides a fitting memorial for those who made the ultimate sacrifice to defend the Trail.

Having met one of Tan's three requirements for completing one's service on the Trail—death—these soldiers, at long last, have finally returned home!

THE WAR DOWN UNDER

If Hanoi's resolve to fight above ground was best epitomized by the commitment of the Truong Son (Ho Chi Minh Trail) soldier, its resolve to fight underground was best epitomized by the Cu Chi fighters. Both groups suffered tremendous hardship; both fought resolutely; both experienced enormous casualties; and both—pitted against a technologically superior enemy—proved to have an uncompromising iron will.

The evolution of tunnel warfare is a testimonial to the patience, dedication and skill of the Cu Chi fighters over a thirty-year span of time. That evolution witnessed a transformation—from the initial use of tunnels in a purely defensive posture to their later use in an offensive one. And, as the enemy, determined to defeat the tunnel fighters, altered tactics to drive them out, the tunnel fighters, exhibiting greater determination, countered with tactical changes to defend themselves. In the battle of wills underground, the tunnel fighters were relentless moles, incapable of being driven out.

✢ ✢ ✢

While several different tunnel systems were constructed during the war in various locations, the one at Cu Chi was most impressive. An extensive system (an underground highway stretching, at its height, more than 340 kilometers, connecting entire villages), its occupation throughout the war on the very doorstep of the enemy's capital made it a source of great embarrassment for the Saigon regime and immense pride for the tunnel fighters. (As pictured at right, immense piles of dirt extracted from digging the tunnels would then have to be camouflaged in some manner.)

The late Major General Tran Hai Phung, who commanded the Cu Chi tunnel forces, gives us a sense of the massiveness of this underground maze: *"One tunnel system alone covered 16,000 hectares—an area*

encompassing six villages." The systems were so vast in fact, that "road" signs were displayed in some so newcomers did not get lost.

Located thirty kilometers northwest of Saigon, the Cu Chi tunnel system emerged in 1945, following the defeat of Japan in World War II and France's renewed effort to keep its Vietnamese colony. Vietnam, however, quickly made it known it would oppose continued French rule.

The French prepared themselves to fight a conventional war against an under-equipped, under-manned Vietnamese army. After all, French leadership reasoned, how long could the Vietminh survive against a larger, better-trained Western army? But the French were ill prepared for what happened. The script envisioned by Paris for fighting the war in Vietnam—one of large engagements in which Vietminh forces were crushed—was never written. Instead, the script was produced by Hanoi—one involving small engagements with the Vietnamese deciding, for the most part, when and where the fighting would take place. As Hanoi settled into a strategy of small unit engagements and Paris became more and more frustrated by its inability to force larger ones, the French found themselves fighting a guerrilla war. Compounding problems further was that the fight became a people's war—a war in which the enemy was not clearly identifiable. The French discovered, the enemy often wore no uniform, crossing gender and age barriers. This created great difficulty in determining (as later, the Americans would encounter) who exactly was friend and who was foe.

General Phung explained the tunnel system's early development:

"The development of the Cu Chi tunnels evolved as a result of our fighting a people's war. By people's war, we do not mean a war in which people go off to fight as an army elsewhere—we mean a war in which the people participate in the fight but then continue to live in their homes. In 1945, we started conducting attacks against targets in Saigon. When the French reacted, we withdrew to the villages. The French then tried to destroy these villages and move our people out. But we were determined to remain, so we dug bunkers in areas where we felt fighting might take place. Then we needed to connect the bunkers together. So for the next year we expanded the bunker system and the connecting tunnels. Our people asked the army to help them build secret

tunnels too. So work began on the Cu Chi system in late 1946, in Tan Thu Trung village."

While this system of bunkers and connecting tunnels was conceptualized initially as a defensive strategy, as explained by General Phung that changed: *"Later, the French army tried to expand the war into the southern part of Vietnam and to occupy our villages. We thought this underground system provided a good mechanism for attacking the French. Eventually, tunnels connecting bunker systems expanded to other hamlets and villages. Tan Thu Trung was the first village tunnel system to be completed. It was finished in January 1947, at which time the French initiated a very fierce ground offensive against us. Due to this and the effectiveness of the tunnels, there was a demand for additional tunnel systems. So other villages undertook the construction of tunnel systems as well. In the beginning, we were more focused on digging—just to get underground—and did not focus on connecting the systems. This was because we first only saw the value of the tunnel system as a defensive measure to hide from the French. Without them, we would have been forced to withdraw further away from the enemy. But we soon saw they could be used offensively as well—for they allowed us to stay close to the enemy, launching attacks at random. Development of our bases below ground paralleled development of the enemy's bases above ground. This offensive role for the tunnels began during the war with the French and continued over into the war with America. The only difference was tunnel bases were expanded more during the American war and were dug deeper."*

General Phung described the Cu Chi tunnel's development as taking place in three distinct phases: *"The tunnel system developed continuously, step-by-step. The first step took place over the nine-year period we fought the French. The second occurred as two small steps:*

"From 1954 to 1959 when the war took on more of a political struggle than a fighting war, there was little expansion of the system as our forces avoided fighting, using the tunnels to hide.

"From 1959 to 1964 when it was clear the struggle against (Ngo Dinh) Diem could no longer be limited to a political one, we began to conduct attacks and expand our operational area.

"The third step occurred at the end of 1964 as the Americans began sending troops to Vietnam and we realized the fighting would become very fierce. We knew we needed to develop tunnel systems quickly, making them bigger, and to develop tunneling techniques to make them more complex. To better defend our tunnels, we organized above ground defenses, developing more dangerous booby traps and using anti-tank mines."

By the time the French were defeated in 1954, only ten percent of the Cu Chi tunnel system existed, as opposed to the 340 kilometers in existence when Saigon fell in 1975. Since minimal construction was undertaken between 1954-1959, and none from 1959-1964, most of tunnel construction took place during America's involvement.

With an ambitious tunneling campaign mounted in late 1964, the Cu Chi tunnels were prepared to greet the first major American incursion into the area—Operation Crimp—in January 1966.

Interestingly, the mission of Crimp was not to ferret Viet Cong forces out of the tunnels, for their existence was not yet known to the Americans. Crimp's mission was to trap guerrilla forces operating in the Cu Chi area. It involved launching an attack through the Ho Bo woods, located west of the "Iron Triangle." (The Iron Triangle was an area dominated by the Viet Cong, situated between the Thi Tinh and Saigon Rivers. The term "Triangle" was used to refer to an area formed by the borders of three different districts—Ben Cat, Trang Bang and Cu Chi. A guerrilla could safely travel to all three of these districts in daytime, without ever setting foot on the surface, through the Cu Chi tunnel system.)

Crimp was a "hammer and anvil" operation—U.S. forces on the Saigon River served as the anvil, while a sweep mounted by the U.S. Army's 1st Division, the "Big Red One," served as the hammer. Landing to the north of Cu Chi, Big Red One was to sweep southeast, towards the Saigon River, to trap the guerrilla forces there.

The plan was simple and seemed likely to ensnare any guerrillas in the area. As U.S. 1st Division forces, flown in by helicopter, landed, they immediately drew small arms fire. This fire continued as the 1st Division advanced towards the Saigon River. However, each time the

Americans gave chase, they were unable to locate their attackers—it was as if the guerrillas had vanished into thin air.

Although some bunkers and trench systems were found, all were unoccupied. By the time U.S. forces had finally reached the Saigon River, they had suffered numerous casualties—without finding a single Viet Cong soldier. Frustration mounted for the Americans as they began to feel like they were fighting an invisible enemy.

The mechanism by which the Viet Cong were affecting their disappearing act soon was uncovered.

As the 1st Division began doubling back through the Iron Triangle again, a carefully concealed trap door, leading to a tunnel below, was discovered by an alert soldier. As a group of 1st Division soldiers stood around examining the tunnel entrance, a guerrilla popped up out of another trap door nearby. With his weapon on automatic, he sprayed the area with gunfire before retreating down into the tunnel. The 1st Division soldiers now descended upon this second tunnel entrance. As they did so, however, a third guerrilla popped up from yet another hidden tunnel entrance, again shooting at the frustrated Americans. It was quickly evident that the 1st Division was facing something it had never encountered before. Nothing in its previous training had prepared the 1st Division to fight guerrilla forces on a subterranean battlefield.

⁂ ⁂ ⁂

Major General Phung shared his personal insights about Operation Crimp: *"Although Crimp took place in January 1966, we were ready for the operation by the previous September. We anticipated it as the U.S. was sending troops into Vietnam since early 1965. It was easy to guess we would have to confront them sometime later that year or early the next. We met regularly with our intelligence people and military analysts who closely monitored developments along the front. They concluded an American sweep into the area was inevitable as Saigon's forces were very weak at that time.*

"I was receiving reports in 1965 on how many U.S. troops were being sent in, when they were arriving and where they were going. I was told the names and structure of forces involved in Crimp and what the strategy was. We knew the direction of attack. We knew all this months ahead of time, although we did not know the precise time Crimp would be initiated. Because Big Red One moved into the base at Long Binh, because large supplies were coming into the base and because reconnaissance aircraft were flying over our positions, we knew an attack would come soon and we were confident that we were the intended target.

"Because the Americans were formidable fighters with technologically superior weapons, we tried to determine during our preparations what their exact offensive tactics would be. We dispatched reconnaissance units for this purpose."

During Crimp, a new breed of American fighting soldier, known as the "tunnel rat," emerged as U.S. forces tried to flush the guerrillas out of their subterranean chambers. The tunnel entrances were very small—much too small for an average-sized American. Therefore, smaller soldiers volunteered to crawl into these tunnels and explore them. If he was lucky, a tunnel rat found an unoccupied tunnel; if he was not, he found himself facing a booby-trap or a guerrilla—under conditions usually favoring the defender.

Colonel Chau Lam was stationed at Cu Chi in 1962, remaining there throughout the war. He was a lieutenant when Operation Crimp was launched. He assessed Crimp's success as follows:

"The U.S. intention during Operation Crimp was not to fight us in the tunnels. It was to trap us against the Saigon River and destroy our base of support in the area. This was the first time the enemy actually realized we had a tunnel system at Cu Chi. For them, and from the standpoint of Crimp's intended purpose, therefore, the operation was a failure."

A principle of war observed for centuries by military commanders on the attack is, whenever possible, to maximize force. This principle was ignored by the guerrillas of Cu Chi. Inside their tunnels, the smaller the attack force, the greater the likelihood of success—for fewer troops meant enhanced mobility underground.

"Because we used fewer soldiers," said Lam, *"we employed tactics that gave the advantage to the smaller force."*

This principle of less being better was employed by the Viet Cong during Crimp. While more than 8,000 U.S. and Allied troops swept towards the Saigon River, several hundred guerrillas, usually operating in groups of three and four, intermittently wreaked havoc with their advance.

"We spread our troops out in small numbers and were ready to fight as soon as the Americans landed," explained Lam. *"They did not know where we were. We shot at them as they advanced. We quickly got back into the tunnel to move to another location to do the same thing again. We inflicted casualties on them and as they stopped to assist the wounded or retrieve their dead, we inflicted more casualties. When they came in after us, by the time they reached us, we were gone. They were surprised by our tactics, not knowing at first from where the attacks were coming."*

The effectiveness of the Viet Cong defense was underscored by Lam's observation, *"With a much smaller force, we were able to tie down a much larger one."* He continued, *"I should add, however, that the tactics used by the Americans against the tunnels were very fierce."*

✻ ✻ ✻

The Americans began using a wide range of counter-tactics against the tunnels. To locate other entrances, smoke was forced into the tunnels. While this tactic did not flush the guerrillas out, it enabled U.S. troops to learn more about the vastness of the system as smoke would seep out through other hidden entrances/exits.

CS or "tear gas"—a non-lethal riot control agent—was also used in an effort to drive the guerrillas out of their underground sanctuary. The use of CS instills panic in its victims, burning the eyes, nostrils and mouth. In the open, many escape routes exist for victims of a CS attack—but for those underground, escape is severely limited and the panic much greater. Unlike their American counterparts, the Viet Cong were not equipped with gas masks. Thus, their only options in the event of a CS attack were to endure the burning discomfort, their screams muffled by the depth of their private hell, or escape through a tunnel exit, where the high risk of death or capture existed.

⁂ ⁂ ⁂

"Initially, the Americans used grenades and explosives to destroy the tunnels but this met with limited success as only a small portion was damaged," said General Phung. *"Later, they used tear gas which was released through a pipe inserted into the tunnel. The purpose of the gas was to suffocate the soldier or make him move to another location inside the tunnel. But even this type of attack became ineffective as we learned to prepare for it."*

Nguyen Thanh Linh, a lieutenant at the time of Operation Crimp, described the tunnel configuration and what was done to defend against CS attacks:

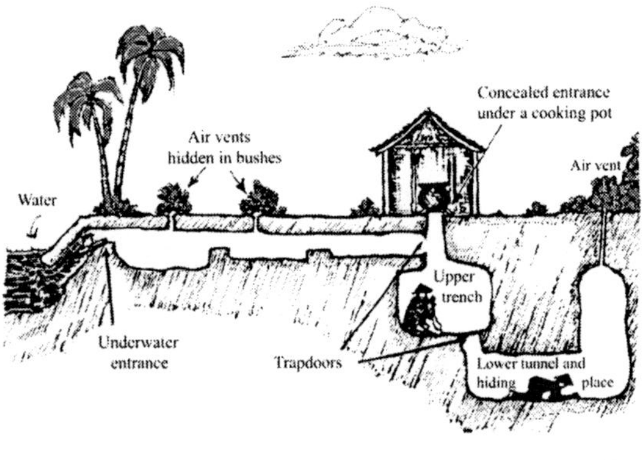

"There were different floors in the tunnels. The first was one and a half to two meters deep. The purpose for the different levels was to protect occupants from explosions. These were not really floors but short lengths of

tunnel dug at different depths. Only our main tunnel systems had them. A main tunnel might run for a distance of five meters before dropping to a lower level, dug to a depth almost two meters below it. Some tunnels contained a third level, which was dug another one and a half to two meters lower than the second. The tunnels barely permitted a person to move in a squatting position. Because of this, a two-kilometer section might take two hours to traverse. And the deeper the level, the more difficult it was to traverse as the tunnels became narrower.

"If gas entered the main tunnel, it had difficulty penetrating to the lower levels. But, if it entered a lower level, it then rose to an adjoining upper level very quickly. If the gas reached all three levels, the situation became very dangerous for those inside. So we began to build airtight trap doors between levels to seal the gas off. If we were on a lower level and heard someone on a higher level screaming from the gas, we immediately shut the trap doors to contain it."

Another tunnel design technique used to defeat CS gas was a U-shaped tunnel connector. Situated at the end of a main tunnel, a U-shaped tunnel was dug into the floor. The tunnel went down a meter and a half, and then leveled off for a short distance before heading back up to the same level as the main tunnel. This served as a detour for a tunnel traveler through the main tunnel. In some cases, the entrance to the U-shaped tunnel connector was simply sealed with a camouflaged trap door so that a tunnel rat would think he had reached the end of the tunnel. But sometimes it was filled with water to prevent CS gas or smoke that had entered into one section of the main tunnel from spreading into another. Effective in doing so, the U-shaped connector presented yet another obstacle for the tunnel dweller moving between main tunnel sections as one had to hold one's breath to pass through the water-filled connector.

There was little a guerrilla could do if caught in the tunnel during a CS attack. *"Our soldiers were taught if they could not escape the gas attack to urinate on a handkerchief and place it over their nose and mouth,"* explained Nguyen Thanh Linh. *"We knew, based on our knowledge of oriental medicine, ammonia in the urine reduced the burning sensation of the gas. This was also a procedure we followed to take the sting out of sunburn. In these cases,"* Linh added, *"it was not difficult for a soldier in such a situation to urinate."*

❊   ❊   ❊

Another tactic employed by Americans to force Viet Cong out of their tunnels was one popular with homeowners back in the U.S. in ridding their yards of moles.

"When tear gas proved unsuccessful against us, the Americans next tried water," explained General Phung. *"For tunnels near the Saigon River, they would connect hoses to pumps and then flush river water through them. But, like a ship, our tunnels were compartmentalized to contain water penetration using watertight doors. We would not stand by idly whenever we observed the Americans setting up their pumps. We shot at the equipment and its operators before the pumps could be put into use."*

❊   ❊   ❊

The Americans were further frustrated during the last days of Operation Crimp, employing another tactic that met with little success in destroying the tunnels.

"After locating a possible tunnel, the Americans repeatedly drove their tanks back and forth over a suspected location to try to collapse it," explained Colonel Lam. But the tactic met with limited success as Viet Cong preparations in anticipation of Crimp resulted in the tunnels being dug at a depth almost impervious to the weight of the steel behemoths.

❊   ❊   ❊

The most effective tactic used against the tunnels was aerial bombardment. This came in the form of the B-52's 500 or 750-pound bombs or the ground penetration bombs dropped by smaller aircraft.

"Most of the time we knew of the bombings ahead of time," said General Phung. *"We looked for indicators a bombing was about to take place. One way was to look for activity at the air bases. Observers let us know when planes were being rearranged on the airfields in preparation for a launch. Another indicator was the sudden withdrawal of South Vietnamese forces from the suspected target area."*

One B-52 bombing survival tactic followed by the tunnel dwellers was based upon the belief lightning would not strike twice in the same place.

"The B-52 left a direct line of bomb craters in its wake as it flew overhead," continued Phung. *"A second run followed some minutes later but subsequent bombs never fell in the same exact spot. Therefore, in between bombing runs, people looked to see where the crater line in the previous bombing fell. If it fell across another bunker system left undamaged, they abandoned their own tunnels and joined the survivors in the bunker system already hit."*

Phung personally attested to the effectiveness of this survival technique. A tunnel he abandoned was destroyed after he relocated to one that survived an earlier bombing run.

❊   ❊   ❊

"After the Cedar Falls Operation (U.S. attack conducted against the Viet Cong headquarters in the Iron Triangle a year after Crimp, January 8-26, 1967)," said Phung, *"the Americans created a new kind of bomb. It did not explode on the surface but penetrated into the ground. It was equipped with a timing device to detonate after penetration. The depth of penetration depended on the ground and soil type. I first encountered this bomb in April 1967. An F-5 went into a steep dive, as the bomb had to be dropped at the right angle to penetrate. Our defensive tactic was to wait until the aircraft went into its dive and then shoot at it with rifles and machine guns. There was no other defense against it. It was not a simple process to drop such a bomb directly into a tunnel system to destroy it which often was required to be most effective."* But a direct hit by such a bomb had devastating consequences. *"In 1969,"* Phung reported, *"a single bomb dropped by an F-5 on a tunnel killed forty men."*

❊   ❊   ❊

While the Americans were able to make life difficult for the guerrillas below ground, the guerrillas were able to make life difficult for the Americans above. U.S. forces operating in Cu Chi were constantly plagued by sniper attacks as they attempted to advance. With the elements of surprise and ability to pick targets freely, the Viet Cong were at an advantage—they made every round count.

"Every man on our sniper teams was issued only 100 rounds of ammunition to fight for a single day," said General Phung. *"Engaging the enemy with this limited supply of ammunition, the teams were able to inflict significant casualties. Our philosophy was that with one bullet we were to inflict one enemy casualty. It a team ran out of rounds, they used their grenades. If one team was involved in heavy fighting and another was not, the latter gave ammunition to the former. We established a competition, giving awards to those snipers who inflicted the most casualties."*

Upon taking sniper fire, U.S. forces usually concentrated their return fire in the same direction—but often it came too late. Inevitably, a guerrilla popped up, fired, and returned to the safety of his tunnel before the Americans knew what had hit them. As Phung claimed, *"Our soldiers were very calm when encountering the enemy, which is why they were so effective."*

Establishing defensive perimeters did not necessarily provide U.S. forces additional protection. Occasionally, a U.S. defensive perimeter was established directly over a tunnel system. Most of the time, the Americans only would learn about this after the fact, as a guerrilla would pop up through a hidden trap door inside the perimeter, fire and quickly disappear.

Operation Crimp concluded on January 14, 1966. Whether it was successful or not depends to whom the question is put. While U.S. Army after action reports suggested it was a success, those on the other side of the battlefield—or, more accurately, those underneath it—suggest it was not. Perhaps the answer lies in one's definition of success.

From the American standpoint, the operation was successful as it provided U.S. forces with new insights into the enemy's capabilities, resulted in the capture of numerous documents, caches of food and weapons, and, temporarily at least, drove the enemy from parts of his underground base. From the Viet Cong standpoint, Crimp was successful as it instilled confidence in their ability to fight the

Americans, enabled them to inflict significant casualties and proved a numerically inferior force at Cu Chi could retain a foothold deep in enemy territory—even if that foothold was underground.

❄ ❄ ❄

Crimp was followed by other U.S. operations through the same area. A year to the day after Crimp, Cedar Falls was initiated, involving most of the same U.S. Army units involved in Crimp. This time the Americans were better prepared for what guerrilla tactics to encounter and brought special equipment to fight accordingly.

"After Operation Crimp was unsuccessful," said General Phung, *"they continued to conduct more operations. The big one was Cedar Falls, which involved more troops and a mechanized force including bulldozers. We followed our same tactics while they employed new ones to find and destroy our tunnels. With bulldozers, they conducted a tactic known as 'boc vo trai dat'* (Vietnamese for 'peeling back the skin of the earth'). *But after Crimp, we learned to make the tunnels more secure by digging them deeper. Not knowing where the tunnels were, the*  *Americans would bring several bulldozers on line at the same time— usually twelve although other times they used an entire battalion simultaneously. If they found nothing, they moved to another location and repeated the tactic. This tactic was very dangerous for them, however, as our soldiers used anti-tank rockets to destroy the bulldozers. So, the Americans committed many troops just to protect their bulldozers."* (Photograph above taken during Operation Cedar Falls.)

The use of bulldozers did not surprise the Viet Cong. Their reconnaissance teams had observed activity at the American bases prior to Cedar Falls. What they saw enabled them to determine bulldozers were going to be employed during the next operation. Phung reported:

"We saw the bulldozers being pre-positioned at the American base before the operation began. Knowing they would be used, we tried to determine what specific areas would be targeted. We then hid mines

and other explosive devices in those areas. While the bulldozers were more effective than tanks against our tunnels, neither really caused us major concern since we had dug our tunnels deeper."

The U.S. Army used dogs in Operation Cedar Falls to try and sniff out Viet Cong hiding places. Again, they met with limited success as the guerrillas were prepared for this too. Deposits of pepper were left on the ground to disrupt the animals' search.

❊   ❊   ❊

On the American side, the tunnel rat who ventured deep into a tunnel system was a unique breed. He entered a world where he fought the enemy on the latter's terms, where uncertainty reigned and death possibly lurked only meters away.

"We intentionally constructed the tunnels in a complex manner," explained General Phung, *"as it was the only way to prevent penetration by the tunnel rats."*

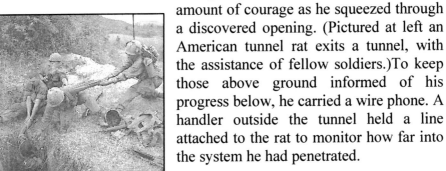

The tunnel rat carried a flashlight, pistol, knife—and an immense amount of courage as he squeezed through a discovered opening. (Pictured at left an American tunnel rat exits a tunnel, with the assistance of fellow soldiers.)To keep those above ground informed of his progress below, he carried a wire phone. A handler outside the tunnel held a line attached to the rat to monitor how far into the system he had penetrated.

Once inside, a cat-and-mouse game ensued between the rat and the guerrilla—with the roles of "cat" and "mouse" occasionally changing. Nguyen Thanh Linh described how the rat's role of cat and defender's role of mouse quickly reversed: *"When we discovered we were being followed in the tunnels, we waited to attack the intruder. Most of the time we waited on an upper level to catch the tunnel rat coming up from a lower level. We constructed the tunnel so an intruder had to lift his hands first and then pull his torso up when attempting to reach an upper level. Preoccupied in this manner,*

the tunnel rat was extremely vulnerable, so we either stabbed him or dropped a grenade down to the lower level when he was in that position." In spite of their adversarial nature, both the tunnel rat and defender maintained a mutual respect for each other. (Pictured at left, a Vietnamese soldier awaits a tunnel rat.)

"The tunnel rats performed a very dangerous mission," General Phung explained. *"They had two objectives upon entering the tunnels: first, to locate documents, supplies, weapons, or anything else of intelligence value; second, to study the best techniques to fight us underground. It was a difficult assignment for them, not only because they had to maneuver within tightly confined spaces but also because our soldiers were waiting for them when they came in...After the war was over, I met an American colonel who shook his head and told me it was impossible to fight our soldiers in the tunnels."*

Booby traps also awaited the tunnel rats. Punji stake pits were the most common form encountered, constructed by placing sharp bamboo stakes at the bottom of a hole camouflaged at the surface. The camouflage consisted of a material light enough so as not to support a man's weight. An inattentive tunnel rat, fell victim to such a pit, impaling him on the stakes. On occasion, the stakes were dipped in animal manure or human feces to promote infectious wounds if the victim happened to survive his impalement.

Explosive devices were also used. Trap doors were often hooked up to explosives, most of which came from unexploded or captured U.S. ordnance. Such explosives served not only to kill or maim intruders but, in partially destroying the tunnel, to confuse the enemy as to the exact location of the rest of the system.

A somewhat less lethal booby-trap consisted of boards with long nails extending out the opposite side. On more than one occasion, a tunnel rat impaled his knee, foot or hand on such a board.

For variety, the Viet Cong used a spring-loaded bow and arrow. A short tunnel was dug, perpendicular to the main one. Inside the short tunnel, a bow was positioned—its string pulled back tight, held in place with a hair-trigger locking device, and loaded with an arrow pointing towards the main tunnel. A trip wire ran across the main tunnel, attached to the locking device. As the tunnel rat crawled through the main tunnel and into the intersection, if not cautious, he would carelessly trip the wire, causing the bow to release the arrow.

"These traps worked well," explained General Phung. *"Although at times they left us with another problem. Sometimes the Americans were unable to recover the bodies of men killed inside a tunnel. I knew of two situations involving booby-traps—one where a tunnel rat fell into a punji stake pit and one where he was hit by an arrow—in which they were killed and their bodies left behind as they could not be recovered. Later, we pulled the bodies out ourselves, leaving them above ground to be retrieved later by the Americans. Our traps were so effective that, after 1966, there was much less activity by the tunnel rats."*

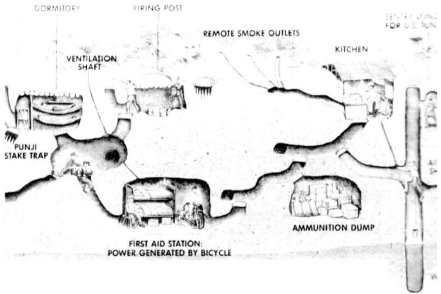

American lives, however, were not the only ones lost to these traps.

"Even our people were afraid of the traps," acknowledged General Phung. *"And there were times we became victims of our own devices. We tried to mark them so this would not happen, but inattentiveness or*

failure to properly mark a trap resulted in the occasional loss of one of our own soldiers."

Some traps instilled more fear than others did, particularly a "live" trap. A poisonous snake or two was sometimes left behind after evacuating a tunnel as a surprise for the rats. Kept in cages until needed, the snakes were released at the last moment to await the tunnel rat's arrival.

"These snakes usually were not very effective," observed General Phung. Perhaps not, but they undoubtedly elevated the fear factor in exploring a tunnel's secrets.

Nguyen Thanh Linh added, *"Even those of us who lived at Cu Chi never knew what we might encounter, for wild animals often found their way into the tunnels. At any time we might be surprised by a bat, fox or snake."*

❉ ❉ ❉

Viet Cong creativity at Cu Chi was not limited to the confines of the tunnels. Traps were prepared on the above ground approaches to the tunnel systems. If the Americans began to develop a proficiency in detecting traps, the guerrillas implemented changes in placement or the types of booby-traps used. This led to the guerrillas' practice of booby-trapping areas they thought were most likely to be used as helicopter landing zones.

"We quickly learned U.S. helicopters looked for open areas to swoop down and off-load troops to conduct surprise attacks against us," said General Phung. *"We countered this by laying mines in those areas we predicted would be so used. Another tactic we employed was to force helicopters to land where we were waiting to ambush them. We forced the Americans to fight our way—not theirs. Later, fearing an area might be mined; pilots were reluctant to land so they would hover over an area while soldiers rappelled down on ropes. Therefore, we designed a new type of booby-trap that exploded if a helicopter hovered ten to fifteen above the landing area. This was done by placing a mine on the ground but positioning a small tree on top of it, directly over the fuse. As the helicopter hovered, the windblast from the blades blew the tree*

over, detonating the mine. The mines used special fuses designed and manufactured by local farmers."

✻ ✻ ✻

The guerrillas relied on manual labor, using shovels and, if necessary, their hands, to dig their tunnel network. Like human earthworms, they burrowed underground with surprising speed. Almost as fascinating as the techniques used for excavating the tunnels were those developed for disguising the tons of earth that had to be removed from carving out the tunnel system.

"We started construction of a tunnel first by digging two 'dry wells,'" described Colonel Chau Lam. *"Each well had a diameter of 0.8 meters. The two were dug about six to fifteen meters apart, depending on the terrain, and excavated to a depth of three to four meters. Upon reaching that depth, the two men in each well began digging towards each other. Each listened for the sound of the other to ensure they met at the right place."* (Digging a dry well is pictured above.)

The depth of the initial dry wells varied, depending on tunnel level. A three to four meter depth was normal for a first tier tunnel, used primarily for rapid transit to other fighting positions. Five to six meters was the normal depth for a second tier tunnel, used as a rest area. Twelve meters was the depth for the third tier tunnel, used as shelter from enemy bombings and tanks/bulldozers. The average horizontal distance for a first or second tier tunnel was 50 to 100 meters; third tier tunnels were limited to about 15 meters.

To access the deeper dry wells, steps were cut into the well walls. The well's small diameter limited the digging activity to one person at a time. A five man digging team was normally involved: while one member would dig, one followed behind to scoop loose soil into a basket, and three remained above ground—one to pull the basket up, one to carry it to the dumpsite, and one to camouflage the excavated

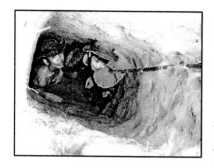

soil. These responsibilities were rotated among team members. (Photo at left shows a basket with excess soil being raised from a dry well.)

The most important aspect of the tunneling operation actually took place above ground—hiding the excavated soil. Careless dumping of soil gave rise to enemy suspicions of nearby tunneling activity—leading to an immediate search for the system.

"We had many different ways of hiding the soil," explained Nguyen Thanh Linh. *"The usual way was to scatter it on the ground, covering it with leaves. Another was to use soil as fill-in for B-52 bomb craters. At times, we even used the soil to construct man-made termite mounds, standing about one-and-a-half meters high."*

Upon completion of the tunnel between the two dry wells, the first well was back-filled. A third dry well was then excavated at a distance from the second equal to the distance between the first two. Upon completion of the third, the men at the bottom of the second and third wells began digging towards each other. Upon completion of this new section of tunnel, the process was repeated as the second well was back-filled and construction on a fourth dry well began. Such a technique required the digging and back filling of thousands of dry wells, one-by-one, as the tunnels connecting them were completed.

One problem that arose over time was the settlement of surface soil in the back-filled dry wells, leaving indentations on the ground. An alert observer would recognize that the cause of these indentations was from tunneling activity. Therefore, the surface area above was regularly checked and capped off with additional soil when actual settlement occurred.

In constructing tunnels, the rate of advance varied depending on the time of season.

"In dry season," said Lam, *"with the soil more difficult to penetrate, it took an entire day to dig one dry well or to advance a tunnel six meters.*

In rainy season, the daily pace was considerably quicker as two dry wells and the connecting tunnel could be completed." With sufficient manpower, several dry wells were dug simultaneously.

A completed tunnel's diameter was usually so small that two people approaching from different directions had great difficulty in passing. One was required to lay prone on the tunnel floor so the other could crawl over him.

Before digging the first dry well, the surface area was carefully inspected. *"We looked for the best location to place a tunnel entrance and exit,"* said Nguyen Thanh Linh. *"Then the first tier would be constructed, after which a second or third tier could be planned."*

Trap doors leading to the tunnels were carefully concealed. Made of wood, the doors were camouflaged by gluing dirt and leaves to the exposed side. The tunnel entrances/exits were kept extremely small, not only to limit detection but also to make entry difficult if discovered.

A tunnel entrance/exit did not always lead to the surface. Some, located near a river, had underwater entrances/exits.

"It was very difficult getting in and out of such an entrance or exit," said General Phung. *"We would have to hold our breath for more than one minute. It was more difficult entering than leaving as one often spent time searching underwater for the entrance before being able to find it. Underwater tunnel entrances were larger than normal surface entrances to assist in locating it. The existence of these entrances/exits were kept secret so few people ever knew about them."*

The tunnels obviously required ventilation shafts for oxygen flow. Construction of these shafts depended on depth.

"For tunnels on the first or second level," said Lam, *"the shaft was dug from below, up to the surface. The handle of a short shovel or a bamboo stake was used to get the shaft started. Then a long length of bamboo was inserted in sections, into the hole, pushing the first section up to the surface. If the ventilation shaft was for a third level tunnel, normally we just left a length of bamboo in the dry well when we back-filled it."*

Cu Chi was a good location for a tunnel system. While the area was known politically as a center of revolutionary activity, there was a "deeper" reason for its selection—its soil. *"The soil composition in Cu Chi was firm, favoring tunnel construction,"* shared Colonel Lam.

Added General Phung, *"It was a porous soil with a water table situated 25 meters beneath the surface. Sometimes we dug 30 meters deep to reach the water table."*

Underground lighting took various forms. Kerosene or diesel fuel lamps provided lighting in the main meeting areas. Some fuel lamps used a particular type of French liquor bottle popular among the guerrillas because of its difficult-to-tip-over design. (When the Saigon regime learned this, it prohibited sale of the bottle.) For tunnel travelers, flashlights or candles were the norm. However, many times, they were in short supply, so travelers transited in total darkness.

Whenever possible, tunnel designers sought to include some creature comforts to minimize the need to go outside. Each system had its own water supply. For cooking, a "smokeless" kitchen was built. This involved a very long series of ventilation shafts, specially constructed so as to dissipate smoke from cooking fires inside the tunnel in such a way so as to make it barely discernible when it reached the surface. Large underground chambers allowed meetings or limited entertainment. Some tunnels contained munition labs for constructing mines. Additionally, facilities were provided for raising poultry and other small farm animals.

"Our life underground was safe and comfortable," said General Phung. *"As we were not always fighting, there were times we took turns going above ground to exercise. Occasionally we brought some of our livestock up with us to exercise, as if they were people."*

While the Viet Cong controlled the subsurface world at Cu Chi, control of the surface changed depending upon the time of day. During daylight hours, U.S. and South Vietnamese forces ruled; in the late afternoon, however, roles were reversed. U.S. and South Vietnamese forces in Cu Chi normally withdrew by 5:00 P.M. Upon doing so, the guerrillas emerged from their tunnels, becoming nocturnal hunters.

"During daylight, most our activities took place underground," said General Phung. *"We held meetings and rested. Some of our ordnance units surfaced to plant mines. If an enemy unit was encountered, we engaged it; but usually we did not initiate a daytime attack on our own."* Nighttime was a different story.

"As darkness fell, we conducted attacks on enemy bases," continued Phung. *"Our specialty was night fighting. Although the enemy was assisted by aircraft which dropped flares and used infrared detectors to provide security for their bases, these were usually ineffective against us."*

✳ ✳ ✳

The Viet Cong's determination—his "iron will"—to defend Cu Chi was explained by Lam: *"We knew the Americans were determined to find and destroy the tunnel system. They understood, as did we, however Cu Chi went, so did the war; if the tunnels survived, we won; if they did not, the Americans won. It was our determination not to lose even one centimeter of the tunnels. It was a contest of wills resulting in some very fierce fighting. We made a tremendous sacrifice to gain victory."*

The Cu Chi fighter did pay a heavy price for his victory. Thirty years of fighting against the French and Americans claimed over 30,000 casualties. *"More than eighty percent of these came at the hands of the Americans,"* estimated General Phung. *"We are very proud of the tunnels and what we were able to accomplish by our determination and spirit. But that we paid a heavy price in terms of the blood shed by these soldiers cannot be denied."*

GOING IT ALONE

Hanoi received assistance from several Communist Bloc countries during the Vietnam conflict. While such assistance primarily came from the former Soviet Union and China, other Communist Bloc countries contributed as well. The assistance provided normally was of a materiel nature—with one rather extraordinary exception.

Of all Hanoi's alliances during the war, the most intriguing was its relationship with China. For two countries that were such traditional enemies, having fought against each other every century for the past thousand years, a Chinese-Vietnamese alliance seemed, and was, unnatural. Clearly, the historical mistrust between these two was not easily set aside during the Vietnam war. While accepting Chinese weapons, ammunition, vehicles, etc., during the war, the Vietnamese did so with reservation.

Hanoi well knew Beijing's assistance was motivated, not out of concern for an Asian brother's plight but, rather, out of concern over the presence of a Western foe in its backyard. To China, the ideal outcome for the Vietnam war would have been for both sides to lose.

The distrust between the Chinese and the Vietnamese continued throughout the Vietnam war, always making Beijing's actions suspect to Hanoi. Such suspicions were well founded as, four years after Saigon fell and the Americans had been driven out, the Vietnamese tiger and the Chinese dragon were back at it again—embroiled in a bloody thirty-day border dispute.

Hanoi's suspicions of Beijing arose early on during the Vietnam war. China had been supplying the Vietnamese with mortar rounds. But in using the mortar rounds against the Americans, they routinely fell short of their mark. The Vietnamese soon learned why—insufficient amounts of gunpowder had been packed into the rounds by the Chinese, significantly reducing their range. When informed, the Chinese made adjustments in their manufacturing process; but Vietnamese doubts lingered as to whether the powder shortage was the result of an intentional act rather than innocent oversight.

At one point during the war, Beijing offered to assist Vietnam in the defense of its airspace along their mutual border. With Vietnam desperately needing its air defense assets deployed around Hanoi and along the Ho Chi Minh Trail, the country's protection of its extreme northern border was tenuous. Despite this, there was clear reluctance on Hanoi's part to allow the Chinese to occupy air defense gun and missile batteries on Vietnamese soil. There was concern as to what obligations such an invitation might give rise. From the Vietnamese perspective, there was no doubt the invitation included a responsibility by the Chinese to withdraw when the war was over. Hanoi's fear, however, was the Chinese perspective might be different, giving rise to a claim by Beijing to maintain a presence in Vietnam since it was formerly Chinese territory. While Beijing's offer was rejected, Hanoi did allow Chinese air defense units, situated on Chinese soil, to fire into Vietnamese airspace at American aircraft.

The Vietnamese saw the Soviets, on the other hand, as trusted allies. During the war, among other things, Moscow provided materiel support and technical training assistance, in particular for surface-to-air missiles (SAMs) they made available to the Vietnamese. However, Russian advisors never operated SAM launchers in Vietnam, limiting their involvement simply to providing on-site training.

As far as Soviet military professionalism was concerned, the Vietnamese had mixed opinions. While some Russian advisors were committed to their jobs, others commanded little respect. Stories were told of advisors—too frightened to remain near the SAMs when an air attack was imminent—who chose to leave their trainees behind to fend for themselves. And, no Soviet advisor ever volunteered to leave the relative comfort of Hanoi to undertake the more dangerous assignment of training air defense personnel along the Ho Chi Minh Trail.

Soviet flight instructors also were sent by Moscow to train the Vietnamese. Again, the reviews were mixed. Colonel Le Thanh Chon, a North Vietnamese tactical flight instructor, recalled a training mission in late 1967/early 1968 that proved to be especially embarrassing for one Soviet instructor. As Chon related, a chance encounter with American warplanes occurred as a Soviet instructor took his Vietnamese student up for a training flight and resulted in a student/teacher role reversal:

"A very experienced Soviet flight instructor took a Vietnamese student pilot up in a MIG-21. They launched from Noi Bai airport with the student pilot in the front seat and the Soviet flight instructor in the back. Soon after they were airborne, they unexpectedly encountered four U.S. aircraft. The Soviet instructor froze at the controls, so the student took over. He engaged the enemy planes, shooting down an F-4 Phantom. When the MIG-21 safely landed, the Soviet instructor turned to his student and addressed him as 'sup hau'—an acknowledgment the student had become teacher of the master."

Cuba dispatched a small contingent of soldiers to Vietnam during the war, although their activities were non-combat related. Primarily engineers, the Cubans earned the respect of the Vietnamese as they, unlike the Soviet advisors, insisted on serving alongside their fellow communist brothers in the most dangerous areas of the Ho Chi Minh Trail. The Cubans endured the same hardships as their Vietnamese hosts, forging a close bond with them that continues to this day—a bond further strengthened during Castro's 1973 transit of a part of the Trail.

Offers to Hanoi from Communist Bloc countries during the war to contribute combat troops to fight the Americans were rejected. While Saigon accepted ground forces from the U.S. and other countries to do its fighting, Hanoi preferred "going it alone." The North Vietnamese leadership recognized the war had to be won by its own forces and on the commitment of its own people—for if the situation got desperate, it would be the Vietnamese and the Vietnamese alone who had to continue the fight.

Hanoi made one brief exception to its "going it alone" policy—one that met with disaster.

In early 1967, North Korea insisted on sending a squadron of its pilots to Vietnam. Pyongyang's proposal was couched in terms of an offer of mutual assistance in which the North Korean pilots would fight only if needed but were primarily there to study U.S. air combat tactics. Hanoi reluctantly accepted the offer and North Korean pilots were dispatched by Pyongyang. For a few of them, it was a one-way trip.

Colonel Chon worked closely with the North Koreans upon their arrival. *"About thirty North Korean pilots arrived,"* he said. *"I was very close to them, teaching them how to guide a fighter to engage Americans in a dogfight. Although I taught those tactics, it was their decision whether to follow my instructions. It was a similar situation to when we were trained in tactics by the Soviets and Chinese—we learned the basics from them and then developed our own tactics to fight the Americans. That is because the realities of actual combat often differ from the structured schoolroom environment. While the Soviets and Chinese had taught us tactics based on the massing of air forces, we learned through our own experiences to use different tactics. I doubt the Americans ever thought we would send just one aircraft up to engage a much larger force. But we did as we discovered there was a greater chance of returning safely if we sent a single plane to intercept several enemy aircraft. We learned to employ guerrilla tactics not only on the ground but in the air as well."*

The North Koreans chose not to follow Chon's instructions. While total Korean combat losses were not disclosed, it was determined from interviews with Vietnamese pilots that several were lost. Their loss was apparently linked to their decision to disregard Chon's instructions and to engage American pilots using the same tactics the North Koreans had employed against them in the Korean War. It proved difficult for the North Koreans to adjust to the significant changes in aviation combat technology that had taken place in the intervening years. Their situation was not enhanced either as the Koreans were flying an older generation MIG against the Americans—the MIG-17. Slower and less maneuverable, the MIG-17 could not operate at the higher elevations and performance levels of American combat aircraft.

"The North Koreans requested to participate in the fighting," acknowledged Nguyen Hong Nhi, a former NVA pilot ace and head of Hanoi's Civil Aviation Administration, *"and did so in 1967. But, after a few months, it was decided their participation would be terminated. While their pilots fought separately from ours, the aircraft they flew were Vietnamese and carried Vietnamese markings on them."*

"We always were opposed to receiving military forces from our allies to fight on our territory," said Colonel Ta Minh Kham, commander of the 9th Viet Cong Division. *"We allowed the North Koreans to come as they wanted to practice their tactics against the Americans. They had their practice—and they died."*

In the first foray the North Koreans made in late April 1967, four MIG-17s—flown by North Korean pilots—and two MIG 21s—flown by Vietnamese pilots—scrambled from Kep Air Base, 60 kilometers northeast of Hanoi, to intercept 24 U.S. F-4Ds and F-4Es on their way to attack the Bac Giang Bridge. (Interestingly, while translators were available to the North Koreans for training purposes, none were provided during combat operations. Hence, there was no way Vietnamese operations personnel on the ground or pilots in the MIG-21s could communicate with the MIG-17 pilots.) As the Americans prepared to engage the two MIG-21s, they spotted the four MIG-17s. Two air battles ensued, one against the MIG-17s and one against the MIG-21s. Two of the MIG-17s were destroyed by the Americans while two F-4Es were allegedly shot down by the Vietnamese. The two North Korean MIG-17 pilots ejected from their planes. However, as they were unfamiliar with proper ejection techniques, both sustained terminal injuries in the process.

(Buried in Vietnam, the Korean pilots received a somewhat bizarre funeral from their fellow countrymen, as shared by Colonel Chon. The bodies were placed inside Vietnamese coffins, on a bed of fried rice and dry tea, with a dried fish at the foot. A small hole was drilled into the lid just above the deceased's mouth. The Koreans slowly paraded around the coffins, eating dog meat and periodically crying out in anguish. Upon reaching the head of the coffin, mourners received a thimble-sized glass of wine. They drank half and poured the remainder into the coffin through the hole in the lid.)

I had been told by the Vietnamese that the North Korean pilots who had been shot down during the war had later, at Pyongyang's request, been returned. But several years later, I happened to read an article in a US newspaper about a visit to Vietnam in April 2000 by North Korean Foreign Minister, Paek Nam-sun. The article indicated Mr. Paek had made a quick trip to a cemetery outside of Hanoi. I realized this had to be the cemetery where the North Korean pilots had been buried during the Vietnam war.

Upon reading the cemetery visited was in Bac Giang Province in Vietnam, I immediately contacted a friend living in Hanoi and asked him to verify whether there were grave markers for any North Koreans there. My friend, Chuck Searcy, after much searching, was able to locate a Korean cemetery in Voi, just off a little used dirt road in the countryside (pictured below).

Unable to reach the cemetery entrance due to ruts in the road, Chuck and two of his friends left their vehicle and driver to continue on foot. It was there his mission would come to a successful conclusion. He found, and photographed, evidence of what is perhaps one of the best-kept secrets of the Vietnam war—i.e., North Korea's participation in that conflict against the Americans. The graves of fourteen pilots who failed to return home were found. He describes what he saw:

"The wooden gate of the cemetery was padlocked, and the wall seemed too high to surmount. The western wall, however, was low enough for me to scramble across.

"The cemetery was surprisingly well maintained. The immediate area of the 14 graves, all above ground in two rows of seven each, was surrounded by a low cement border and paved with cement. The land beyond the burial area was cultivated in neat rows of peanuts, with lychee and peach trees scattered throughout.

"The obelisk in front of the graves is inscribed with a common tribute at veteran cemeteries: 'The nation will always remember your sacrifice.'"

Pictures of 12 of the 14 grave obelisks follow:

Hanoi's willingness to accept assistance from an ally was perhaps best understood by a North Korean officer who Colonel Kham knew. In 1958, Colonel Kham attended a Chinese military academy along with this North Korean officer. A classroom discussion ensued one day about the Korean war and China's contribution of hundreds of thousands of its own troops after the Americans and the South Koreans had successfully repelled an earlier North Korean invasion. The North Korean officer observed, *"For an ally, it is always easy to repay a debt of money but it is never easy to repay a debt of blood."*

Today, there is evidence of North Korea's blood debt to Vietnam in two locations. One is a picture displayed at Hanoi's Air Museum of a group of North Korean pilots being thanked by their Vietnamese counterparts for their service as the Koreans prepare to return home. The second is an isolated cemetery at Bac Giang Province where the grave markers of 14 North Korean pilots who were not included in that photograph can be found.

EPILOGUE: "LEST WE FORGET"

The Vietnam war has had a profound impact upon my life. As a college student in the late 1960s, I saw firsthand the turmoil it created on campuses across the Nation. As a member of a family with a deep-rooted military history, I was proud to serve alongside other family members in that conflict. I lost friends and classmates on its battlefields—and a brother who survived the war only to fight—and lose—another battle to cancers caused by his exposure to Agent Orange.

This sensitized me to the suffering the war inflicted upon Americans—the brave men and women who had fought in it and the families who awaited their return. But not until I went back to Vietnam years later did I come to understand that such suffering also had been inflicted upon the equally brave men and women who had fought on the other side of the battlefield—and their families as well.

History shows we made many mistakes in forging our policies towards Vietnam. In the aftermath of World War II, we supported French colonialism, contrary to Vietnam's right for self-determination. This support for France was contrary to President Roosevelt's belief, expressed just before his death, that following the defeat of Japan, the French should not be allowed to reassert themselves in Vietnam as a colonial power. (While Roosevelt was sensitive to the issue of French colonialism, an indication of even his failure to truly understand the issue of Vietnamese nationalism was evidenced by his support for the occupation of Vietnam by the Chinese instead of the French.) By failing to recognize Vietnam's right to self-determination at the end of World War II, we sealed America's fate in Southeast Asia. In the process, we transformed a World War II friend into a post-World War II foe.

✳ ✳ ✳

Should Vietnam have been where America drew its line in the sand to confront communism in Southeast Asia? The argument can be made, had it not been drawn in Vietnam, Soviet and/or Chinese adventurism in the region would most assuredly have caused us to draw it elsewhere in the region. Thailand, or the Philippines, or Malaysia, or any other country in the region with a struggling economy at that time, could well have become a "Vietnam" equivalent. Unfortunately, for the people of Vietnam, it was their country in which we chose to take our stand against communism.

⁂ ⁂ ⁂

It is not my intent to suggest by what I have written that we should feel a deep sense of remorse over Vietnam—we, as a people, did what we thought was the right thing to do to contain the communist threat. A strong case can be made in taking the stand we did, and in spite of our defeat, that we did achieve a grander, strategic victory. By drawing the line in the sand against communism in Vietnam, we were able to buy additional time for those other countries in the region to stabilize their economies, denying them the fertile soil of economic unrest necessary for the seed of communism to take root.

I wrote this book to build a foundation for healing. Hopefully, by better understanding the suffering our enemy endured during the war, those of us still bearing the pain from its wounds might find in our hearts, the power to heal. It is my hope that those of us having problems with the healing process will be able to set aside our ideological differences to allow that to happen.

⁂ ⁂ ⁂

As Americans, we must understand we were not alone in the anguish created by the Vietnam conflict. In that war, we fought an enemy who suffered at least as much as we did and who was just as committed to his beliefs as we were to ours. Despite our cultural and political differences, their suffering is deserving of our recognition; their commitment is deserving of our respect.

⁂ ⁂ ⁂

It is a frailty of human nature to maximize our own suffering and to minimize that of others. A critique of the 1998 movie release "Saving Private Ryan" bears this out. The film is about a squad of American soldiers during World War II sent to rescue Private Ryan from behind German lines. Ryan's three brothers had been killed in action, so the

U.S. War Department was seeking to avoid the loss of the Ryan family's sole remaining son. Viewing audiences are given a most realistic view of the carnage that occurs on the battlefield. As to that carnage, a film critic made the observation:

"There are many heart-wrenching deaths in 'Saving Private Ryan,' but they are all American deaths. When Germans are shot, they go down like tenpins, and they stay down. Their deaths are movie deaths. And the more agonizingly the Americans suffer, the happier we are to see the Germans slaughtered."

We have a tendency to overly simplify warfare as a conflict between "white hats" and "black hats." Our side wears the white; therefore, the other side, by definition, wears the black. Thus, the death or wounding of a white hat is always more devastating, more brutal, than that of a black hat. But the reality is that death and dying and suffering are just as agonizing for one as for the other. For the black hats of the Vietnam war it was, quantitatively, much worse as more than fifty Vietnamese soldiers died for every American who fell in battle. The Private Ryan film critic seems to suggest that black hats are incapable of suffering as much as white. However, by reading the stories related by the Vietnamese veterans in this book—stories which clearly show that the enemy did suffer greatly in that conflict—perhaps we can try to overcome such insensitivity to the tragedies of others and, by so doing, allow for healing.

❊ ❊ ❊

While we may not agree with the political motivations to which those on the other side of the battlefield adhered, we must respect their commitment and belief to die for them. Perhaps this message was no more eloquently stated than by U.S. Supreme Court Justice Oliver Wendell Holmes, Jr., in a Memorial Day speech he gave in 1884. A Union veteran of America's Civil War, he noted that he and his fellow Union comrades had been driven during that conflict by a belief their cause was a just and noble one. *"But,"* he explained, *"we equally believed that those who stood against us held, just as sacred, convictions that were the opposite of ours—and we respected them as every man with a heart must respect those who give all for their belief...You could not stand up day after day in those indecisive contests where overwhelming victory was impossible...without getting at last something of the same brotherhood for the enemy that the north pole of a magnet has for the south—each working in an opposite sense to the other, but each unable to get along without the other. As it was then, it is now. The soldiers of the war need no explanations; they can join in commemorating a soldier's death with feelings not different in kind, whether he fell toward them or by his side."*

America's first ambassador to Vietnam after the war, Douglas "Pete" Peterson, undoubtedly would agree with Holmes' statement. Having spent nearly seven years as a POW in Vietnam, Peterson is a man with a reason to be bitter towards his former enemies—yet he is not. On September 10, 1997—the 31st anniversary of the day he was shot down near the village of An Doai—Peterson visited the site of that memorable event in his life. With two of the men involved in his capture at the time standing before him, the Ambassador said, *"I return here not to relive what was probably the most unhappy day of my life, but to signify to the entire world that reconciliation with a former enemy is not only possible but absolutely the right way to reach out."*

⁂ ⁂ ⁂

Before meeting veterans who stood on the other side of the battlefield in Vietnam, I will freely acknowledge my ignorance as to the suffering they experienced during the war. The 19th century British statesman Benjamin Disraeli noted, ignorance is *"a great step to knowledge."* My numerous return trips to Vietnam and discussions with the Vietnamese people about the war and what they endured during it have enabled me now to climb that step.

Undoubtedly, this book will be criticized for its effort to humanize an enemy some may feel was brutal. Clearly, atrocities did occur on Vietnam's battlefields. It has long been recognized that while war can bring out the best in man, it can also bring out the worst. When it does, ethnicity is not a factor, for even combatants linked by a common culture and heritage have exhibited the capability to brutalize their fellow man. Our own Civil War has demonstrated that to us.

In must be recognized that heinous acts during the Vietnam war were committed on both sides. The My Lai massacre will long remain a black mark in American military history—and My Lai was not an isolated event on the U.S. side. Other war crimes by Americans have been recorded, such as the murder of 16 women and children by five U.S. Marines at Son Thang, only three months after My Lai. But, just as My Lai and Son Thang were not representative of the moral fiber of the vast majority of American fighting men, neither were those acts of brutality committed by the enemy, representative of theirs. Both sides were innocent victims of brutality; both were perpetrators of it. The fact that more incidents may have occurred on one side than on the other is of no consequence—for brutality simply cannot be quantitatively dismissed. It is criminal whether committed once or many times.

We must keep in mind that while evil individuals exist, evil nations do not. The sins of a few, therefore, should not be held against an entire nation.

※ ※ ※

For those still struggling to put the Vietnam war behind them, they should heed the words of a young Jewish girl, wise beyond her years, who met death tragically at the age of fifteen. Living in Nazi-occupied Amsterdam during World War II, Anne Frank was sent to a concentration camp after she and her family were discovered hiding in a secret annex of her father's office. She died at the camp only two months before Germany's surrender, leaving behind a diary that provided tremendous insight into the phenomenal character of this young girl and her amazing capacity to forgive. In the face of her terrible ordeal, her faith in humanity never wavered. *"In spite of everything,"* she wrote, *"I still believe that people are really good at heart."*

We can learn much from Anne Frank. As Americans, a good start is not to let our Vietnam experience dampen our belief in the basic goodness of all people, even our former enemies. The wounds of war—the pain it inflicts—are never one-sided. Good people served in the Vietnam war on both sides and similarly suffered.

❋   ❋   ❋

The vast majority of soldiers who fought in the war, both Vietnamese and American, were courageous men and women who believed their cause was right and fought an honorable fight. We have heard much to date about the American side. This book seeks to provide a forum by which we might now hear about the Vietnamese side—a people whose suffering has largely gone unrecognized.

This was not an easy book to write.

At times, there was an element of fascination in hearing the war stories of enemy veterans. There was also an element of emotion in knowing a battle won on their side was one lost on ours. That the survival of one of their soldiers often meant the death of one of ours. Over the years, in listening to my fellow veterans share their stories of an enemy left dead or dying on Vietnam's battlefields, I had never felt sadness. After getting to know my former enemies, and now being able to put a face on a previously unknown foe, I feel a sense of sadness for all the battlefield's dead.

In writing this book I have not sought to make a political statement. I believe ideological differences should not preclude us from recognizing the commitment, ingenuity and courage a former enemy exhibited in pursuing that in which they believed—nor should such differences preclude us from recognizing the suffering and hardship they endured.

❋   ❋   ❋

While significant differences in ideologies exist even today between the Vietnamese and American governments, there is a commonality of interest in what the people of both countries want out of life. It is upon that commonality of interest we must now build a solid foundation for a new relationship with Hanoi.

On the occasion, of America's Independence Day, a newspaper article once posed the question: *"What is an American?"* One writer defined an American as *"anyone who loves life enough to want the best that it has to offer."* I would submit such a definition is just as applicable to the Vietnamese for, in spite of our differences, we—as individuals—

both cherish the same things in life: the peaceful pursuit of happiness, the exercise of one's free will from intervention, the right to live as one chooses. While the governmental means by which these ends are achieved for its people differ, we cannot ignore the fact our two peoples are driven by similar desires.

The Vietnam conflict was the only war in which Americans and Vietnamese opposed each other. To ensure such a tragedy is not repeated, we need to have a better appreciation for one another. A stepping-stone to doing so is to overcome our mutual ignorance in better understanding what each side had to endure.

※ ※ ※

As I listened to these Vietnamese veterans tell their stories, I wondered from what inner source they were able to draw their strength—their will—to overcome such adversity. Perhaps it was just a writer's folly—simply fueled by the emotions of the moment as these proud veterans relived their wartime experiences—but I observed something after one interview that gave me particular pause to reflect on a possible source.

I had interviewed a retired colonel at his home. A very distinguished looking gentleman in his early seventies, he shared with me his activities during the war. He provided me with a detailed account about an engagement in which he fought against American soldiers. It was a series of firefights that took place over several days involving attacks and counter-attacks that left heavy casualties on both sides. There was a certain fire in the colonel's eyes as he related his story, seemingly unaffected by the significant loss of life he described as having taken place during the fighting.

When the interview concluded, the colonel walked me to the door; we shook hands and I headed to my car. As my driver pulled away from the house, I glanced back at the colonel who remained at the front door. He waved good-bye and then gently reached down to pick up his three-year old grandchild standing next to him. Holding the child in his arms, he gently hugged and kissed her. I was immediately struck by the irony of the moment—for this tender sight bore quite a contrast, I thought, to the dispassionate old warrior who only moments earlier had been sharing his bloody battlefield account.

As the colonel disappeared from view, I found myself reflecting. I thought for a moment, perhaps idealistically, if man could be reduced to his base elements, among those making up an essential part of his character and crossing all cultural boundaries would be one's love for a child.

The scene of the colonel and his grandchild remained etched on my mind. Such love for a child, I reflected, could motivate a people to do the impossible. It could instill within them an inhuman source of strength to overcome any adversity, and to defeat a superpower. By the same token, the absence of such motivation could doom them to failure.

This colonel, and the millions of other Vietnamese veterans who fought with him, saw the reunification of their country as a moral responsibility—as their legacy to their children and grandchildren. Most of them were driven by a common ideology—national survival.

Yet, for Americans, there was no perception of a threat to their own national survival; consequently, no similar legacy was perceived to be at risk. Vietnam was a war different from World War II when American fighting men clearly understood that their own national survival—and, as a result, their legacy to their children—hung in the balance. It was that recognition of our national survival in World War II that gave rise to what newsman and author Tom Brokaw has described as our "greatest generation"—the generation of Americans who sacrificed so much to fight and win that war. Perhaps our biggest mistake in Vietnam was our failure to understand we were fighting its "greatest generation"—a generation that proved it was committed to reunification and national survival as it tallied defeats against one foreign occupier after another. Between 1945 and 1979, that tally included Japan, France, America, Cambodia and China.

∗ *∗* *∗*

It is important to recognize too, that a reunified Vietnam, under Hanoi's leadership, contrary to the rhetoric of U.S. government officials during the war, never really posed a threat to America. The proof lies in the fact that, even today, Hanoi's victory poses no real threat, direct or indirect, to us. Our willingness finally to accept this is what enabled

America to normalize relations with Hanoi after a hiatus of four decades. I believe most Americans sensed that our national survival was never really threatened by what was going on in Vietnam. As General Fred Weyand, the last commander of U.S. forces in Vietnam, observed, *"Vietnam was a reaffirmation of the peculiar relationship between the American Army and the American people. When the Army is committed, the American people are committed. When the American people lose their commitment, it is futile to try to keep the Army committed."* To stay the course in Vietnam, the American people had to perceive their national security was at risk. They did not and such a commitment, therefore, could not and would not be made.

✻ ✻ ✻

That the Vietnamese people were fighting for a legacy to leave their children in the war against America was shared by Colonel Nguyen Van:

"We are very proud of what we accomplished. But what we did we had to do to continue the resistance against foreign occupiers, to gain our independence, to protect and safeguard our country. Although we experienced many losses in doing so, we do not regret what we did. For what we were doing was continuing our heritage. President Ho said it was the responsibility of the people to preserve a single country. The people are the children of the nation who all have—in Vietnam—a common mother. Thus, the Vietnamese people were fighting for the survival of their family."

The Vietnamese are a forgiving people. This has been ingrained as a part of their culture for centuries as shown by their humility in victory—even seeking forgiveness from those they vanquished.

That same humility exists today. In the wake of their victory in the war against America, the Vietnamese harbor no animosity towards us. Instead, they welcome Americans with open arms and high expectations of forging a new relationship mutually beneficial to both. In the tradition of Anne Frank, the Vietnamese people, largely, see only the goodness in mankind. We need do likewise.

✻ ✻ ✻

In late 1968, during a Viet Cong mortar attack against Tan Son Nhut Air Base in Saigon, a memorial chapel was destroyed. A few days later as a chaplain passed by its ruins, his eye caught the glimmer of an object amongst the rubble. It was a board upon which was inscribed a poem of unknown origin.

As I read the poem, I was struck by its simple message and applicability to all combatants and victims of the Vietnam war.

The words are just as applicable to my brother, Elmo, as they are to the brother of Dr. Phan—the surgeon who had spent 17 years looking for his brother's remains.

They are just as applicable to the thousands of Americans who died in Vietnam for what they believed in as they are to the millions of Vietnamese who died with a similar belief.

They are just as applicable to the Americans who bravely served in Vietnam and survived as they are to the Vietnamese survivors as well.

Entitled *"Lest We Forget,"* the poem (on the following page) is a fitting tribute by which to remember all victims of a terrible war that represents a terrible mistake in the history of American/Vietnamese relations.

Only by not forgetting those who made sacrifices in that war can we hope to avoid making such a mistake again:

"*Lest We Forget*"

Not for fame or reward,

Not for place or rank,

Not lured by ambition

or goaded by necessity,

But in simple obedience

as they understood it.

These men suffered all,

dared all, and died.

Lest we forget...lest we forget.

CPSIA information can be obtained
at www.ICGtesting.com
Printed in the USA
FFOW05n0942220515